AF654756

HANDBOOK OF CONSERVATION BIOLOGY

HANDBOOK OF CONSERVATION BIOLOGY

By

Dr. Govind Prasad

M.A., Ph.D., D.litt., F.A.MSE (France)

Senior Reader

Deptt. of Geography

Rana Pratap Postgraduate College

Sultanpur (U.P.)

(India)

DPH

DISCOVERY PUBLISHING HOUSE PVT. LTD.

NEW DELHI-110 002

Published by:
Tilak Wasan
DISCOVERY PUBLISHING HOUSE PVT. LTD.
4383/4A, Ansari Road, Darya Ganj
New Delhi-110 002 (India)
Phone : +91-11-23279245, 43596064-65
Fax : +91-11-23253475
E-mail : parul.wasan@gmail.com
discoverypublishinghouse@gmail.com
web : www.discoverypublishinggroup.com

***First Edition:* 2012**
ISBN: 978-93-5056-003-7

Handbook of Conservation Biology
© 2012, **Author**

All rights reserved. No part of this publication should be reproduced, stored in a retrieval system, or transmitted in any form or by any means: electronic, mechanical, photocopying, recording or otherwise, without the prior written permission of the author and the publisher.

This book has been published in good faith that the material provided by authors is original. Every effort is made to ensure accuracy of material, but the publisher and printer will not be held responsible for any inadvertent error(s). In case of any dispute, all legal matters are to be settled under Delhi jurisdiction only.

Printed at:
Shree Balaji Art Press
Delhi

Preface

Conservation biology is the scientific study of the nature and status of Earth's biodiversity with the aim of protecting species, their habitats, and ecosystems from excessive rates of extinction. It is an interdisciplinary subject drawing on sciences, economics, and the practice of natural resource management. The term *conservation biology* was introduced as the title of a conference held at the University of California in La Jolla, California in 1978 organized by biologists Bruce Wilcox and Michael Soulé. The meeting was prompted by the concern among scientists over tropical deforestation, disappearing species, eroding genetic diversity within species. The conference and proceedings that resulted sought to bridge a gap existing at the time between theory in ecology and population biology on the one hand and conservation policy and practice on the other. Conservation biology and the concept of biological diversity (biodiversity) emerged together, helping crystallize the modern era of conservation science and policy.

The rapid decline of established biological systems around the world means that conservation biology is often referred to as a 'Discipline with a deadline'. Conservation biology is tied closely to ecology in researching the dispersal, migration, demographics, effective population size, inbreeding depression, and minimum population viability of rare or endangered species. Conservation biology is concerned with phenomena that affect the maintenance, loss, and restoration of biodiversity and the science of sustaining evolutionary processes that engender genetic, population, species, and ecosystem diversity. The concern stems from estimates suggesting that up to 50 per cent of all species on the planet will disappear within the next 50 years which has contributed to poverty, starvation, and will reset the course of evolution on this planet.

Conservation biologists research and educate on the trends and process of biodiversity loss, species extinctions, and the negative affect this is having on our capabilities to sustain the well-being of human society. Conservation biologists work in the field and office, in government, universities, non-profit organizations and industry. They are funded to research, monitor, and catalog every angle of the earth and its relation to society. The topics are diverse, because this is an interdisciplinary network with professional alliances in the biological as well as social sciences. Those dedicated to the cause and profession advocate for a global response to the current biodiversity crisis based on morals, ethics, and scientific reason. Organizations and citizens are responding to the biodiversity crisis through conservation action plans that direct research, monitoring, and education programmes that engage concerns at local through global scales.

Conservation biologists study trends and process from the paleontological past to the ecological present as they gain an understanding of the context related to species extinction. It is generally accepted that there have been five major global mass extinctions that register in Earth's history.

Author

Contents

1 Introduction

Conservation biology is the scientific study of the nature and status of Earth's biodiversity with the aim of protecting species, their habitats, and ecosystems from excessive rates of extinction. It is an interdisciplinary subject drawing on sciences, economics, and the practice of natural resource management. The term *conservation biology* was introduced as the title of a conference held at the University of California in La Jolla, California in 1978 organized by biologists Bruce Wilcox and Michael Soulé. The meeting was prompted by the concern among scientists over tropical deforestation, disappearing species, eroding genetic diversity within species. The conference and proceedings that resulted sought to bridge a gap existing at the time between theory in ecology and population biology on the one hand and conservation policy and practice on the other. Conservation biology and the concept of biological diversity (biodiversity) emerged together, helping crystallize the modern era of conservation science and policy.

The rapid decline of established biological systems around the world means that conservation biology is often referred to as a 'Discipline with a deadline'. Conservation biology is tied closely to ecology in researching the dispersal, migration, demographics, effective population size, inbreeding depression, and minimum population viability of rare or endangered species. Conservation biology is concerned with phenomena that affect the maintenance, loss, and restoration of biodiversity and the science of sustaining evolutionary processes that engender genetic, population, species, and ecosystem diversity. The concern stems from estimates suggesting that up to 50 per cent of all species on the planet will disappear within the next 50 years which has contributed to poverty, starvation, and will reset the course of evolution on this planet.

Conservation biologists research and educate on the trends and process of biodiversity loss, species extinctions, and the negative affect this is having on our capabilities to sustain the well-being of human society. Conservation biologists work in the field and office, in government, universities, non-profit organizations and industry. They are funded to research, monitor, and catalog every angle of the earth and its relation to society. The topics are diverse, because this is an interdisciplinary network with professional alliances in the biological as well as social sciences. Those dedicated to the cause and profession advocate for a global response to the current biodiversity crisis based on morals, ethics, and scientific reason. Organizations and citizens are responding to the biodiversity crisis through conservation action plans that direct research, monitoring, and education programmes that engage concerns at local through global scales.

Conservation biologists study trends and process from the paleontological past to the ecological present as they gain an understanding of the context related to species extinction. It is generally accepted that there have been five major global mass extinctions that register in Earth's history. These include: the Ordovician (440 mya), Devonian (370 mya), Permian–Triassic (245 mya), Triassic–Jurassic (200 mya), and Cretaceous (65 mya) extinction spasms. Within the last 10,000 years, human influence over the

Earth's ecosystems has been so extensive that scientists have difficulty estimating the number of species lost; that is to say the rates of deforestation, reef destruction, wetland draining and other human acts are proceeding much faster than human assessment of species. The latest *Living Planet Report* by the World Wide Fund for Nature estimates that we have exceeded the bio-regenerative capacity of the planet, requiring 1.5 Earths to support the demands placed on our natural resources.

Global assessments of coral reefs of the world continue to report drastic and rapid rates of decline. By 2000, 27 per cent of the world's coral reef ecosystems had effectively collapsed. The largest period of decline occurred in a dramatic 'bleaching' event in 1998, where approximately 16 per cent of all the coral reefs in the world disappeared in less than a year. *Coral bleaching* is caused by a mixture of environmental stresses, including increases in ocean temperatures and acidity, causing both the release of symbiotic algae and death of corals . Decline and extinction risk in coral reef biodiversity has risen dramatically in the past ten years. The loss of coral reefs, which are predicted to go extinct in the next century, will have huge economic impacts, threatens the balance of global biodiversity, and endangers food security for hundreds of millions of people. Conservation biology plays an important role in international agreements covering the world's oceans (and other issues pertaining to biodiversity.

These predictions will undoubtedly appear extreme, but it is difficult to imagine how such changes will not come to pass without fundamental changes in human behaviour.

The oceans are threatened by acidification due to an increase in CO_2 levels. This is a most serious threat to societies relying heavily upon oceanic natural resources. A concern is that the majority of all marine species will not be able to evolve or acclimate in response to the changes in the ocean chemistry.

The prospects of averting mass extinction seems unlikely when "90 per cent of all of the large (average approximately =50 kg), open ocean tuna, billfishes, and sharks in the ocean" are reportedly gone. Given the scientific review of current trends, the ocean is predicted to have few surviving multi-cellular organisms with only microbes left to dominate marine ecosystems.

There are serious concerns also being hailed from taxonomic groups that do not receive the same degree of social attention or attract funds as the vertebrates do, including fungi, lichen, plant and insect communities where the vast majority of biodiversity is represented. Insect conservation, in particular, is of pivotal importance for conservation biology. The value of insects in the biosphere is enormous because they outnumber all other living groups in measure of species richness. The greatest bulk of biomass on land is found in plants, which is sustained by insect relations. This great ecological value of insects is countered by a society that oftentimes reacts negatively toward these aesthetically 'unpleasant' creatures.

One area of concern in the insect world that has caught the public eye is the mysterious case of missing honey bees (*Apis mellifera*). Honey bees provide an indispensable ecological services through their acts of pollination supporting a huge variety of agriculture crops. The sudden disappearance of bees leaving empty hives or colony collapse disorder (CCD) is not uncommon. However, in a 16-month period from 2006 through 2007, 29 per cent of 577 beekeepers across the United States reported CCD losses in up to 76 per cent of their colonies. This sudden demographic loss in bee numbers is placing a strain on the agricultural sector. The cause behind the massive declines is puzzling scientists. Pests, pesticides, and global warming are all being considered as possible causes.

Another highlight that links conservation biology to insects, forests, and climate change is the mountain pine beetle (*Dendroctonus ponderosae*) epidemic of British Columbia, Canada, which has infested 470,000 km^2 (180,000 sq mi) of forested land since 1999. An action plan has been prepared by the Government of British Columbia to address this problem.

This impact [*pine beetle epidemic*] converted the forest from a small net carbon sink to a large net carbon source both during and immediately after the outbreak. In the worst year, the impacts resulting from the beetle outbreak in British Columbia were equivalent to 75 per cent of the average annual direct forest fire emissions from all of Canada during 1959-1999.

A large proportion of parasite species are threatened by extinction. A few of them are being eradicated as pests of humans or domestic animals, however, most of them are harmless. Threats include the decline or fragmentation of host populations, or the extinction of host species.

Threats to Biodiversity

Many of the threats to biodiversity, including disease and climate change, are reaching inside borders of protected areas, leaving them 'not-so protected' (e.g. Yellowstone National Park . Climate change, for example, is often cited as a serious threat in this regard, because there is a feedback loop between species extinction and the release of carbon dioxide into the atmosphere. Ecosystems store and cycle large amounts of carbon to regulate global conditions. The effects of global warming adds a catastrophic threat toward a mass extinction of global biological diversity. The extinction threat is estimated to range from 15 to 37 per cent of all species by 2050, or 50 per cent of all species over the next 50 years.

Some of the most significant and insidious threats to biodiversity and ecosystem processes include climate change, mass agriculture, deforestation, overgrazing, slash-and-burn agriculture, urban development, wildlife trade, light pollution and pesticide use. Habitat fragmentation poses one of the more difficult challenges, because the global network of protected areas only covers 11.5 per cent of the Earth's surface. A significant consequence of fragmentation and lack of linked protected areas is the reduction of animal migration on a global scale. Considering that billions of tonnes of biomass are responsible for nutrient cycling across the earth, the reduction of migration is a serious matter for conservation biology.

These figures do not imply, however, that human activities must necessarily cause irreparable harm to the biosphere. With conservation management and planning for biodiversity at all levels, from genes to ecosystems, there are examples where humans mutually coexist in a sustainable way with nature. However, it may be too late for human intervention to reverse the current mass extinction.

Extinction rates are measured in a variety of ways. Conservation biologists measure and apply statistical measures of fossil records, rates of habitat loss, and a multitude of other variables such as loss of biodiversity as a function of the rate of habitat loss and site occupancy to obtain such estimates. The Theory of Island Biogeography is possibly the most significant contribution toward the scientific understanding of both the process and how to measure the rate of species extinction. The current background extinction rate is estimated to be one species every few years.

The measure of ongoing species loss is made more complex by the fact that most of the Earth's species have not been described or evaluated. Estimates vary greatly on how many species actually exist (estimated range: 3,600,000-111,700,000) to how many have received a species binomial (estimated range: 1.5-8 million). Less than 1 per cent of all species that have been described have been studied beyond simply noting its existence. From these figures, the IUCN reports that 23 per cent of vertebrates, 5 per cent of invertebrates and 70 per cent of plants that have been evaluated are designated as endangered or threatened.

Systematic Conservation Planning

Systematic conservation planning is an effective way to seek and identify efficient and effective types of reserve design to capture or sustain the highest priority biodiversity values and to work with communities in support of local ecosystems. Margules and Pressey identify six interlinked stages in the systematic planning approach:

- Compile data on the biodiversity of the planning region
- Identify conservation goals for the planning region
- Review existing conservation areas
- Select additional conservation areas
- Implement conservation actions
- Maintain the required values of conservation areas

Conservation biologists regularly prepare detailed conservation plans for grant proposals or to effectively coordinate their plan of action and to identify best management practices (e.g.). Systematic strategies generally employ the services of Geographic Information Systems to assist in the decision making process.

Conservation Biology as a Profession

The Society for Conservation Biology is a global community of conservation professionals dedicated to advancing the science and practice of conserving biodiversity. Conservation biology as a discipline reaches beyond biology, into subjects such as philosophy, law, economics, humanities, arts, anthropology, and education. Within biology, conservation genetics and evolution are immense fields unto themselves, but these disciplines are of prime importance to the practice and profession of conservation biology.

Is conservation biology an objective science when biologists advocate for an inherent value in nature? Do conservationists introduce bias when they support policies using qualitative description, such as habitat *degradation*, or *healthy* ecosystems? As all scientists hold values, so do conservation biologists. Conservation biologists advocate for reasoned and sensible management of natural resources and do so with a disclosed combination of science, reason, logic, and values in their conservation management plans. This sort of advocacy is similar to the medical profession advocating for healthy lifestyle options, both are beneficial to human well-being yet remain scientific in their approach. Many conservation biologists, in addition to having a Bachelors of Science (or extensive natural experience) often receive professional accreditation during their career.

There is a movement in conservation biology suggesting a new form of leadership is needed to mobilize conservation biology into a more effective discipline that is able to communicate the full scope of the problem to society at large. The movement proposes an adaptive leadership approach that parallels an adaptive management approach. The concept is based on a new philosophy or leadership theory steering away from historical notions of power, authority, and dominance. Adaptive conservation leadership is reflective and more equitable as it applies to any member of society who can mobilize others toward meaningful change using communication techniques that are inspiring, purposeful, and collegial. Adaptive conservation leadership and mentoring programmes are being implemented by conservation biologists through organizations such as the Aldo Leopold Leadership Programme.

Preservation

A preservationist differs from a conservation biologist through the principal of non-interference. Preservationists advocate for giving areas of nature and species a protected existence that halts interference from the humans. In this regard, conservationists differ from preservationists in the social dimension, as conservation biology engages society and seeks equitable solutions for both society and ecosystems.

Ethics and Values

Conservation biologists are interdisciplinary researchers that practice ethics in the biological and social sciences. Chan states that conservationists must advocate for biodiversity and can do so in a scientifically ethical manner by not promoting simultaneous advocacy against other competing values. A conservationist researches biodiversity and reasons through a Resource Conservation Ethic, which identify what measures will deliver 'the greatest good for the greatest number of people for the longest time'.

Some conservation biologists argue that nature has an intrinsic value that is independent of anthropocentric usefulness or utilitarianism. Intrinsic value advocates that a gene, or species, be valued because they have a utility for the ecosystems they sustain. Aldo Leopold was a classical thinker and writer on such conservation ethics whose philosophy, ethics and writings are still valued and revisited by modern conservation biologists. His writing is oftentimes required reading for those in the profession.

While most in the community of conservation science 'stress the importance' of sustaining biodiversity there is debate on how to prioritize genes, species, or ecosystems, which are all components of biodiversity. While the predominant approach to date has been to focus efforts on endangered species by conserving *biodiversity hotspots*, some scientists (e.g.) and conservation organizations, such as the Nature Conservancy, argue that it is more cost effective, logical, and socially relevant to invest in *biodiversity coldspots*. The costs of discovering, naming, and mapping out the distribution every species, they argue, is an ill advised conservation venture. They reason it is better to understand the significance of the ecological roles of species.

Biodiversity hotspots and coldspots are a way of recognizing that the spatial concentration of genes, species, and ecosystems is not uniformly distributed on the Earth's surface. For example, "[...] 44 per cent of all species of vascular plants and 35 per cent of all species in four vertebrate groups are confined to 25 hotspots comprising only 1.4 per cent of the land surface of the Earth."

Those arguing in favour of setting priorities for coldspots point out that there are other measures to consider beyond biodiversity. They point out that emphasizing hotspots downplays the importance of the social and ecological connections to vast areas of the Earth's ecosystems where biomass, not biodiversity, reigns supreme. It is estimated that 36 per cent of the Earth's surface, encompassing 38.9 per cent of the worlds vertebrates, lacks the endemic species to qualify as biodiversity hotspot. Moreover, measures show that maximizing protections for biodiversity does not capture ecosystem services any better than targeting randomly chosen regions. Population level biodiversity (i.e. coldspots) are disappearing at a rate that is ten times that at the species level. The level of importance in addressing biomass versus endemism as a concern for conservation biology is highlighted in literature measuring the level of threat to global ecosystem carbon stocks that do not necessarily reside in areas of endemism. A hotspot priority approach would not invest so heavily in places such as steppes, the Serengeti, the Arctic, or taiga. These areas contribute a great abundance of population (not species) level biodiversity and ecosystem services, including cultural value and planetary nutrient cycling.

Those in favour of the hotspot approach point out that species are irreplaceable components of the global ecosystem, they are concentrated in places that are most threatened, and should therefore receive maximal strategic protections. The IUCN Red List categories, which appear on Wikipedia species articles, is an example of the hotspot conservation approach in action; species that are not rare or endemic are listed the least concern and their wikipedia articles tend to be ranked low on the importance scale. This is a hotspot approach because the priority is set to target species level concerns over population level or biomass. Species richness and genetic biodiversity contributes to and engenders ecosystem stability, ecosystem processes, evolutionary adaptability, and biomass. Both sides agree, however, that conserving biodiversity is necessary to reduce the extinction rate and identify an inherent value in nature; the debate hinges on how to prioritize limited conservation resources in the most cost effective way.

Economic Values and Natural Capital

Conservation biologists have started to collaborate with leading global economists to determine how to measure the wealth and services of nature and to make these values apparent in global market transactions. This system of accounting is called *natural capital* and would, for example, register the value of an ecosystem before it is cleared to make way for development. The WWF publishes its *Living Planet Report* and provides a global index of biodiversity by monitoring approximately 5,000 populations in 1,686 species of vertebrate (mammals, birds, fish, reptiles, and amphibians) and report on the trends in much the same way that the stock market is tracked.

This method of measuring the global economic benefit of nature has been endorsed by the G8+5 leaders and the European Commission. Nature sustains many ecosystem services that benefit humanity. Many of the earths ecosystem services are public goods without a market and therefore no price or value. When the *stock market* registers a financial crisis, traders on Wall Street are not in the business of trading stocks for much of the planet's living natural capital stored in ecosystems. There is no natural stock market with investment portfolios into sea horses, amphibians, insects, and other creatures that provide a sustainable supply of ecosystem services that are valuable to society The ecological footprint of society has exceeded the bio-regenerative capacity limits of the planet's ecosystems by about 30 per cent, which is the same percentage of vertebrate populations that have registered decline from 1970 through 2005.

The inherent natural economy plays an essential role in sustaining humanity, including the regulation of global atmospheric chemistry, pollinating crops, pest control, cycling soil nutrients, purifying our water supply, supplying medicines and health benefits, and unquantifiable quality of life improvements. There is a relationship, a correlation, between markets and natural capital, and social income inequity and biodiversity loss. This means that there are greater rates of biodiversity loss in places where the inequity of wealth is greatest.

Although a direct market comparison of natural capital is likely insufficient in terms of human value, one measure of ecosystem services suggests the contribution amounts to trillions of dollars yearly. For example, one segment of North American forests has been assigned an annual value of 250 billion dollars; as another example, honey-bee pollination is estimated to provide between 10 and 18 billion dollars of value yearly. The value of ecosystem services on one New Zealand island has been imputed to be as great as the GDP of that region. This planetary wealth is being lost at an incredible rate as the demands of human society is exceeding the bio-regenerative capacity of the Earth. While biodiversity and ecosystems are resilient, the danger of losing them is that humans cannot recreate many ecosystem functions through technological innovation.

Some species, called a *keystone species*, form a central supporting hub in the ecosystem. The loss of such a species results in a collapse in ecosystem function, as well as the loss of coexisting species. The importance of a keystone species was shown by the extinction of the Steller's Sea Cow (*Hydrodamalis gigas*) through its interaction with sea otters, sea urchins, and kelp. Kelp beds grow and form nurseries in shallow waters to shelter creatures that support the food chain. Sea urchins feed on kelp, while sea otters feed on sea urchins. With the rapid decline of sea otters due to overhunting, sea urchin populations grazed unrestricted on the kelp beds and the ecosystem collapsed. Left unchecked, the urchins destroyed the shallow water kelp communities that supported the Steller's Sea Cow's diet and hastened their demise. The sea otter is a keystone species because the coexistence of many ecological associates in the kelp beds relied upon otters for their survival.

Indicator Species

The NAMOS BC logo is an example of an ecosystem *umbrella* concept (forests and wetlands) combined with amphibians as *indicator* and *flagship species.*

An *indicator species* has a narrow set of ecological requirements, therefore they become useful targets for observing the health of an ecosystem. Some animals, such as amphibians with their semi-permeable skin and linkages to wetlands, have an acute sensitivity to environmental harm and thus may serve as a *miner's canary.* Indicator species are monitored in an effort to capture environmental degradation through pollution or some other link to proximate human activities. Monitoring an indicator species is a measure to determine if there is a significant environmental impact that can serve to advise or modify practice, such as through different forestsilviculture treatments and management scenarios, or to measure the degree of harm that a pesticide may impart on the health of an ecosystem.

Government regulators, consultants, or NGOs regularly monitor indicator species, however, there are limitations coupled with many practical considerations that must be followed for the approach to be effective. It is generally recommended that multiple indicators (genes, populations, species, communities, and landscape) be monitored for effective conservation measurement that prevents harm to the complex, and oftentimes unpredictable, response from ecosystem dynamics.

Umbrella and Flagship Species

An example of an *umbrella species* is the Monarch butterfly, because of its lengthy migrations and aesthetic value. The Monarch migrates across North America, covering multiple ecosystems and so requires a large area to exist. Any protections afforded to the Monarch butterfly will at the same time umbrella many other species and habitats. An umbrella species is often used as *flagship species*, which are species, such as the Giant Panda, the Blue Whale, the tiger, the mountain gorilla and the Monarch butterfly, that capture the public's attention and attract support for conservation measures.

Efforts to conserve and protect *global* biodiversity are a recent phenomenon. Prior to the global conservation era, there was the coming of the age of conservation. Some historians have linked this with the 1916 National Parks Act, which included the 'use without impairment' clause, sought by John Muir. This eventually resulted in the removal of a proposal to build a dam in Dinosaur National Monument in 1959.

Natural resource conservation, however, has a history that extends prior to the age of conservation. Resource ethics grew out of necessity through direct relations with nature. Regulation or communal restraint became necessary to prevent selfish motives from taking more than could be locally sustained, therefore compromising the long-term supply for the rest of the community. This social dilemma with respect to natural resource management is often called the 'Tragedy of the Commons'. From this principal, conservation biologists can trace communal resource based ethics throughout cultures as a solution to communal resource conflict. For example, the Alaskan Tlingit peoples and the Haida of the Pacific Northwest had resource boundaries, rules, and restrictions among clans with respect to the fishing of Sockeye Salmon. These rules were guided by clan elders who knew life-long details of each river and stream they managed. There are numerous examples in history where cultures have followed rules, rituals, and organized practice with respect to communal natural resource management.

Conservation ethics are also found in early religious and philosophical writings. There are examples in the Tao, Shinto, Hindu, Islamic and Buddhist traditions. In Greek philosophy, Plato lamented about pasture land degradation: "What is left now is, so to say, the skeleton of a body wasted by disease; the rich, soft soil has been carried off and only the bare framework of the district left." In the bible, through Moses, God commanded to let the land rest from cultivation every seventh year. Before the 18th century, however, much of European culture considered it a pagan view to admire nature. Wilderness was denigrated while agricultural development was praised. However, as early as AD 680 a wildlife sanctuary was founded on the Farne Islands by St Cuthbert in response to his religious beliefs.

Natural history was a major preoccupation in the 18th century, with grand expeditions and the opening of popular public displays in Europe and North America. By 1900 there were 150 natural history museums in Germany, 250 in Great Britain, 250 in the United States, and 300 in France. Preservationist or conservationist sentiments are a development in the late 18th to early 20th century. The 19th century fascination with natural history engendered a fervor to be the first to collect rare specimens with the goal of doing so before they became extinct by other such collectors. Although his artistic works and romantic depiction of avian life inspired many bird enthusiasts and conservation organizations, the writings of John James Audubon, by modern standards, show insensitivity toward bird conservation as he shot and collected hundreds of specimens. Inspired by him, however, the first chapter of the Audubon Society started in 1905 for the purpose of protecting birds.

Coming of the Age of Conservation

The modern concept of ecosystem services can be found in the late 19th century. "The utility of Natural History or its applicability to promote the material wealth of the State cannot be doubted. It was a great mistake to suppose that the subjects of Zoology, Botany, and Geology did not involve much that affects our comfort, convenience, health and wealth." However, the article continues and discusses the dread of agricultural pests and the utility of understanding their natural history for the purpose of facilitating their destruction.

By the early 1800s biogeography was ignited through efforts of Alexander von Humboldt, DeCandolle, Lyell and Darwin their efforts, while important in relating species to their environments, were part of the naturalist tradition and fell short of conservation biology proper. Darwin, for example, hunted and shot birds and kept natural history cabinets in line with Victorian tradition.

Modern roots of conservation biology can be found in the late 19th century Enlightenment period particularly in England and Scotland. A number of thinkers, among them notably Lord Monboddo, described the importance of 'preserving nature'; much of this early emphasis had its origins in Christian theology.

In the 20th century, actions in the United Kingdom, United States, and Canada emphasized the protection of habitat areas pursuant to visions of such people as John

Muir, Theodore Roosevelt, and Aldo Leopold. While the Canadian nor the United Kingdom governments did not pioneer the creation of National Parks as the United States did in the late 19th century, there were many far-sighted civil servants who were dedicated to wildlife conservation and of notable mention. Some of these historical figures include Charles Gordon Hewitt and James Harkin.

The term *conservation* came into use in the late 19th century and referred to the management, mainly for economic reasons, of such natural resources as timber, fish, game, topsoil, pastureland, and minerals. In addition it referred to the preservation of forests (forestry), wildlife (wildlife refuge), parkland, wilderness, and watersheds. Western Europe was the source of much 19th century progress for conservation biology, particularly the British Empire with the Sea Birds Preservation Act 1869. However, the United States made contributions to this field starting with thinking of Thoreau and taking form with the Forest Act of 1891, John Muir's founding of the Sierra Club in 1892, the founding of the New York Zoological Society in 1895 and establishment of a series of national forests and preserves by Theodore Roosevelt from 1901 to 1909.

Not until the mid 20th century did efforts arise to target individual species for conservation, notably efforts in big cat conservation in South America led by the New York Zoological Society. In the early 20th century the New York Zoological Society was instrumental in developing concepts of establishing preserves for particular species and conducting the necessary conservation studies to determine the suitability of locations that are most appropriate as conservation priorities; the work of Henry Fairfield Osborn Jr., Carl E. Akeley, Archie Carr and Archie Carr III is notable in this era Akeley for example, having led expeditions to the Virunga Mountains and observed the mountain gorilla in the wild, became convinced that the species and the area were conservation priorities. He was instrumental in persuading Albert I of Belgium to act in defense of the mountain gorilla and establish Albert National Park (since renamed Virunga National Park) in what is now Democratic Republic of Congo By the 1970s, led primarily by work in the United States under the Endangered Species Act along with the Species at Risk Act (SARA) of Canada, Biodiversity Action Plans developed in Australia, Sweden, the United Kingdom, hundreds of species specific protection plans ensued. Notably the United Nations acted to conserve sites of outstanding cultural or natural importance to the common heritage of mankind. The programme was adopted by the General Conference of UNESCO in 1972. As of 2006, a total of 830 sites are listed: 644 cultural, 162 natural. The first country to pursue aggressive biological conservation through national legislation was the United States, which passed back to back legislation in the Endangered Species Act (1966) and National Environmental Policy Act (1970) which together injected major funding and protection measures to large scale habitat protection and threatened species research. Other conservation developments, however, have taken hold throughout the world. India, for example, passed the Wildlife Protection Act of 1972.

In 1980 a significant development was the emergence of the urban conservation movement. A local organization was established in Birmingham, UK, a development followed in rapid succession in cities across the UK, then overseas. Although perceived as a grassroots movement, its early development was driven by academic research into urban wildlife. Initially perceived as radical, the movement's view of conservation being inextricably linked with other human activity has now become mainstream in conservation thought. Considerable research effort is now directed at urban conservation biology. The Society for Conservation Biology originated in 1985.

By 1992 most of the countries of the world had become committed to the principles of conservation of biological diversity with the Convention on Biological Diversity subsequently many countries began programmes of Biodiversity Action Plans to identify and conserve threatened species within their borders, as well as protect associated habitats. The late 1990s saw increasing professionalism in the sector, with the maturing of organisations such as the Institute of Ecology and Environmental Management and the Society for the Environment.

Since 2000 the concept of landscape scale conservation has risen to prominence, with less emphasis being given to single-species or even single-habitat focussed actions. Instead an ecosystem approach is advocated by most mainstream conservationist, although concerns have been expressed by those working to protect some high-profile species.

Ecology has clarified the workings of the biosphere; i.e., the complex interrelationships among humans, other species, and the physical environment. The burgeoning human population and associated agriculture, industry, and the ensuing pollution, have demonstrated how easily ecological relationships can be disrupted.

The last word in ignorance is the man who says of an animal or plant: "What good is it?" If the land mechanism as a whole is good, then every part is good, whether we understand it or not. If the biota, in the course of aeons, has built something we like but do not understand, then who but a fool would discard seemingly useless parts? To keep every cog and wheel is the first precaution of intelligent tinkering."

2 Biodiversity

Biodiversity is the variation of life forms within a given ecosystem, biome, or for the entire Earth. Biodiversity is often used as a measure of the health of biological systems. The biodiversity found on Earth today consists of many millions of distinct biological species, which is the product of nearly 3.5 billion years of evolution.

The term was used first by wildlife scientist and conservationist Raymond F. Dasmann in a lay book advocating nature conservation. The term was not widely adopted for more than a decade, when in the 1980s it and 'biodiversity' came into common usage in science and environmental policy. Use of the term by Thomas Lovejoy in the Foreword to the book credited with launching the field of conservation biology introduced the term along with 'conservation biology' to the scientific community. Until then the term 'natural diversity' was used in conservation science circles, including by the Science Division of the Nature Conservancy in an important 1975 study, 'The Preservation of Natural Diversity'. By the early 1980s TNC's Science programme and its head Robert E. Jenkins, Lovejoy, and other leading conservation scientists at the time in America advocated the use of 'biological diversity' to embrace the object of biological conservation.

The term's contracted form *biodiversity* may have been coined by W.G. Rosen in 1985 while planning the *National Forum on Biological Diversity* organized by the National Research Council (NRC) which was to be held in 1986, and first appeared in a publication in 1988 when entomologist E. O. Wilson used it as the title of the proceedings of that forum.

Since this period both terms and the concept have achieved widespread use among biologists, environmentalists, political leaders, and concerned citizens worldwide. The term is sometimes used to equate to a concern for the natural environment and nature conservation. This use has coincided with the expansion of concern over extinction observed in the last decades of the 20th century.

A similar concept in use in the United States, besides natural diversity, is the term 'natural heritage'. It pre-dates both terms though it is a less scientific term and more easily comprehended in some ways by the wider audience interested in conservation. Furthermore it may be misleading if used to refer only to biodiversity, as natural heritage also includes geology and landforms (geodiversity). The term 'Natural Heritage' was used when Jimmy Carter set up the Georgia Heritage Trust while he was governor of Georgia; Carter's trust dealt with both natural and cultural heritage. It would appear that Carter picked the term up from Lyndon Johnson, who used it in a 1966 Message to Congress. 'Natural Heritage' was picked up by the Science Division of the US Nature Conservancy when, under Jenkins, it launched in 1974 the network of State Natural Heritage Programmes. This network took on a life of its own in the 1990s when it became an independent non-profit organization named NatureServe. When NatureServe was extended outside the USA, the term 'Conservation Data Centre' was suggested by Guillermo Mann is now also used by several programmes, for example those that operate as part of NatureServe Canada.

'Biological diversity' or 'biodiversity' can have many interpretations and it is most commonly used to replace the more clearly defined and long established terms, species diversity and species richness. Biologists most often define biodiversity as the 'totality of genes, species, and ecosystems of a region'. An advantage of this definition is that it seems to describe most circumstances and present a unified view of the traditional three levels at which biological variety has been identified:

- genetic diversity
- species diversity
- ecosystem diversity

But Professor Anthony Campbell at Cardiff University, UK and the Darwin Centre, Pembrokeshire, has defined a fourth, and critical one: Molecular Diversity.

This multilevel conception is consistent with the early use of 'biological diversity' in Washington D.C. and international conservation organizations in the late 1960s through 1970's, by Raymond F. Dasmann who apparently coined the term and Thomas E. Lovejoy who later introduced it to the wider conservation and science communities. An explicit definition consistent with this interpretation was first given in a paper by Bruce A. Wilcox commissioned by the International Union for the Conservation of Nature and Natural Resources (IUCN) for the 1982 World National Parks Conference in Bali. The definition Wilcox gave is 'Biological diversity is the variety of life forms...at all levels of biological systems (i.e., molecular, organismic, population, species and ecosystem)..." Subsequently, the 1992 United Nations Earth Summit in Rio de Janeiro defined 'biological diversity' as 'the variability among living organisms from all sources, including, 'inter alia', terrestrial, marine, and other aquatic ecosystems, and the ecological complexes of which they are part: this includes diversity within species, between species and of ecosystems".

This is, in fact, the closest thing to a single legally accepted definition of biodiversity, since it is the definition adopted by the United Nations Convention on Biological Diversity.

The current textbook definition of 'biodiversity' is 'variation of life at all levels of biological organization'.

For geneticists, *biodiversity* is the diversity of genes and organisms. They study processes such as mutations, gene exchanges, and genome dynamics that occur at the DNA level and generate evolution. Consistent with this, along with the above definition the Wilcox paper stated "genes are the ultimate source of biological organization at all levels of biological systems..."

Measurement

A variety of objective measures have been created in order to empirically measure biodiversity. Each measure of biodiversity relates to a particular use of the data. For practical conservationists, measurements should include a quantification of values that are commonly-shared among locally affected organisms, including humans. For others, a more economically defensible definition should allow the ensuring of continued possibilities for both adaptation and future use by humans, assuring environmental sustainability.

Nevertheless, biodiversity is not distributed evenly on Earth. It is consistently richer in the tropics and in other localized regions such as the Cape Floristic Province. As one approaches polar regions one generally finds fewer species. Flora and fauna diversity depends on climate, altitude, soils and the presence of other species. In the year 2006 large numbers of the Earth's species were formally classified as rare or endangered or threatened species; moreover, many scientists have estimated that there are millions more species actually endangered which have not yet been formally recognized. About 40 per cent of the 40,177 species assessed using the IUCN Red List criteria, are now listed as threatened species with extinction - a total of 16,119 species.

Even though biodiversity declines from the equator to the poles in terrestrial ecoregions, whether this is so in aquatic ecosystems is still a hypothesis to be tested, especially in marine ecosystems where causes of this phenomenon are unclear. In addition, particularly in marine ecosystems, there are several well stated cases where diversity in higher latitudes actually increases. Therefore, the lack of information on biodiversity of Tropics and Polar Regions prevents scientific conclusions on the distribution of the world's aquatic biodiversity.

A biodiversity hotspot is a region with a high level of endemic species. These biodiversity hotspots were first identified in 1988 by Dr. Norman Myers in two articles in the scientific journal *The Environmentalist.* Dense human habitation tends to occur near hotspots. Most hotspots are located in the tropics and most of them are forests.

Brazil's Atlantic Forest is considered a hotspot of biodiversity and contains roughly 20,000 plant species, 1350 vertebrates, and millions of insects, about half of which occur nowhere else in the world. The island of Madagascar including the unique Madagascar dry deciduous forests and lowland rainforests possess a very high ratio of species endemism and biodiversity, since the island separated from mainland Africa 65 million years ago, most of the species and ecosystems have evolved independently producing unique species different from those in other parts of Africa.

Biodiversity found on Earth today is the result of 3.5 billion years of evolution. The origin of life has not been definitely established by science, however some evidence suggests that life may already have been well-established a few hundred million years after the formation of the Earth. Until approximately 600 million years ago, all life consisted of archaea, bacteria, protozoans and similar single-celled organisms.

The history of biodiversity during the Phanerozoic (the last 540 million years), starts with rapid growth during the Cambrian explosion—a period during which nearly every phylum of multicellular organisms first appeared. Over the next 400 million years or so, global diversity showed little overall trend, but was marked by periodic, massive losses of diversity classified as mass extinction events.

The apparent biodiversity shown in the fossil record suggests that the last few million years include the period of greatest biodiversity in the Earth's history. However, not all scientists support this view, since there is considerable uncertainty as to how strongly the fossil record is biased by the greater availability and preservation of recent geologic sections. Some argue that, corrected for sampling artifacts, modern biodiversity is not much different from biodiversity 300 million years ago. Estimates of the present global macroscopic species diversity vary from 2 million to 100 million species, with a best estimate of somewhere near 13-14 million, the vast majority of them arthropods.

The existence of a global carrying capacity has been debated, that is to say that there is a limit to the number of species that can live on this planet. While records of life in the sea shows a logistic pattern of growth, life on land (insects, plants and tetrapods) shows an exponential rise in diversity. As one author states, "Tetrapods have not yet invaded 64 per cent of potentially habitable modes, and it could be that without human influence the ecological and taxonomic diversity of tetrapods would continue to increase in an exponential fashion until most or all of the available ecospace is filled."

Many regions of high biodiversity (as well as high endemism) arise from very specialized habitats which require unusual adaptation mechanisms, for example alpine environments in high mountains, or the peat bogs of Northern Europe.

Distribution

Selection bias amongst researchers may contribute to biased empirical research for modern estimates of biodiversity. In 1768 Rev. Gilbert White succinctly observed of his Selborne, Hampshire 'all nature is so full, that that district produces the most variety which is the most examined'.

Most biologists agree however that the period since the emergence of humans is part of a new mass extinction, the Holocene extinction event, caused primarily by the impact humans are having on the environment. It has been argued that the present rate of extinction is sufficient to eliminate most species on the planet Earth within 100 years.

New species are regularly discovered (on average between 5-10,000 new species each year, most of them insects) and many, though discovered, are not yet classified (estimates are that nearly 90 per cent of all arthropods are not yet classified). Most of the terrestrial diversity is found in tropical forests.

Biodiversity also supports a number of natural ecosystem processes and services. Some ecosystem services that benefit society are air quality, climate (both global CO_2 sequestration and local), water purification, pollination, and prevention of erosion.

Since the stone age, species loss has been accelerated above the geological rate by human activity. The rate of species extinction is difficult to estimate, but it has been estimated that species are now being lost at a rate approximately 100 times as fast as is typical in the geological record, or perhaps as high as 10000 times as fast. To feed such a large population, more land is being transformed from wilderness with wildlife into agricultural, mining, lumbering, and urban areas for humans.

Non-material benefits that are obtained from ecosystems include spiritual and aesthetic values, knowledge systems and the value of education.

The economic value of the reservoir of genetic traits present in wild varieties and traditionally grown landraces is extremely important in improving crop performance. Important crops, such as the potato and coffee, are often derived from only a few genetic strains. Improvements in crop plants over the last 250 years have been largely due to harnessing the genetic diversity present in wild and domestic crop plants. Interbreeding crops strains with different beneficial traits has resulted in more than doubling crop production in the last 50 years as a result of the Green Revolution.

Crop diversity is also necessary to help the system recover when the dominant crop type is attacked by a disease:

- The Irish potato blight of 1846, which was a major factor in the deaths of a million people and migration of another million, was the result of planting only two potato varieties, both of which were vulnerable.
- When rice grassy stunt virus struck rice fields from Indonesia to India in the 1970s, 6273 varieties were tested for resistance. One was found to be resistant, an Indian variety, known to science only since 1966. This variety formed a hybrid with other varieties and is now widely grown.

Coffee rust attacked coffee plantations in Sri Lanka, Brazil, and Central America in 1970. A resistant variety was found in Ethiopia. Although the diseases are themselves a form of biodiversity.

Monoculture, the lack of biodiversity, was a contributing factor to several agricultural disasters in history, the European wine industry collapse in the late 1800s, and the US Southern Corn Leaf Blight epidemic of 1970. Higher biodiversity also controls the spread of certain diseases as pathogens will need to adapt to infect different species.

Biodiversity provides food for humans . Although about 80 per cent of our food supply comes from just 20 kinds of plants, humans use at least 40,000 species of plants and animals a day. Many people around the world depend on these species for their food, shelter, and clothing. There is untapped potential for increasing the range of food products suitable for human consumption, provided that the high present extinction rate can be stopped.

One of the key health issues associated with biodiversity is that of drug discovery and the availability of medicinal resources. A significant proportion of drugs are derived, directly or indirectly, from biological sources; Chivian and Bernstein report that at least 50 per cent of the pharmaceutical compounds on the market in the US are derived from natural compounds found in plants, animals, and microorganisms, while about 80 per cent of the world population depends on medicines from nature (used in either modern or traditional medical practice) for primary healthcare. Moreover, only a tiny proportion of the total diversity of wild species has been investigated for potential sources of new drugs. Through the field of bionics, considerable technological advancement has occurred which would not have without a rich biodiversity. It has been argued, based on evidence from market analysis and biodiversity science, that the decline in output from the pharmaceutical sector since the mid-1980s can be attributed to a move away from natural product exploration ('bioprospecting') in favour of R & D programmes based on genomics and synthetic chemistry, neither of which have yielded the expected product outputs; meanwhile, there is evidence that natural product chemistry can provide the basis for innovation which can yield significant economic and health benefits. Marine ecosystems are of particular interest in this regard, however unregulated and inappropriate bioprospecting can be considered a form of over-exploitation which has the potential to degrade ecosystems and increase biodiversity loss, as well as impacting on the rights of the communities and states from which the resources are taken.

A wide range of industrial materials are derived directly from biological resources. These include building materials, fibers, dyes, resirubber and oil. There is enormous potential for further research into sustainably utilizing materials from a wider diversity of organisms. In addition, biodiversity and the ecosystem goods and services it provides are considered to be fundamental to healthy economic systems. The degree to which biodiversity supports business varies between regions and between economic sectors, however the importance of biodiversity to issues of resource security (water quantity and quality, timber, paper and fibre, food and medicinal resources etc) are increasingly recognized as universal. As a result, the loss of biodiversity is increasingly recognized as a significant risk factor in business development and a threat to long term economic sustainability. A number of case studies recently compiled by the World Resources Institute demonstrate some of these risks as identified by specific industries.

Human Health

The diverse forest canopy on Barro Colorado Island, Panama, yielded this display of different fruit.

The relevance of biodiversity to human health is becoming a major international political issue, as scientific evidence builds on the global health implications of biodiversity loss. This issue is closely linked with the issue of climate change, as many of the anticipated health risks of climate change are associated with changes in biodiversity (e.g. changes in populations and distribution of disease vectors, scarcity of fresh water, impacts on agricultural biodiversity and food resources etc). Some of the health issues influenced by biodiversity include dietary health and nutrition security, infectious diseases, medical science and medicinal resources, social and psychological health, and spiritual well-being. Biodiversity is also known to have an important role in reducing disaster risk, and in post-disaster relief and recovery efforts.

Biodiversity provides many ecosystem services that are often not readily visible. It plays a part in regulating the chemistry of our atmosphere and water supply. Biodiversity is directly involved in water purification, recycling nutrients and providing fertile soils. Experiments with controlled environments have shown that humans cannot easily build ecosystems to support human needs; for example insect pollination cannot be mimicked by human-made construction, and that activity alone represents tens of billions of dollars in ecosystem services per year to humankind.

The stability of ecosystems is also related to biodiversity, with higher biodiversity producing greater stability over time, reducing the chance that ecosystem services will be disrupted as a result of disturbances such as extreme weather events or human exploitation.

Leisure, Cultural and Aesthetic Value

Many people derive value from biodiversity through leisure activities such as hiking, birdwatching or natural history study. Biodiversity has inspired musicians, painters, sculptors, writers and other artists. Many cultural groups view themselves as an integral part of the natural world and show respect for other living organisms.

Popular activities such as gardening, caring for aquariums and collecting butterflies are all strongly dependent on biodiversity. The number of species involved in such pursuits is in the tens of thousands, though the great majority do not enter mainstream commercialism.

The relationships between the original natural areas of these often 'exotic' animals and plants and commercial collectors, suppliers, breeders, propagators and those who promote their understanding and enjoyment are complex and poorly understood. It seems clear, however, that the general public responds well to exposure to rare and unusual organisms—they recognize their inherent value at some level. A family outing to the botanical garden or zoo is as much an aesthetic or cultural experience as it is an educational one.

Philosophically it could be argued that biodiversity has intrinsic aesthetic and spiritual value to mankind *in and of itself.* This idea can be used as a counterweight to the notion that tropical forests and other ecological realms are only worthy of conservation because they may contain medicines or useful products.

An interesting point is that evolved DNA embodies knowledge, and therefore destroying a species resembles burning a book, with the caveat that the book is of uncertain depth and importance and may in fact be best used as fuel.

Number of Species

According to the Global Taxonomy Initiative and the European Distributed Institute of Taxonomy, the *total* number of species for some phyla may be much higher as what we know currently:

- 10-30 million insects of some 0.9 we know today;
- 5-10 million bacteria;
- 1.5 million fungi of some 0.4 million we know today;
- ~1 million mites

Due to the fact that we know but a portion of the organisms in the biosphere, we do not have a complete understanding of the workings of our environment. To make matters worse, according to professor James Mallet, we are wiping out these species at an unprecedented rate. This means that even before a species has had the chance of being discovered, studied and classified, it may already be extinct.

During the last century, decreases in biodiversity have been increasingly observed. Studies show that 30 per cent of all natural species will be extinct by 2050. Of these, about one eighth of the known plant species are threatened with extinction. Some estimates put the loss at up to 1,40,000 species per year (based on Species-area theory) and subject to discussion. This figure indicates unsustainable ecological practices, because only a small number of species come into being each year. Almost all scientists acknowledge that the rate of species loss is greater now than at any time in human history, with extinctions occurring at rates hundreds of times higher than background extinction rates.

The factors that threaten biodiversity have been variously categorized. Jared Diamond describes an 'Evil Quartet' of habitat destruction, overkill, introduced species, and secondary extensions. Edward O. Wilson prefers the acronym HIPPO, standing for Habitat destruction, Invasive species, Pollution, Human Over Population, and Overharvesting.

Most of the species extinctions from 1000 AD to 2000 AD are due to human activities, in particular destruction of plant and animal habitats. Raised rates of extinction are being driven by human consumption of organic resources, especially related to tropical forest destruction. While most of the species that are becoming extinct are not food species, their biomass is converted into human food when their habitat is transformed into pasture, cropland, and orchards. It is estimated that more than a third of the Earth's biomass is tied up in only the few species that represent humans, livestock and crops. Because an ecosystem decreases in stability as its species are made extinct, these studies warn that the global ecosystem is destined for collapse if it is further reduced in complexity. Factors contributing to loss of biodiversity are: overpopulation, deforestation, pollution (air pollution, water pollution, soil contamination) and global warming or climate change, driven by human activity.

These factors, while all stemming from overpopulation, produce a cumulative impact upon biodiversity.

There are systematic relationships between the area of a habitat and the number of species it can support, with greater sensitivity to reduction in habitat area for species of larger body size and for those living at lower latitudes or in forests or oceans. Some characterize loss of biodiversity not as ecosystem degradation but by conversion to trivial standardized ecosystems (e.g., monoculture following deforestation). In some countries lack of property rights or access regulation to biotic resources necessarily leads to biodiversity loss (degradation costs having to be supported by the community).

A September 14, 2007 study conducted by the National Science Foundation found that biodiversity and genetic diversity are dependent upon each other—that diversity within a species is necessary to maintain diversity among species, and vice versa. According to the lead researcher in the study, Dr. Richard Lankau, "If any one type is removed from the system, the cycle can break down, and the community becomes dominated by a single species."

At present, the most threathened ecosystems are those found in fresh water. The marking of fresh water ecosystems as the ecosystems most under threat was done by the Millennium Ecosystem Assessment 2005, and was confirmed again by the project '*Freshwater Animal Diversity Assessment*', organised by the biodiversity platform, and the French Institut de recherche pour le dévelopement (MNHNP).

Exotic Species

The rich diversity of unique species across many parts of the world exist only because they are separated by barriers, particularly large rivers, seas, oceans, mountains and deserts from other species of other land masses, particularly the highly fecund, ultra-competitive, generalist 'super-species'. These are barriers that couldn't have been easily crossed by natural processes, except through continental drift. However, humans have invented transportation with the ability to bring into contact species that they've never met in their evolutionary history; also, this is done on a time scale of days, unlike the centuries that historically have accompanied major animal migrations. As these species that never met before come in contact with each other, the rate at which species are extincting is increasing still. See below for an example.

The widespread introduction of exotic species by humans is a potent threat to biodiversity. When exotic species are introduced to ecosystems and establish self-sustaining populations, the endemic species in that ecosystem that have not evolved to cope with the exotic species may not survive. The exotic organisms may be either predators, parasites, or simply aggressive species that deprive indigenous species of nutrients, water and light. These invasive species often have features, due to their evolutionary background and new environment, that make them highly competitive; able to become well-established and spread quickly, reducing the effective habitat of endemic species.

Exotic species are introduced by human, either unwillingly or intentionally. Examples on unwilling introduction are fore example ladybugs. ... These were bred to help in combating pests in agriculture (for greenhouses). Other examples of unwilling introduction are species that are unknowingly brought in by vessel or automotive. These include certain bacteria, spiders, seeds of certain plants. Examples of intentional introduction are the planting of exotic plants in gardens. It is clear that with simple measures the preventing of the spread of exotic plants, yet as of present, trying to reduce the inflow of exotic species has remained low on the political agenda. Also, the intentional planting of species that are marked as 'indigenous', yet are from a non-indigenous strain can be considered exotic and create problems in the ecosystem. For example in Belgium, Prunus spinosa (an indigenous species) that originates from Eastern Europe has been introduced. This has created problems, as the this tree species comes into leave much sooner than their West European counterparts, bringing the Thecla betulae butterfly (which feed on the leaves) into trouble.

As a consequence of the above, if humans continue to combine species from different ecoregions, there is the potential that the world's ecosystems will end up dominated by relatively a few, aggressive, cosmopolitan 'super-species'.

At present, several countries have already imported so much exotic species, that the own indigenous fauna/flora is greatly outnumbered. For example, in Belgium, only 5 per cent of the indigenous trees remain.

In 2004, an international team of scientists estimated that 10 per cent of species would become extinct by 2050 because of global warming. "We need to limit climate change or we wind up with a lot of species in trouble, possibly extinct," said Dr. Lee Hannah, a co-author of the paper and chief climate change biologist at the Center for Applied Biodiversity Science at Conservation International.

Purebred naturally evolved region specific wild species can be threatened with extinction through the process of genetic pollution i.e. uncontrolled hybridization, introgression and genetic swamping which leads to homogenization or replacement of local genotypes as a result of either a numerical and/or fitness advantage of introduced plant or animal. Non-native species can bring about a form of extinction of native plants and animals by hybridization and introgression either through purposeful introduction by humans or through habitat modification, bringing previously isolated species into contact. These phenomena can be especially detrimental for rare species coming into contact with more abundant ones. The abundant species can interbreed with the rarer, swamping the entire gene pool and creating hybrids, thus driving the entire native stock to complete extinction. Attention has to be focused on the extent of this under appreciated problem that is not always apparent from morphological (outward appearance) observations alone. Some degree of gene flow may be a normal, evolutionarily constructive, process, and all constellations of genes and genotypes cannot be preserved. However, hybridization with or without introgression may, nevertheless, threaten a rare species' existence.

Hybridization and Genetics

The Yecoro wheat (right) cultivar is sensitive to salinity, plants resulting from a hybrid cross with cultivar W4910 (left) show greater tolerance to high salinity.

In agriculture and animal husbandry, the green revolution popularized the use of conventional hybridization to increase yield by creating 'high-yielding varieties'. Often the handful of hybridized breeds originated in developed countries and were further hybridized with local varieties in the rest of the developing world to create high yield strains resistant to local climate and diseases. Local governments and industry have been pushing hybridization which has resulted in several of the indigenous breeds becoming extinct or threatened. Disuse because of unprofitability and uncontrolled intentional and unintentional cross-pollination and crossbreeding (genetic pollution), formerly huge gene pools of various wild and indigenous breeds have collapsed causing widespread genetic erosion and genetic pollution. This has resulted in loss of genetic diversity and biodiversity as a whole.

A genetically modified organism (GMO) is an organism whose genetic material has been altered using the genetic engineering techniques generally known as recombinant DNA technology. Genetically Modified (GM) crops today have become a common source for genetic pollution, not only of wild varieties but also of other domesticated varieties derived from relatively natural hybridization.

Genetic erosion coupled with genetic pollution may be destroying unique genotypes, thereby creating a hidden crisis which could result in a severe threat to our food security. Diverse genetic material could cease to exist which would impact our ability to further hybridize food crops and livestock against more resistant diseases and climatic changes.

Climate Change

The recent phenomenon of global warming is also considered to be a major threat to global biodiversity. For example coral reefs — which are biodiversity hotspots — will be lost in 20 to 40 years if global warming continues at the current trend.

Conservation biology matured in the mid- 20th century as ecologists, naturalists, and other scientists began to collectively research and address issues pertaining to global declines in biodiversity. The conservation ethic differs from the preservationist ethic, historically lead by John Muir, who advocate for protected areas devoid of human exploitation or interference for profit The conservation ethic advocates for wise stewardship and management of natural resource production for the purpose of protecting and sustaining biodiversity in species, ecosystems, the evolutionary process, and human culture and society. Conservation biologists are concerned with the trends in biodiversity being reported in this era, which has been labeled by science as the Holocene extinction period, also known as the sixth mass extinction. Rates of decline in biodiversity in this sixth mass extinction match or exceed rates of loss in the five previous mass extinction events recorded in the fossil record. Loss of biodiversity results in the loss of natural capital that supplies ecosystem goods and services. The economic value of 17 ecosystem services for the entire biosphere (calculated in 1997) has an estimated average value of US$ 33 trillion (10^{12}) per year!

A schematic image illustrating the relationship between biodiversity, ecosystem services, human well-being, and poverty. The illustration shows where conservation action, strategies and plans can influence the drivers of the current biodiversity crisis at local, regional, to global scales.

In response to the extinction crisis, the research of conservation biologists is being organized into strategic plans that include principles, guidelines, and tools for the purpose of protecting biodiversity. Conservation biology is a crisis orientated discipline and it is multi-disciplinary, including ecological, social, education, and other scientific disciplines outside of biology. Conservation biologists work in both the field and office, in government, universities, non-profit organizations and in industry. The conservation of biological diversity is a global priority in strategic conservation plans that are designed to engage public policy and concerns affecting local, regional and global scales of communities, ecosystems, and cultures. Conserving biodiversity and action plans identify ways of sustaining human well-being and global economics, including natural capital, market capital, and ecosystem services.

One of the strategies involves placing a monetary value on biodiversity through biodiversity banking, of which one example is the Australian Native Vegetation Management Framework. Other approaches are the creation of gene banks, as well as the creation of gene banks that have the intention of growing the indigenous species for reintroduction to the ecosystem (eg via tree nurseries, ...) The eradication of exotic species is also an important method to preserve the local biodiversity. Exotic species that have become a pest can be identified using taxonomy (eg with DAISY, barcode of life, ...) and can then be eradicated. This method however can only be used against a large group of a certain exotic organism due to the econimic cost. Other measures contributing to the preservation of biodiversity include: the reduction of pesticide use and/or a switching to organic pesticides. ... These measures however, are of less importance than the preserving of rural lands, reintroduction of indigenous species and the removal of exotic species. Finally, if the continued preservation of native organisms in an area can be guaranteed, efforts can be made in trying to reintroduce eliminated native species back into the environment. This can be done by first determining which species were indigenous to the area, and then reintroducing them. This determination can be done using databases as the Encyclopedia of life, Global Biodiversity Information Facility. ... Extermination is usually done with either (ecological) pesticides, or natural predators.

Strategies

As noted above (Distribution), biodiversity is not as rich everywhere on the planet. Regions as the tropics and subtropics are considerably much richer in biodiversity than regions in temperate climates. In addition, in temperate climates, a lot of countries are located which are already vastly urbanised, and require -in addition- great amounts of space for the growing of crops. As rehabilitating the biodiversity within these countries would again require the clearing and redeveloping of spaces, it has been proposed of some that efforts are best instead directed unto the tropics. Arguments include economics, it would be far less costly and more efficient to preserve the biodiversity in the tropics, especially as many countries in these areas are only now beginning to urbanise.

However, only directing the efforts into these areas would not be enough, as many species still need to migrate at certain times of the year, requiring a connection to other regions/countries. In the more urbanised countries in temperate climates, this would mean that wildlife corridors need to be made. However, making wildlife corridors would still be considerably cheaper and easier than clearing/ preserving entirely new areas.

Judicial Status

A great deal of work is occurring to preserve the natural characteristics of Hopetoun Falls, Australia while continuing to allow visitor access.

Biodiversity is beginning to be evaluated and its evolution analysed (through observations, inventories, conservation...) as well as being taken into account in political and judicial decisions:

The relationship between law and ecosystems is very ancient and has consequences for biodiversity. It is related to property rights, both private and public. It can define protection for threatened ecosystems, but also some rights and duties (for example, fishing rights, hunting rights).

Law regarding species is a more recent issue. It defines species that must be protected because they may be threatened by extinction. The U.S. Endangered Species Act is an example of an attempt to address the 'law and species' issue.

Laws regarding gene pools are only about a century old. While the genetic approach is not new (domestication, plant traditional selection methods), progress made in the genetic field in the past 20 years have led to a tightening of laws in this field. With the new technologies of genetic analysis and genetic engineering, people are going through gene patenting, processes patenting, and a totally new concept of genetic resources. A very hot debate today seeks to define whether the resource is the gene, the organism itself, or its DNA.

The 1972 UNESCO World Heritage convention established that biological resources, such as plants, were the common heritage of mankind. These rules probably inspired the creation of great public banks of genetic resources, located outside the source-countries.

New global agreements (e.g.Convention on Biological Diversity), now give sovereign national rights over biological resources (not property). The idea of static conservation of biodiversity is disappearing and being replaced by the idea of dynamic conservation, through the notion of resource and innovation.

The new agreements commit countries to conserve biodiversity, develop resources for sustainability and share the benefits resulting from their use. Under new rules, it is expected that bioprospecting or collection of natural products has to be allowed by the biodiversity-rich country, in exchange for a share of the benefits.

Sovereignty principles can rely upon what is better known as Access and Benefit Sharing Agreements (ABAs). The Convention on Biodiversity spirit implies a prior informed consent between the source country and the collector, to establish which resource will be used and for what, and to settle on a fair agreement on benefit sharing. Bioprospecting can become a type of biopiracy when those principles are not respected.

Uniform approval for use of biodiversity as a legal standard has not been achieved, however. At least one legal commentator has argued that biodiversity should not be used as a legal standard, arguing that the multiple layers of scientific uncertainty inherent in the concept of biodiversity will cause administrative waste and increase litigation without promoting preservation goals.

Taxonomic and Size Bias

Less than one per cent of all species that have been described have been studied beyond simply noting their existence. Biodiversity researcher Sean Nee points out that the vast majority of Earth's biodiversity is microbial, and that contemporary biodiversity physics is 'firmly fixated on the visible world' (Nee uses 'visible' as a synonym for macroscopic). For example, microbial life is very much more metabolically and environmentally diverse than multicellular life. Nee has stated: "On the tree of life, based on analyses of small-subunit ribosomal RNA, visible life consists of barely noticeable twigs.

The size bias is not restricted to consideration of microbes. Entomologist Nigel Stork states that "to a first approximation, all multicellular species on Earth are insects". Even in insects, however, the extinction rate is high and indicative of the general trend of the sixth greatest extinction period that human society is faced with. Moreover, there are species co-extinctions, such as plants and beetles, where the extinction or decline in one is reciprocated in the other.

3 Species

In biology, a species is:

- a taxonomic rank (the basic rank of biological classification); or
- a unit at that rank (in which case the *plural* is 'species'. This is sometimes abbreviated: 'spec.' or 'sp.' *singular*, or 'spp.' *plural*).

There are many definitions of what kind of unit a species is (or should be). A common definition is that of a group of organisms capable of interbreeding and producing fertile offspring of both genders, and separated from other such groups with which interbreeding does not (normally) happen. Other definitions may focus on similarity of DNA or morphology. Some species are further subdivided into subspecies, and here also there is no close agreement on the criteria to be used.

Biologists' Working Definition

A usable definition of the word 'species' and reliable methods of identifying particular species is essential for stating and testing biological theories and for measuring biodiversity. Traditionally, multiple examples of a proposed species must be studied for unifying characters before it can be regarded as a species. It is generally difficult to give precise taxonomic rankings to extinct species known only from fossils.

Some biologists may view species as statistical phenomena, as opposed to the traditional idea, with a species seen as a class of organisms. In that case, a species is defined as a separately evolving lineage that forms a single gene pool. Although properties such as DNA-sequences and morphology are used to help separate closely-related lineages, this definition has fuzzy boundaries. However, the exact definition of the term "species" is still controversial, particularly in prokaryotes, and this is called the species problem. Biologists have proposed a range of more precise definitions, but the definition used is a pragmatic choice that depends on the particularities of the species concerned.

Common Names and Species

The commonly used names for plant and animal taxa sometimes correspond to species: for example, 'lion', 'walrus', and 'Camphor tree' — each refers to a species. In other cases common names do not: for example, 'deer' refers to a family of 34 species, including Eld's Deer, Red Deer and Elk (Wapiti). The last two species were once considered a single species, illustrating how species boundaries may change with increased scientific knowledge.

Because of the difficulties with both defining and tallying the total numbers of different species in the world, it is estimated that there are anywhere between 2 and 100 million different species.

Placement within Genera

Ideally, a species is given a formal, scientific name, although in practice there are very many unnamed species (which have only been described, not named). When a species is named, it is placed within a genus. From a scientific point of view this can be regarded as a hypothesis that the species is more closely related to other species within its genus (if any) than to species of other genera. A genus is commonly included in a hierarchy, with as the best-known taxonomic ranks: life, domain, kingdom, phylum, class, order, family, genus, and species. This assignment to a genus is not immutable; later a different (or the same) taxonomist may assign it to a different genus, in which case the name will also change.

In biological nomenclature, the name for a species is a two-part name (a binomial name), treated as Latin, although roots from any language can be used as well as names of locales or individuals. The generic name is listed first (with its leading letter capitalized), followed by a second term, the specific name (or specific epithet). For example, the species commonly known as the Longleaf Pine is *Pinus palustris*; gray wolves belong to the species *Canis lupus*, coyotes to *Canis latrans*, golden jackals to *Canis aureus*, etc., and all of those belong to the genus *Canis* (which also contains many other species). The name of the species is the whole binomial, not just the second term (which may be called the specific name for animals).

This binomial naming convention, later formalized in the biological codes of nomenclature, was first used by Leonhart Fuchs and introduced as the standard by Carolus Linnaeus in his 1753, *Species Plantarum* (followed by his, 1758 *Systema Naturae*, 10th edition). At that time, the chief biological theory was that species represented independent acts of creation by God and were therefore considered objectively real and immutable, so the hypothesis of common descent did not apply.

Abbreviated Names

Books and articles sometimes intentionally do not identify species fully and use the abbreviation 'sp.' in the singular or 'spp.' in the plural in place of the specific epithet: for example, *Canis* sp. This commonly occurs in the following types of situations:

- The authors are confident that some individuals belong to a particular genus but are not sure to which exact species they belong. This is particularly common in paleontology.
- The authors use 'spp.' as a short way of saying that something applies to many species within a genus, but do not wish to say that it applies to all species within that genus. If scientists mean that something applies to all species within a genus, they use the genus name without the specific epithet.

In books and articles, genus and species names are usually printed in italics. If using 'sp.' and 'spp.', these should not be italicized.

It is surprisingly difficult to define the word 'species' in a way that applies to all naturally occurring organisms, and the debate among biologists about how to define 'species' and how to identify actual species is called the species problem.

Most textbooks follow Ernst Mayr's definition of a species as "groups of actually or potentially interbreeding natural populations, which are reproductively isolated from other such groups".

Various parts of this definition serve to exclude some unusual or artificial matings:

- Those which occur only in captivity (when the animal's normal mating partners may not be available) or as a result of deliberate human action.
- Animals which may be physically and physiologically capable of mating but do not normally do so in the wild, for various reasons.

The typical textbook definition above works well for most multi-celled organisms, but there are several types of situations in which it breaks down:

- By definition it applies only to organisms that reproduce sexually. So it does not work for asexually reproducing single-celled organisms and for the relatively few parthenogenetic multi-celled organisms. The term 'phylotype' is often applied to such organisms.

Biologists frequently do not know whether two morphologically similar groups of organisms are 'potentially' capable of interbreeding.

There is considerable variation in the degree to which hybridization may succeed under natural conditions, or even in the degree to which some organisms use sexual reproduction between individuals to breed.

In ring species, members of adjacent populations interbreed successfully but members of some non-adjacent populations do not.

In a few cases it may be physically impossible for animals that are members of the same species to mate. However, these are cases in which human intervention has caused gross morphological changes, and are therefore excluded by the biological species concept.

Horizontal gene transfer makes it even more difficult to define the word 'species'. There is strong evidence of horizontal gene transfer between very dissimilar groups of prokaryotes, and at least occasionally between dissimilar groups of eukaryotes; and Williamson argues that there is evidence for it in some crustaceans and echinoderms. All definitions of the word 'species' assume that an organism gets all its genes from one or two parents which are very like that organism, but horizontal gene transfer makes that assumption false.

Definitions of Species

The question of how best to define 'species' is one that has occupied biologists for centuries, and the debate itself has become known as the species problem.

No one definition has satisfied all naturalists; yet every naturalist knows vaguely what he means when he speaks of a species. Generally the term includes the unknown element of a distinct act of creation.

But later, in *The Descent of Man*, when addressing "The question whether mankind consists of one or several species", Darwin revised his opinion to say:

> It is a hopeless endeavour to decide this point on sound grounds, until some definition of the term 'species' is generally accepted; and the definition must not include an element which cannot possibly be ascertained, such as an act of creation.

The modern theory of evolution depends on a fundamental redefinition of 'species'. Prior to Darwin, naturalists viewed species as ideal or general types, which could be exemplified by an ideal specimen bearing all the traits general to the species. Darwin's theories shifted attention from uniformity to variation and from the general to the particular. According to intellectual historian Louis Menand.

Once our attention is redirected to the individual, we need another way of making generalizations. We are no longer interested in the conformity of an individual to an ideal type; we are now interested in the relation of an individual to the other individuals with which it interacts. To generalize about groups of interacting individuals, we need to drop the language of types and essences, which is prescriptive (telling us what finches should be), and adopt the language of statistics and probability, which is predictive (telling us what the average finch, under specified conditions, is likely to do). Relations will be more important than categories; functions, which are variable, will be more important than purposes; transitions will be more important than boundaries; sequences will be more important than hierarchies.

This shift results in a new approach to 'species'; Darwin concluded that species are what they appear to be: ideas, which are provisionally useful for naming groups of interacting individuals. 'I look at the term species', he wrote, "as one arbitrarily given for the sake of convenience to a set of individuals closely resembling each other. ... It does not essentially differ from the word variety, which is given to less distinct and more fluctuating forms. The term variety, again, in comparison with mere individual differences, is also applied arbitrarily, and for convenience sake."

Practically, biologists define species as *populations of organisms that have a high level of genetic similarity.* This may reflect an adaptation to the same niche, and the transfer of genetic material from one individual to others, through a variety of possible means. The exact level of similarity used in such a definition is arbitrary, but this is the most common definition used for organisms that reproduce asexually (asexual reproduction), such as some plants and microorganisms.

This lack of any clear species concept in microbiology has led to some authors arguing that the term 'species' is not useful when studying bacterial evolution. Instead they see genes as moving freely between even distantly-related bacteria, with the entire bacterial domain being a single gene pool. Nevertheless, a kind of rule of thumb has been established, saying that species of *Bacteria* or *Archaea* with 16S rRNA gene sequences more similar than 97 per cent to each other need to be checked by DNA-DNA Hybridization if they belong to the same species or not. This concept has been updated recently, saying that the border of 97 per cent was too low and can be raised to 98.7 per cent.

In the study of sexually reproducing organisms, where genetic material is shared through the process of reproduction, the ability of two organisms to interbreed and produce fertile offspring of both genders is generally accepted as a simple indicator that the organisms share enough genes to be considered members of the same species. Thus a 'species' is a group of interbreeding organisms.

This definition can be extended to say that a species is a group of organisms that could potentially interbreed — fish could still be classed as the same species even if they live in different lakes, as long as they could still interbreed were they ever to come into contact with each other. On the other hand, there are many examples of series of three or more distinct populations, where individuals of the population in the middle can interbreed with the populations to either side, but individuals of the populations on either side cannot interbreed. Thus, one could argue that these populations constitute a single species, or two distinct species. This is not a paradox; it is evidence that species are defined by gene frequencies, and thus have fuzzy boundaries.

Consequently, any single, universal definition of 'species' is necessarily arbitrary. Instead, biologists have proposed a range of definitions; which definition a biologists uses is a pragmatic choice, depending on the particularities of that biologist's research.

Typological Species

A group of organisms in which individuals are members of the species if they sufficiently conform to certain fixed properties. The clusters of variations or phenotypes within specimens (i.e. longer and shorter tails) would differentiate the species. This method was used as a 'classical' method of determining species, such as with Linnaeus early in evolutionary theory. However, we now know that different phenotypes do not always constitute different species (e.g.: a 4-winged Drosophila born to a 2-winged mother is not a different species). Species named in this manner are called *morphospecies.*

Morphological Species

A population or group of populations that differs morphologically from other populations. For example, we can distinguish between a chicken and a duck because they have different shaped bills and the duck has webbed feet. Species have been defined in this way since well before the beginning of recorded history. This species concept is much criticised because more recent genetic data reveal that genetically distinct populations may look very similar and, contrarily, large morphological differences sometimes exist between very closely-related populations. Nonetheless, most species known have been described solely from morphology.

Biological/Isolation Species

A set of actually or potentially interbreeding populations. This is generally a useful formulation for scientists working with living examples of the higher taxa like mammals, fish, and birds, but more problematic for organisms that do not reproduce sexually. The results of breeding experiments done in artificial conditions may or may not reflect what would happen if the same organisms encountered each other in the wild, making it difficult to gauge whether or not the results of such experiments are meaningful in reference to natural populations.

Biological/Reproductive Species

Two organisms that are able to reproduce naturally to produce fertile offspring of both genders. Organisms that can reproduce but almost always make infertile hybrids of at least one gender, such as a mule, hinny or F1 male cattalo are not considered to be the same species.

Recognition Species

It is based on shared reproductive systems, including mating behaviour. The Recognition concept of species has been introduced by Hugh E. H. Paterson.

Mate-recognition Species

A group of organisms that are known to recognize one another as potential mates. Like the isolation species concept above, it applies only to organisms that reproduce sexually. Unlike the isolation species concept, it focuses specifically on pre-mating reproductive isolation.

Evolutionary/Darwinian Species

A group of organisms that shares an ancestor; a lineage that maintains its integrity with respect to other lineages through both time and space. At some point in the progress of such a group, some members may diverge from the main population and evolve into a subspecies, a process that eventually will lead to the formation of a new full species if isolation (geographical or ecological) is maintained.

Phylogenetic (Cladistic)

A group of organisms that shares an ancestor; a lineage that maintains its integrity with respect to other lineages through both time and space. At some point in the progress of such a group, members may diverge from one another: when such a divergence becomes sufficiently clear, the two populations are regarded as separate species. This differs from evolutionary species in that the parent species goes extinct taxonomically when a new species evolve, the mother and daughter populations now forming two new species. Subspecies as such are not recognized under this approach; either a population is a phylogenetic species or it is not taxonomically distinguishable.

Ecological Species

A set of organisms adapted to a particular set of resources, called a niche, in the environment. According to this concept, populations form the discrete phenetic clusters that we recognize as species because the ecological and evolutionary processes controlling how resources are divided up tend to produce those clusters.

Genetic Species

It is based on similarity of DNA of individuals or populations. Techniques to compare similarity of DNA include DNA-DNA hybridization, and genetic fingerprinting (or DNA barcoding).

Phenetic Species

It is based on phenotypes.

Microspecies

Species that reproduce without meiosis or fertilization so that each generation is genetically identical to the previous generation. See also apomixis.

Cohesion Species

Most inclusive population of individuals having the potential for phenotypic cohesion through intrinsic cohesion mechanisms. This is an expansion of the mate-recognition species concept to allow for post-mating isolation mechanisms; no matter whether populations can hybridize successfully, they are still distinct cohesion species if the amount of hybridization is insufficient to completely mix their respective gene pools.

Evolutionarily Significant Unit (ESU)

An evolutionarily significant unit is a population of organisms that is considered distinct for purposes of conservation. Often referred to as a species or a *wildlife species*, an ESU also has several possible definitions, which coincide with definitions of species.

In practice, these definitions often coincide, and the differences between them are more a matter of emphasis than of outright contradiction. Nevertheless, no species concept yet proposed is entirely objective, or can be applied in all cases without resorting to judgment. Given the complexity of life, some have argued that such an objective definition is in all likelihood impossible, and biologists should settle for the most practical definition.

For most vertebrates, this is the biological species concept (BSC), and to a lesser extent (or for different purposes) the phylogenetic species concept (PSC). Many BSC subspecies are considered species under the PSC; the difference between the BSC and the PSC can be summed up insofar as that the BSC defines a species as a consequence of manifest evolutionary *history*, while the PSC defines a species as a consequence of manifest evolutionary *potential*. Thus, a PSC species is 'made' as soon as an evolutionary lineage has started to separate, while a BSC species starts to exist only when the lineage separation is complete. Accordingly, there can be considerable conflict between alternative classifications based upon the PSC versus BSC, as they differ completely in their treatment of taxa that would be considered subspecies under the latter model (e.g., the numerous subspecies of honey bees)

Life Support Species: Many species display distinct adaptations to environmental extreme, as they are able to grow and reproduce under such conditions as drought, desertification, flood, soil toxicity, soil sailinity among them a number already provide source of food, materials and energy to humans, livestock and other animals, are of considerable potential benefit to man. and these are known as Life support species. As such they mutually include keystone species since these hold the key to the integrity of landscapes which include both the diversity of living biota and the human communities. Both ecological and socio-economic species are Life support species.

Numbers of Species

Bearing in mind the aforementioned problems with categorising species, the following numbers are only a soft guide. In 2007, they broke down as follows:

Total number of species (estimated): 7–100 millions (identified and unidentified), including:

- 5-10 million bacteria

- 74,000-1,20,000 fungi

Of the *identified* eukaryote species we have:

- 1.6 million

2,97,326 plants, including:

- 15,000 mosses
- 13,025 Ferns and horsetails
- 980 gymnosperms
- 2,58,650 angiosperms
- 1,99,350 dicotyledons
- 59,300 monocotyledons
- 9,671 Red and green algae

28,849 fungi and other non-animals, including:

- 10,000 lichens
- 16,000 mushrooms
- 2,849 brown algae

12,50,000 animals, including:

- 1,203,375 invertebrates
- 9,50,000 insects
- 81,000 mollusks
- 40,000 crustaceans
- 2,175 corals
- 1,30,200 others
- 59,811 vertebrates
- 29,300 fish
- 6,199 amphibians
- 8,240 reptiles
- 9,956 birds
- 5,416 mammals.

At present, organisations such as the Global Taxonomy Initiative, the European Distributed Institute of Taxonomy and the Census of Marine Life (the latter only for marine organisms) are trying to improve taxonomy and implement previously undiscovered species to the taxonomy system. Due to the fact that we know but a portion of the organisms in the biosphere, we do not have a complete understanding of the workings of our environment. To make matters worse, despite the discovery of new species, according to professor James Mallet, we are wiping out these species at an unprecedented rate .This means that even before a new species has had the chance of being studied and classified, it may already be extinct.

Importance in Biological Classification

The idea of *species* has a long history. It is one of the most important levels of classification, for several reasons:

- It often corresponds to what lay people treat as the different basic kinds of organism — dogs are one species, cats another.
- It is the standard binomial nomenclature (or trinomial nomenclature) by which scientists typically refer to organisms.
- It is the highest taxonomic level which mostly cannot be made more or less inclusionary.

After years of use, the concept remains central to biology and a host of related fields, and yet also remains at times ill-defined.

Implications of Assignment of Species Status

The naming of a particular species should be regarded as a *hypothesis* about the evolutionary relationships and distinguishability of that group of organisms. As further information comes to hand, the hypothesis may be confirmed or refuted. Sometimes, especially in the past when communication was more difficult, taxonomists working in isolation have given two distinct names to individual organisms later identified as the same species. When two named species are discovered to be of the same species, the older species name is usually retained, and the newer species name dropped, a process called *synonymization*, or colloquially, as lumping. Dividing a taxon into multiple, often new, taxons is called splitting. Taxonomists are often referred to as 'lumpers' or 'splitters' by their colleagues, depending on their personal approach to recognizing differences or commonalities between organisms (see lumpers and splitters).

Traditionally, researchers relied on observations of anatomical differences, and on observations of whether different populations were able to interbreed successfully, to distinguish species; both anatomy and breeding behaviour are still important to assigning species status. As a result of the revolutionary (and still ongoing) advance in microbiological research techniques, including DNA analysis, in the last few decades, a great deal of additional knowledge about the differences and similarities between species has become available. Many populations which were formerly regarded as separate species are now considered to be a single taxon, and many formerly grouped populations have been split. Any taxonomic level (species, genus, family, etc.) can be synonymized or split, and at higher taxonomic levels, these revisions have been still more profound.

From a taxonomical point of view, groups within a species can be defined as being of a taxon hierarchically lower than a species. In zoology only the subspecies is used, while in botany the variety, subvariety, and form are used as well. In conservation biology, the concept of evolutionary significant units (ESU) is used, which may be define either species or smaller distinct population segments.

The Isolation Species Concept in more detail

In general, for large, complex organisms that reproduce sexually (such as mammals and birds), one of several variations on the *isolation* or *biological* species concept is employed. Often, the distinction between different species, even quite closely related ones, is simple. Horses (*Equus caballus*) and donkeys (*Equus asinus*) are easily told apart even without study or training, and yet are so closely related that they can interbreed after a fashion. Because the result, a mule or hinny, is not fertile, they are clearly separate species.

But many cases are more difficult to decide. This is where the isolation species concept diverges from the evolutionary species concept. Both agree that a species is a lineage that maintains its integrity over time, that is diagnosably different from other lineages (else we could not recognise it), is reproductively isolated (else the lineage would merge into others, given the chance to do so), and has a working intra-species recognition system (without which it could not continue). In practice, both also agree that a species must have its own independent evolutionary history—otherwise the characteristics just mentioned would not apply. The species concepts differ in that the evolutionary species concept does not make predictions about the future of the population: it simply records that which is already known. In contrast, the isolation species concept refuses to assign the rank of species to populations that, in the best judgement of the researcher, would recombine with other populations if given the chance to do so.

The Isolation Question

There are, essentially, two questions to resolve. First, is the proposed species consistently and reliably distinguishable from other species? Second, is it likely to remain so in the future? To take the second question first, there are several broad geographic possibilities.

The proposed species are sympatric—they occupy the same habitat. Observation of many species over the years has failed to establish even a single instance of two diagnostically different populations that exist in sympatry and have then merged to form one united population. Without reproductive isolation, population differences cannot develop, and given reproductive isolation, gene flow between the populations cannot merge the differences. This is not to say that cross breeding does not take place at all, simply that it has become negligible. Generally, the hybrid individuals are less capable of successful breeding than pure-bred individuals of either species.

The proposed species are allopatric—they occupy different geographical areas. Obviously, it is not possible to observe reproductive isolation in allopatric groups directly. Often it is not possible to achieve certainty by experimental means either: even if the two proposed species interbreed in captivity, this does not demonstrate that they would freely interbreed in the wild, nor does it always provide much information about the evolutionary fitness of hybrid individuals. A certain amount can be inferred from other experimental methods: for example, do the members of population A respond appropriately to playback of the recorded mating calls of population B? Sometimes, experiments *can* provide firm answers. For example, there are seven pairs of apparently almost identical marine snapping shrimp (*Alpheus*) populations on either side of the Isthmus of Panama, which did not exist until about 3 million years ago. Until then, it is assumed, they were members of the same seven species. But when males and females from opposite sides of the isthmus are placed together, they fight instead of mating. Even if the isthmus were to sink under the waves again, the populations would remain genetically isolated: therefore they are now different species. In many cases, however, neither observation nor experiment can produce certain answers, and the determination of species rank must be made on a 'best guess' basis from a general knowledge of other related organisms.

The proposed species are parapatric—they have breeding ranges that abut but do not overlap. This is fairly rare, particularly in temperate regions. The dividing line is often a sudden change in habitat (an ecotone) like the edge of a forest or the snow line on a mountain, but can sometimes be remarkably trivial. The parapatry itself indicates that the two populations occupy such similar ecological roles that they cannot coexist in the same area. Because they do not crossbreed, it is safe to assume that there is a mechanism, often behavioral, that is preventing gene flow between the populations, and that therefore they should be classified as separate species.

There is a hybrid zone where the two populations mix. Typically, the hybrid zone will include representatives of one or both of the 'pure' populations, plus first-generation and back-crossing hybrids. The strength of the barrier to genetic transmission between the two pure groups can be assessed by the width of the hybrid zone relative to the typical dispersal distance of the organisms in question. The dispersal distance of oaks, for example, is the distance that a bird or squirrel can be expected to carry an acorn; the dispersal distance of Numbats is about 15 kilometres, as this is as far as young Numbats will normally travel in search of vacant territory to occupy after leaving the nest. The narrower the hybrid zone relative to the dispersal distance, the less gene flow there is between the population groups, and the more likely it is that they will continue on separate evolutionary paths. Nevertheless, it can be very difficult to predict the future course of a hybrid zone; the decision to define the two hybridizing populations as either the same species or as separate species is difficult and potentially controversial.

The variation in the population is clinal, at either extreme of the population's geographic distribution, typical individuals are clearly different, but the transition between them is seamless and gradual. For example, the Koalas of northern Australia are clearly smaller and lighter in colour than those of the south, but there is no particular dividing line: the further south an individual Koala is found, the larger and darker it is likely to be; Koalas in intermediate regions are intermediate in weight and colour. In contrast, over the same geographic range, black-backed (northern) and white-backed (southern) Australian Magpies do not blend from one type to another: northern populations have black backs, southern populations white backs, and there is an extensive hybrid zone where both 'pure' types are common, as are crossbreeds. The variation in Koalas is clinal (a smooth transition from north to south, with populations in any given small area having a uniform appearance), but the variation in magpies is *not* clinal. In both cases, there is some uncertainty regarding correct classification, but the consensus view is that species rank is not justified in either. The gene flow between northern and southern magpie populations is judged to be sufficiently restricted to justify terming them subspecies (not full species); but the seamless way that local Koala populations blend one into another shows that there is substantial gene flow between north and south. As a result, experts tend to reject even subspecies rank in this case.

The Difference Question

Obviously when defining a species, the geographic circumstances become meaningful only if the population groups in question are clearly different: if they are not consistently and reliably distinguishable from one another, then we have no grounds for believing that they might be different species. The key question in this context, is 'how different is different?' and the answer is usually 'it all depends'.

In theory, it would be possible to recognise even the tiniest of differences as sufficient to delineate a separate species, provided only that the difference is clear and consistent (and that other criteria are met). There is no universal rule to state the smallest allowable difference between two species, but in general, very trivial differences are ignored on the twin grounds of simple practicality, and genetic similarity: if two population groups are so close that the distinction between them rests on an obscure and microscopic difference in morphology, or a single base substitution in a DNA sequence, then a demonstration of restricted gene flow between the populations will probably be difficult in any case.

More typically, one or other of the following requirements must be met:

- It is possible to reliably measure a *quantitative* difference between the two groups that *does not overlap.* A population has, for example, thicker fur, rougher bark, longer ears, or larger seeds than another population, and although this characteristic may vary within each population, the two do not grade into one another, and given a reasonably large sample size, there is a definite discontinuity between them. Note that this applies to *populations*, not individual organisms, and that a small number of exceptional individuals within a population may 'break the rule' without invalidating it. The less a quantitative difference varies *within* a population and the more it varies *between* populations, the better the case for making a distinction. Nevertheless, borderline situations can only be resolved by making a 'best-guess' judgement.
- It is possible to distinguish a *qualitative* difference between the populations; a feature that does not vary continuously but is either entirely present or entirely absent. This might be a distinctively shaped seed pod, an extra primary feather, a particular courting behaviour, or a clearly different DNA sequence.

Sometimes it is not possible to isolate a single difference between species, and several factors must be taken in combination. This is often the case with plants in particular.

In eucalypts, for example, *Corymbia ficifolia* cannot be reliably distinguished from its close relative *Corymbia calophylla* by any single measure (and sometimes individual trees cannot be definitely assigned to either species), but populations of *Corymbia* can be clearly told apart by comparing the colour of flowers, bark, and buds, number of flowers for a given size of tree, and the shape of the leaves and fruit.

When using a combination of characteristics to distinguish between populations, it is necessary to use a reasonably small number of factors (if more than a handful are needed, the genetic difference between the populations is likely to be insignificant and is unlikely to endure into the future), and to choose factors that are functionally independent (height and weight, for example, should usually be considered as one factor, not two).

Historical Development of the Species Concept

In the earliest works of science, a species was simply an individual organism that represented a group of similar or nearly identical organisms. No other relationships beyond that group were implied. Aristotle used the words *genus* and *species* to mean generic and specific categories. Aristotle and other pre-Darwinian scientists took the species to be distinct and unchanging, with an 'essence', like the chemical elements. When early observers began to develop systems of organization for living things, they began to place formerly isolated species into a context. Many of these early delineation schemes would now be considered whimsical and these included consanguinity based on colour (all plants with yellow flowers) or behaviour (snakes, scorpions and certain biting ants).

In the 18th century swedish scientist Carolus Linnaeus classified organisms according to differences in the form of reproductive apparatus. Although his system of classification sorts organisms according to degrees of similarity, it made no claims about the relationship between similar species. At that time, it was still widely believed that there was no organic connection between species, no matter how similar they appeared. This approach also suggested a type of idealism: the notion that each species existed as an 'ideal form'. Although there are always differences (although sometimes minute) between individual organisms, Linnaeus considered such variation problematic. He strove to identify individual organisms that were exemplary of the species, and considered other non-exemplary organisms to be deviant and imperfect.

By the 19th century most naturalists understood that species could change form over time, and that the history of the planet provided enough time for major changes. Jean-Baptiste Lamarck, in his 1809 *Zoological Philosophy*, offered one of the first logical arguments against creationism. The new emphasis was on determining *how* a species could change over time. Lamarck suggested that an organism could pass on an acquired trait to its offspring, i.e., the giraffe's long neck was attributed to generations of giraffes stretching to reach the leaves of higher treetops (this well-known and simplistic example, however, does not do justice to the breadth and subtlety of Lamarck's ideas). With the acceptance of the natural selection idea of Charles Darwin in the 1860s, however, Lamarck's view of goal-oriented evolution, also known as a teleological process, was eclipsed. Recent interest in inheritance of acquired characteristics centers around epigenetic processes, e.g. methylation, that do not affect DNA sequences, but instead alter expression in an inheritable manner. Thus, neo-lamarckism, as it is sometimes termed, is not a challenge to the theory of evolution by natural selection.

Charles Darwin and Alfred Wallace provided what scientists now consider as the most powerful and compelling theory of evolution. Darwin argued that it was populations that evolved, not individuals. His argument relied on a radical shift in perspective from that of Linnaeus: rather than defining species in ideal terms (and searching for an ideal representative and rejecting deviations), Darwin considered variation among individuals to be natural. He further argued that variation, far from being problematic, actually provides the *explanation* for the existence of distinct species.

Darwin's work drew on Thomas Malthus' insight that the rate of growth of a biological population will always outpace the rate of growth of the resources in the environment, such as the food supply. As a result, Darwin argued, not all the members of a population will be able to survive and reproduce. Those that did will, on average, be the ones possessing variations—however slight—that make them slightly better adapted to the environment. If these variable traits are heritable, then the offspring of the survivors will also possess them. Thus, over many generations, adaptive variations will accumulate in the population, while counter-adaptive traits will tend to be eliminated.

It should be emphasized that whether a variation is adaptive or non-adaptive depends on the environment: different environments favour different traits. Since the environment effectively selects which organisms live to reproduce, it is the environment (the 'fight for existence') that selects the traits to be passed on. This is the theory of evolution by natural selection. In this model, the length of a giraffe's neck would be explained by positing that proto-giraffes with longer necks would have had a significant reproductive advantage to those with shorter necks. Over many generations, the entire population would be a species of long-necked animals.

In 1859, when Darwin published his theory of natural selection, the mechanism behind the inheritance of individual traits was unknown. Although Darwin made some speculations on how traits are inherited (pangenesis), his theory relies only on the fact that inheritable traits *exist*, and are variable (which makes his accomplishment even more remarkable.) Although Gregor Mendel's paper on genetics was published in 1866, its significance was not recognized. It was not until 1900 that his work was rediscovered by Hugo de Vries, Carl Correns and Erich von Tschermak, who realised that the 'inheritable traits' in Darwin's theory are genes.

The theory of the evolution of species through natural selection has two important implications for discussions of species–consequences that fundamentally challenge the assumptions behind Linnaeus' taxonomy. First, it suggests that species are not just similar, they may actually be related. Some students of Darwin argue that *all* species are descended from a common ancestor. Second, it supposes that 'species' are not homogeneous, fixed, permanent things; members of a species are all different, and over time species change. This suggests that species do not have any clear boundaries but are rather momentary statistical effects of constantly changing gene-frequencies. One may still use Linnaeus' taxonomy to identify individual plants and animals, but one can no longer think of species as independent and immutable.

The rise of a new species from a parental line is called speciation. There is no clear line demarcating the ancestral species from the descendant species.

Although the current scientific understanding of species suggests that there is no rigorous and comprehensive way to distinguish between different species in *all* cases, biologists continue to seek concrete ways to operationalize the idea. One of the most popular biological definitions of species is in terms of reproductive isolation; if two creatures cannot reproduce to produce fertile offspring of both genders, then they are in different species. This definition captures a number of intuitive species boundaries, but it remains imperfect. It has nothing to say about species that reproduce asexually, for example, and it is very difficult to apply to extinct species. Moreover, boundaries between species are often fuzzy: there are examples where members of one population can produce fertile offspring of both genders with a second population, and members of the second population can produce fertile offspring of both genders with members of a third population, but members of the first and third population cannot produce fertile offspring, or can only produce fertile offspring of the homozygous gender. Consequently, some people reject this definition of a species.

Richard Dawkins defines two organisms as conspecific if and only if they have the same number of chromosomes and, for each chromosome, both organisms have the same number of nucleotides. However, most if not all taxonomists would strongly disagree. For example, in many amphibians, most notably in New Zealand's *Leiopelma* frogs, the genome consists of 'core' chromosomes which are mostly invariable and accessory chromosomes, of which exist a number of possible combinations. Even though the chromosome numbers are highly variable between populations, these can interbreed successfully and form a single evolutionary unit. In plants, polyploidy is extremely commonplace with few restrictions on interbreeding; as individuals with an odd number of chromosome sets are usually sterile, depending on the actual number of chromosome sets present, this results in the odd situation where some individuals of the same evolutionary unit can interbreed with certain others and some cannot, with all populations being eventually linked as to form a common gene pool.

The classification of species has been profoundly affected by technological advances that have allowed researchers to determine relatedness based on molecular markers, starting with the comparatively crude blood plasma precipitation assays in the mid-20th century to Charles Sibley's ground-breaking DNA-DNA hybridization studies in the 1970s leading to DNA sequencing techniques. The results of these techniques caused revolutionary changes in the higher taxonomic categories (such as phyla and classes), resulting in the reordering of many branches of the phylogenetic tree. For taxonomic categories below genera, the results have been mixed so far; the pace of evolutionary change on the molecular level is rather slow, yielding clear differences only after considerable periods of reproductive separation. DNA-DNA hybridization results have led to misleading conclusions, the Pomarine Skua — Great Skua phenomenon being a famous example. Turtles have been determined to evolve with just one-eighth of the speed of other reptiles on the molecular level, and the rate of molecular evolution in albatrosses is half of what is found in the rather closely related storm-petrels. The hybridization technique is now obsolete and is replaced by more reliable computational approaches for sequence comparison. Molecular taxonomy is not directly based on the evolutionary processes, but rather on the overall change brought upon by these processes. The processes that lead to the generation and maintenance of variation such as mutation, crossover and selection are not uniform (see also molecular clock). DNA is only extremely rarely a direct target of natural selection rather than changes in the DNA sequence enduring over generations being a result of the latter; for example, silent transition-transversion combinations would alter the melting point of the DNA sequence, but not the sequence of the encoded proteins and thus are a possible example where, for example in microorganisms, a mutation confers a change in fitness all by itself.

4 Ecosystem

The term 'ecosystem' refers to the combined physical and biological components of an environment. An ecosystem is generally an area within the natural environment in which physical (abiotic) factors of the environment, such as rocks and soil, function together along with interdependent (biotic) organisms, such as plants and animals, within the same habitat. Ecosystems can be permanent or temporary. Ecosystems usually form a number of food webs.

Central to the ecosystem concept is the idea that living organisms interact with every other element in their local environment. Eugene Odum, a founder of ecology, stated: "Any unit that includes all of the organisms (ie: the 'community') in a given area interacting with the physical environment so that a flow of energy leads to clearly defined trophic structure, biotic diversity, and material cycles (ie: exchange of materials between living and non-living parts) within the system is an ecosystem." The human ecosystem concept is then grounded in the deconstruction of the human/nature dichotomy and the premise that all species are ecologically integrated with each other, as well as with the abiotic constituents of their biotope.

Etymology

The term ecosystem was coined in 1930 by Roy Clapham to mean the combined physical and biological components of an environment. British ecologist Arthur Tansley later refined the term, describing it as "The whole system,... including not only the organism-complex, but also the whole complex of physical factors forming what we call the environment". Tansley regarded ecosystems not simply as natural units, but as mental isolates. Tansley later defined the spatial extent of ecosystems using the term ecotope.

Biomes

Biomes are a classification of globally similar areas, including ecosystems, such as ecological communities of plants and animals, soil organisms and climatic conditions. Biomes are in part defined based on factors such as plant structures (such as trees, shrubs, and grasses), leaf types (such as broadleaf and needleleaf), plant spacing (forest, woodland, savanna), and climate. Unlike ecozones, biomes are not defined by genetic, taxonomic, or historical similarities. Biomes are often identified with particular patterns of ecological succession and climax vegetation.

A fundamental classification of biomes is:

- Terrestrial (land) biomes
- Freshwater biomes
- Marine biomes

Ecosystems have become particularly important politically, since the Convention on Biological Diversity (CBD) — ratified by 192 countries — defines "the protection of ecosystems, natural habitats and the maintenance of viable populations of species in natural surroundings" as a commitment of ratifying countries. This has created the political necessity to spatially identify ecosystems and somehow distinguish among them. The CBD defines an 'ecosystem' as a "dynamic complex of plant, animal and micro-organism communities and their non-living environment interacting as a functional unit".

With the need of protecting ecosystems, the political need arose to describe and identify them efficiently. Vreugdenhil et al. argued that this could be achieved most effectively by using a physiognomic-ecological classification system, as ecosystems are easily recognizable in the field as well as on satellite images. They argued that the structure and seasonality of the associated vegetation, complemented with ecological data (such as elevation, humidity, and drainage), are each determining modifiers that separate partially distinct sets of species. This is true not only for plant species, but also for species of animals, fungi and bacteria. The degree of ecosystem distinction is subject to the physiognomic modifiers that can be identified on an image and/or in the field. Where necessary, specific fauna elements can be added, such as seasonal concentrations of animals and the distribution of coral reefs.

Several physiognomic-ecological classification systems are available:

- Physiognomic-Ecological Classification of Plant Formations of the Earth: a system based on the 1974 work of Mueller-Dombois and Heinz Ellenberg and developed by UNESCO. This classificatie "describes the above-ground or underwater vegetation structures and cover as observed in the field, described as plant life forms. This classification is fundamentally a species—independent physiognomic, hierarchical vegetation classification system which also takes into account ecological factors such as climate, elevation, human influences such as grazing, hydric regimes, and survival strategies such as seasonality. The system was expanded with a basic classification for open water formations"

- Land Cover Classification System (LCCS), developed by the Food and Agriculture Organization (FAO).

Forest-Range Environmental Study Ecosystems (FRES) developed by the United States Forest Service for use in the United States.

Several aquatic classification systems are available, and an effort is being made by the United States Geological Survey (USGS) and the Inter-American Biodiversity Information Network (IABIN) to design a complete ecosystem classification system that will cover both terrestrial and aquatic ecosystems.

From a philosophy of science perspective, ecosystems are not discrete units of nature that simply can be identified using "the right" classification approach. In agreement with the definition by Tansley ('mental isolates'), any attempt to delineate or classify ecosystems should be explicit about the observer/analyst input in the classification including its normative rationale.

Two Giant Sequoias, Sequoia National Park. Note the large fire scar at the base of the right-hand tree; fires do not kill the trees but do remove competing thin-barked species, and aid Giant Sequoia regeneration.

Ecosystem Services

Ecosystem services are "fundamental life-support services upon which human civilization depends,"[i] and can be direct or indirect. Examples of direct ecosystem services are: pollination, wood, and erosion prevention. Indirect services could be considered climate moderation, nutrient cycles, and detoxifying natural substances.

The services and goods an ecosystem provides are often undervalued as many of them are without market value. Broad examples include:

- regulating (climate, floods, nutrient balance, water filtration)

- cultural (science, spiritual, ceremonial, recreation, aesthetic)
- supporting (nutrient cycling, photosynthesis, soil formation).

Ecuador's new constitution of 2008 is the first in the world to recognize legally enforceable Rights of Nature, or ecosystem rights.

The borough of Tamaqua, Pennsylvania passed a law giving ecosystems legal rights. The ordinance establishes that the municipal government or any Tamaqua resident can file a lawsuit on behalf of the local ecosystem. Other townships, such as Rush, followed suit and passed their own laws.

This is part of a growing body of legal opinion proposing 'wild law'. Wild law, a term coined by Cormac Cullinan (a lawyer based in South Africa), would cover birds and animals, rivers and deserts.

Function and Biodiversity

From an anthropocentric point of view, some people perceive ecosystems as production units that produce goods and services, such as wood by forest ecosystems and grass for cattle by natural grasslands. Meat from wild animals, often referred to as bush meat in Africa, has proven to be extremely successful under well-controlled management schemes in South Africa and Kenya. Much less successful has been the discovery and commercialization of substances of wild organism for pharmaceutical purposes. Services derived from ecosystems are referred to as ecosystem services. They may include:

1. facilitating the enjoyment of nature, which may generate many forms of income and employment in the tourism sector, often referred to as eco-tourisms;
2. water retention, thus facilitating a more evenly distributed release of water;

3. soil protection, open-air laboratory for scientific research, etc.

A greater degree of species or biological diversity — popularly referred to as Biodiversity — of an ecosystem may contribute to greater resilience of an ecosystem, because there are more species present at a location to respond to change and thus 'absorb' or reduce its effects. This reduces the effect before the ecosystem's structure is fundamentally changed to a different state. This is not universally the case and there is no proven relationship between the species diversity of an ecosystem and its ability to provide goods and services on a sustainable level: Humid tropical forests produce very few goods and direct services and are extremely vulnerable to change, while many temperate forests readily grow back to their previous state of development within a lifetime after felling or a forest fire. Some grasslands have been sustainably exploited for thousands of years (Mongolia, Africa, European peat and mooreland communities).

Introduction of new elements, whether biotic or abiotic, into an ecosystem tend to have a disruptive effect. In some cases, this can lead to ecological collapse or 'trophic cascading' and the death of many species within the ecosystem. Under this deterministic vision, the abstract notion of ecological health attempts to measure the robustness and recovery capacity for an ecosystem; i.e. how far the ecosystem is away from its steady state.

Often, however, ecosystems have the ability to rebound from a disruptive agent. The difference between collapse or a gentle rebound is determined by two factors—the toxicity of the introduced element and the resiliency of the original ecosystem.

Ecosystems are primarily governed by stochastic (chance) events, the reactions these events provoke on non-living materials, and the responses by organisms to the conditions surrounding them. Thus, an ecosystem results from the sum of individual responses of organisms to stimuli from elements in the environment. The presence or absence of populations merely depends on reproductive and dispersal success, and population levels fluctuate in response to stochastic events. As the number of species in an ecosystem is higher, the number of stimuli is also higher. Since the beginning of life organisms have survived continuous change through natural selection of successful feeding, reproductive and dispersal behavior. Through natural selection the planet's species have continuously adapted to change through variation in their biological composition and distribution. Mathematically it can be demonstrated that greater numbers of different interacting factors tend to dampen fluctuations in each of the individual factors.

Given the great diversity among organisms on earth, most ecosystems only changed very gradually, as some species would disappear while others would move in. Locally, sub-populations continuously go extinct, to be replaced later through dispersal of other sub-populations. Stochastists do recognize that certain intrinsic regulating mechanisms occur in nature. Feedback and response mechanisms at the species level regulate population levels, most notably through territorial behaviour. Andrewatha and Birch suggest that territorial behaviour tends to keep populations at levels where food supply is not a limiting factor. Hence, stochastists see territorial behaviour as a regulatory mechanism at the species level but not at the ecosystem level. Thus, in their vision, ecosystems are not regulated by feedback and response mechanisms from the (eco)system itself and there is no such thing as a balance of nature.

If ecosystems are governed primarily by stochastic processes, through which its subsequent state would be determined by both predictable and random actions, they may be more resilient to sudden change than each species individually. In the absence of a balance of nature, the species composition of ecosystems would undergo shifts that would depend on the nature of the change, but entire ecological collapse would probably be infrequent events.

The theoretical ecologist Robert Ulanowicz has used information theory tools to describe the structure of ecosystems, emphasizing mutual information (correlations) in studied systems. Drawing on this methodology and prior observations of complex ecosystems, Ulanowicz depicts approaches to determining the stress levels on ecosystems and predicting system reactions to defined types of alteration in their settings (such as increased or reduced energy flow, and eutrophication.

Ecosystem Ecology

Ecosystem ecology is the integrated study of biotic and abiotic components of ecosystems and their interactions within an ecosystem framework. This science examines how ecosystems work and relates this to their components such as chemicals, bedrock, soil, plants, and animals. Ecosystem ecology examines physical and biological structure and examines how these ecosystem characteristics interact.

5 Ecology

Ecology (from Greek:, 'house' or 'living relations'; - , 'study of') is the interdisciplinary scientific study of the distributions, abundance and relations of organisms and their interactions with the environment. Ecology is also the study of ecosystems. Ecosystems describe the web or network of relations among organisms at different scales of organization. Since ecology refers to any form of biodiversity, ecologists research everything from tiny bacteria's role in nutrient recycling to the effects of tropical rain forest on the Earth's atmosphere. The discipline of ecology emerged from the natural sciences in the late 19th century. Ecology is not synonymous with environment, environmentalism, or environmental science. Ecology is closely related to the disciplines of physiology, evolution, genetics and behaviour.

Like many of the natural sciences, a conceptual understanding of ecology is found in the broader details of study, including:

- life processes explaining adaptations;
- distribution and abundance of organisms;
- the movement of materials and energy through living communities;

- the successional development of ecosystems; and
- the abundance and distribution of biodiversity in context of the environment.

Ecology is distinguished from natural history, which deals primarily with the descriptive study of organisms. It is a sub-discipline of biology, which is the study of life.

There are many practical applications of ecology in conservation biology, wetland management, natural resource management (agriculture, forestry , fisheries), city planning (urban ecology), community health, economics, basic & applied science and it provides a conceptual framework for understanding and researching human social interaction (human ecology).

Because ecology deals with ever changing ecosystems, both time and space must be taken into account when describing ecological phenomena. In regards to time, it can take thousands of years for ecological processes to mature. The life-span of a tree, for example, can pass through different successional or seral stages leading to mature old-growth forests. The ecological process is extended even further through time as trees topple over and decay.

Ecosystems are also classified at different spatial scales: the area of an ecosystem can vary greatly from tiny to vast. For instance, several generations of an aphid population and their predators might exist on a single leaf. Inside each of those aphids exist diverse communities of bacteria. The scale of study must at times be quite large, when studying the life of the tree in the forest where bacteria and aphids live. To understand tree growth, for example, soil type, moisture content, slope of the land, forest canopy closure, and other local site variables must all be examined; to understand the ecology of the forest, complex global factors such as climate must be considered.

Long-term ecological studies provide important track records to better understand ecosystems over space and time. The International Long Term Ecological Network manages and exchanges scientific information among research sites. The longest experiment in existence is the Park Grass Experiment that was initiated in 1856. Another example includes the Hubbard Brook study in operation since 1960. Ecology is also complicated by the fact that small scale patterns do not necessarily explain large scale phenomena, otherwise captured in the expression 'the sum is greater than the parts'. These emergent phenomena operate at different environmental scales of influence, ranging from molecular to planetary scales, and require different sets of scientific explanation.

To structure the study of ecology into a manageable framework of understanding, the biological world is conceptually organized as a nested hierarchy of organization, ranging in scale from genes, to cells, to tissues, to organs, to organisms, to species and up to the level of the biosphere Ecosystems are primarily researched at (but not restricted to) three key levels of organization, including organisms, populations, and communities. Ecologists study ecosystems by sampling a certain number of individuals that are representative of a population. Ecosystems consist of communities interacting with each other and the environment. In ecology, communities are created by the interaction of the populations of different species in an area.

Biodiversity is an attribute of a site or area that consists of the variety within and among biotic communities, whether influenced by humans or not, at any spatial scale from microsites and habitat patches to the entire biosphere.

Biodiversity (an amalgamation of the words biological diversity) describes all varieties of life from genes to ecosystems and spans every level of biological organization. There are many ways to index, measure, and represent biodiversity. Biodiversity includes species diversity, ecosystem diversity, genetic diversity and the complex processes operating at and among these respective levels. Biodiversity plays an important role in ecological health as much as it does for human health. Preventing or prioritizing species extinctions is one way to preserve biodiversity, but populations, the genetic diversity within them and ecological processes, such as migration, are being threatened on global scales and disappearing rapidly as well. Conservation priorities and management techniques require different approaches and considerations to address the full ecological scope of biodiversity. Populations and species migration, for example, are more sensitive indicators of ecosystem services that sustain and contribute natural capital toward the well-being of humanity. An understanding of biodiversity has practical application for ecosystem-based conservation planners as they make ecologically responsible decisions in management recommendations to consultant firms, governments and industry.

The ecological niche is a central concept in the ecology of organisms. There are many definitions of the niche dating back to 1917, but George Evelyn Hutchinson made conceptual advances in 1957 and introduced the most widely accepted definition: "The niche is the set of biotic and abiotic conditions in which a species is able to persist and maintain stable population sizes". The ecological niche is divided into the *fundamental* and the *realized* niche. The fundamental niche is the set of environmental conditions under which a species is able to persist. The realized niche is the set of environmental plus ecological conditions under which a species is able to persist Organisms have functional traits that are uniquely adapted to the ecological niche. A trait is a measurable property of an organism that strongly influences its performance. Biogeographical patterns and range distributions are explained or predicted through knowledge and understanding of a species niche requirements. For example, the uniquely adapted nature of each species to their ecological niche means that they are able to competitively exclude other similarly adapted species from having an overlapping geographic range. This is called the competitive exclusion principle. Important to the concept of niche is habitat. The habitat describes the environment over which a species is known to occur and the type of community that is formed as a result. For example, habitat might refer to an aquatic or terrestrial environment that can be further categorized as montane or alpine ecosystems.

Organisms are subject to environmental pressures, but they are also modifiers of their habitats. The regulatory feedback between organisms and their environment can modify conditions from local (e.g., a pond) to global scales (e.g., Gaia) and over time and even after death, such as decaying logs or silica skeleton deposits from marine organisms. This process of ecosystem engineering has also been called niche construction. Ecosystem engineers are defined as: "...organisms that directly or indirectly modulate the availability of resources to other species, by causing physical state changes in biotic or abiotic materials. In so doing they modify, maintain and create habitats."

The ecological engineering concept has stimulated a new appreciation for the degree of influence that organisms have on the ecosystem and evolutionary process. The niche construction concept highlights a previously under-appreciated feedback mechanism of natural selection imparting forces on the abiotic niche. An example of natural selection through ecosystem engineering occurs in the nests of social insects, including ants, bees, wasps, and termites. There is an emergent homeostasis in the structure of the nest that regulates, maintains and defends the physiology of the entire colony. Termite mounds, for example, maintain a constant internal temperature through the design of air-conditioning chimneys. The structure of the nests themselves are subject to the forces of natural selection. Moreover, the nest can survive over successive generations, which means that ancestors inherit both genetic material and a legacy niche that was constructed before their time.

The population is the unit of analysis in population ecology. A population consists of individuals of the same species that live, interact and migrate through the same niche and habitat. A primary law of population ecology is the Malthusian growth model This law states that:

> "... a population will grow (or decline) exponentially as long as the environment experienced by all individuals in the population remains constant."

This Malthusian premise provides the basis for formulating predictive theories and tests that follow. Simplified population models usually start with four variables including death, birth, immigration, and emigration. Mathematical models are used to calculate changes in population demographics using a null model. A null model is used as a null hypothesis for statistical testing. The null hypothesis states that random processes create observed patterns. Alternatively the patterns differ significantly from the random model and require further explanation. Models can be mathematically complex where "...several competing hypotheses are simultaneously confronted with the data." An example of an introductory population model describes a closed population, such as on an island, where immigration and emigration does not take place.

An important concept in population ecology is *r/K*-selection theory. The concept was introduced in 1967 in a book entitled The Theory of Island Biogeography and was one of the first predictive models to explain life-history evolution. The premise behind this model is that forces of natural selection change according to the density of the population. When an island is first colonized, the density of individuals is low and the population size increases with reduced levels of competition and an abundance of available resources. Under such circumstances a population experiences density independent forces of natural selection, which is called *r*-selection. When the population becomes crowded it has reached the carrying capacity for the island and individuals compete more heavily for limited resources. Under crowded conditions the population experiences density dependent forces of natural selection, which is called *K*-selection.

In the *r/K*-selection model, the first variable *r* is called the intrinsic rate of natural increase in population size and the second variable *K* is called the carrying capacity of a population. Different species evolve different life-histories strategies spanning a continuum between these two selective forces. An *r*-selected species is one that has high birth rates, low levels of parental investment, and high rates of mortality before individuals reach maturity. Evolution favours high rates of fecundity in *r*-selected species. Many kinds of insects and invasive species exhibit *r*-selected characteristics. In contrast, a *K*-selected species has low rates of fecundity, high levels of parental investment in the young, and low rates of mortality as individuals mature. Humans and elephants are examples of species exhibiting *K*-selected characteristics, including longevity and efficiency in the conversion of more resources into fewer offspring.

Metapopulation Ecology

Populations are also studied and conceptualized through the metapopulation concept. The metapopulation concept was introduced in 1969: "as a population of populations which go extinct locally and recolonize.": Metapopulation ecology is another statistical approach that is often used in conservation research. Metapopulation research simplifies the landscape into patches of varying levels of quality. Like the r/K-selection model, metapopulation models have also been used to explain life-history evolution, such as the ecological stability of amphibian metamorphosis shifting life stages out of aquatic patches and into terrestrial patches. In metapopulation terminology there are emigrants (individuals that leave a patch), immigrants (individuals that move into a patch) and sites are classed either as sources or sinks. A site is a generic term that refers to places where ecologists sample populations, such as ponds or defined sampling areas in a forest. Source patches are productive sites that generate a seasonal supply of juveniles that migrate to other patch locations. Sink patches are unproductive sites that only receive migrants and will go extinct unless rescued by an adjacent source patch or environmental conditions become more favourable. Metapopulation models examine patch dynamics over time to answer questions about spatial and demographic ecology. The ecology of metapopulations is a dynamic process of extinction and colonization. Small patches of lower quality (i.e., sinks) are maintained or rescued by a seasonal influx of new immigrants. A dynamic metapopulation structure evolves from year to year, where some patches are sinks in dry years and become sources when conditions are more favourable. Ecologists utilize a mixture of computer models and field studies to explain metapopulation structure.

Community ecology is a subdiscipline of ecology which studies the distribution, abundance, demography, and interactions between coexisting populations. An example of a study in community ecology might measure primary production in a wetland in relation to decomposition and consumption rates. This requires a understanding of the community connections between plants (i.e., primary producers) and the decomposers (e.g., fungi and bacteria). or the analysis of predator-prey dynamics affecting amphibian biomass. Food webs and trophic levels are two widely employed conceptual models used to explain the linkages among species.

Food Webs

Food webs are a type of concept map that illustrate ecological pathways, usually starting with solar energy being used by plants during photosynthesis. As plants grow, they accumulate carbohydrates and are eaten by grazing herbivores. Step by step lines or relations are drawn until a web of life is illustrated.

There are different ecological dimensions that can be mapped to create more complicated food webs, including: species composition (type of species), richness (number of species), biomass (the dry weight of plants and animals), productivity (rates of conversion of energy and nutrients into growth), and stability (food webs over time). A food web diagram illustrating species composition shows how change in a single species can directly and indirectly influence many others. Microcosm studies are used to simplify food web research into semi-isolated units such as small springs, decaying logs, and laboratory experiments using organisms that reproduce quickly, such as daphnia feeding on algae grown under controlled environments in jars of water.

Principles gleaned from food web microcosm studies are used to extrapolate smaller dynamic concepts to larger systems. Food webs are limited because they are generally restricted to a specific habitat, such as a cave or a pond. The food web illustration (right) only shows a small part of the complexity connecting the aquatic system to the adjacent terrestrial land. Many of these species migrate into other habitats to distribute their effects on a larger scale. In other words, food webs are incomplete, but are nonetheless a valuable tool in understanding community ecosystems.

Food chain length is another way of describing food webs as a measure of the number of species encountered as energy or nutrients move from the plants to top predators. There are different ways of calculating food chain length depending on what parameters of the food web dynamic are being considered: connectance, energy, or interaction. In a simple predator-prey example, a deer is one step removed from the plants it eats (chain length = 1) and a wolf that eats the deer is two steps removed (chain length = 2). The relative amount or strength of influence that these parameters have on the food web address questions about:

- the identity or existence of a few dominant species (called strong interactors or keystone species);
- the total number of species and food-chain length (including many weak interactors); and
- how community structure, function and stability is determined.

The Greek root of the word *troph*, trophe, means food or feeding. Links in food-webs primarily connect feeding relations or trophism among species. Biodiversity within ecosystems can be organized into vertical and horizontal dimensions. The vertical dimension represents feeding relations that become further removed from the base of the food chain up toward top predators. The horizontal dimension represents the abundance or biomass at each level. When the relative abundance or biomass of each functional feeding group is stacked into their respective trophic levels they naturally sort into a 'pyramid of numbers'. Functional groups are broadly categorized as autotrophs (or primary producers), heterotrophs (or consumers), and detrivores (or decomposers). Heterotrophs can be further sub-divided into different functional groups, including: primary consumers (strict herbivores), secondary consumers (predators that feed exclusively on herbivores) and tertiary consumers (predators that feed on a mix of herbivores and predators). Omnivores do not fit neatly into a functional category because they eat both plant and animal tissues. It has been suggested, however, that omnivores have a greater functional influence as predators because relative to herbivores they are comparatively inefficient at grazing.

Ecologist collect data on trophic levels and food webs to statistically model and mathematically calculate parameters, such as those used in other kinds of network analysis (e.g., graph theory), to study emergent patterns and properties shared among ecosystems. The emergent pyramidal arrangement of trophic levels with amounts of energy transfer decreasing as species become further removed from the source of production is one of several patterns that is repeated amongst the planets ecosystems. The size of each level in the pyramid generally represents biomass, which can be measured as the dry weight of an organism. Autotrophs may have the highest global proportion of biomass, but they are closely rivaled or surpassed by microbes.

The decomposition of dead organic matter, such as leaves falling on the forest floor, turns into soils that feed plant production. The total sum of the planet's soil ecosystems is called the pedosphere where a very large proportion of the Earth's biodiversity sorts into other trophic levels. Invertebrates that feed and shred larger leaves, for example, create smaller bits for smaller organisms in the feeding chain. Collectively, these are the detrivores that regulate soil formation. Tree roots, fungi, bacteria, worms, ants, beetles, centipedes, spiders, mammals, birds, reptiles, amphibians and other less familiar creatures all work to create the trophic web of life in soil ecosystems. As organisms feed and migrate through soils they physically displace materials, which is an important ecological process called bioturbation. Biomass of soil microorganisms are influenced by and feed back into the trophic dynamics of the exposed solar surface ecology. Paleoecological studies of soils places the origin for bioturbation to a time before the Cambrian period. Other events, such as the evolution of trees and amphibians moving into land in the Devonian period played a significant role in the development of soils and ecological trophism.

Producers or Autotrophs

Usually plants or cyanobacteria that are capable of photosynthesis but could be other organisms such as the bacteria near ocean vents that are capable of chemosynthesis.

Consumers or Heterotrophs

Animals, which can be primary consumers (herbivorous), or secondary or tertiary consumers (carnivorous and omnivoures).

Decomposers or Detritivoures

Bacteria, fungi, and insects which degrade organic matter of all types and restore nutrients to the environment. The producers will then consume the nutrients, completing the cycle.

Functional trophic groups sort out hierarchically into pyramidic trophic levels because it requires specialized adaptations to become a photosynthesizer or a predator, so few organisms have the adaptations needed to combine both abilities. This explains why functional adaptations to trophism (feeding) organizes different species into emergent functional groups. Trophic levels are part of the holistic or complex systems view of ecosystems. Each trophic level contains unrelated species that grouped together because they share common ecological functions. Grouping functionally similar species into a trophic system gives a macroscopic image of the larger functional design.

Links in a food-web illustrate direct trophic relations among species, but there are also indirect effects that can alter the abundance, distribution, or biomass in the trophic levels. For example, predators eating herbivoures indirectly influence the control and regulation of primary production in plants. Although the predators do not eat the plants directly, they regulate the population of herbivoures that are directly linked to plant trophism. The net effect of direct and indirect relations is called trophic cascades. Trophic cascades are separated into species-level cascades, where only a subset of the food-web dynamic is impacted by a change in population numbers, and community-level cascades, where a change in population numbers has a dramatic effect on the entire food-web, such as the distribution of plant biomass.

Keystone Species

A keystone species is a species that is disproportionately connected to more species in the food-web. Keystone species have lower levels of biomass in the trophic pyramid relative to the importance of their role. The many connections that a keystone species holds means that it maintains the organization and structure of entire communities. The loss of a keystone species results in a range of dramatic cascading effects that alters trophic dynamics, other food-web connections and can cause the extinction of other species in the community.

Sea otters (*Enhydra lutris*) are commonly cited as an example of a keystone species because they limit the density of sea urchins that feed on kelp. If sea otters are removed from the system, the urchins graze until the kelp beds disappear and this has a dramatic effect on community structure. Hunting of sea otters, for example, is thought to have indirectly lead to the extinction of the Steller's Sea Cow (*Hydrodamalis gigas*). While the keystone species concept has been used extensively as a conservation tool, it has been criticized for being poorly defined from an operational stance. It is very difficult to experimentally determine in each different ecosystem what species may hold a keystone role. Furthermore, food-web theory suggests that keystone species may not be all that common. It is therefore unclear how generally the keystone species model can be applied.

Ecological units of organization are defined through reference to any magnitude of space and time on the planet.

Communities of organisms, for example, are somewhat arbitrarily defined, but the processes of life integrate at different levels and organize into more complex wholes. Biomes, for example, are a larger unit of organization that categorize regions of the Earth's ecosystems mainly according to the structure and composition of vegetation. Different researchers have applied different methods to define continental boundaries of biomes dominated by different functional types of vegetative communities that are limited in distribution by climate, precipitation, weather and other environmental variables. Examples of biome names include: tropical rainforest, Temperate broadleaf and mixed forests, temperate deciduous forest, taiga, tundra, hot desert, and polar desert. Other researchers have recently started to categorize other types of biomes, such as the human and oceanic microbiomes. To a microbe, the human body is a habitat and a landscape. The microbiome has been largely discovered through molecular genetic advances revealing a hidden richness of microbial diversity on the planet. The oceanic microbiome plays a significant role in the ecological biogeochemistry of the planets oceans.

The largest scale of ecological organization is the biosphere. The biosphere is the total sum of ecosystems on the planet. Ecological relations regulate the flux of energy, nutrients, and climate all the way up to the planetary scale. For example, the dynamic history of the planetary CO_2 and O_2 composition of the atmosphere has been largely by the biogenic flux of gases coming from respiration and photosynthesis with levels fluctuating in time and in relation to the ecology and evolution of plants and animals. When sub-component parts are organized into a whole there are oftentimes emergent properties that describe the nature of the system. Ecological theory has been used to explain self emergent regulatory phenomena at the planetary scale. This is known as the Gaia hypothesis. The Gaia hypothesis is an example of holism applied in ecological theory. The ecology of the planet acts as a single regulatory or holistic unit called Gaia. The Gaia hypothesis states that there is an emergent feedback loop generated by the metabolism of living organisms that maintains the temperature of the Earth and atmospheric conditions within a narrow self-regulating range of tolerance.

Ecology and evolution are considered sister disciplines of the life sciences. Natural selection, life history, development, adaptation, populations, and inheritance are examples of concepts that thread equally into ecological and evolutionary theory. Morphological, behavioural and/or genetic traits, for example, can be mapped onto evolutionary trees to study the historical development of a species in relation to their functions and roles in different ecological circumstances. In this framework, the analytical tools of ecologists and evolutionists overlap as they organize, classify and investigate life through common systematic principals, such as phylogenetics or the Linnaean system of taxonomy. The two disciplines often appear together, such as in the title of the journal *Trends in Ecology and Evolution.* There is no sharp boundary separating ecology from evolution and they differ more in their areas of applied focus. Both disciplines discover and explain emergent and unique properties and processes operating across different spatial or temporal scales of organization. While the boundary between ecology and evolution is not always clear, it is understood that ecologists study the abiotic and biotic factors that influence the evolutionary process.

All organisms are motile to some extent. Behavioural ecology is the study of ethology and its ecological and evolutionary implications. Ethology is the study of observable movement or behaviour in nature. This could include investigations of motile sperm of plants and zooplankton swimming toward the female egg, the cultivation of fungi by weevils, the mating dance of a salamander, or social gatherings of amoeba.

Adaptation is the central unifying concept in behavioural ecology. 'International Society for Behavioural Ecology' Behaviours can be recorded as traits and inherited in much the same way that eye and hair colour can. Behaviours evolve and become adapted to the ecosystem because they are subject to the forces of natural selection. Hence, behaviours can be adaptive, meaning that they evolve functional utilities that increases reproductive success for the individuals that inherit such traits. This is also the technical definition for fitness in biology, which is a measure of reproductive success over successive generations.

Predator-prey interactions are an introductory concept into food-web studies as well as behavioural ecology. Prey species can exhibit different kinds of behavioural adaptations to predators, such as avoid, flee or defend. Many prey species are faced with multiple predators that differ in the degree of danger posed. To be adapted to their environment and face predatory threats, organisms must balance their energy budgets as they invest in different aspects of their life history, such as growth, feeding, mating, socializing, or modifying their habitat. Hypotheses posited in behavioural ecology are generally based on adaptive principals of conservation, optimization or efficiency. For example:

> "The threat-sensitive predator avoidance hypothesis predicts that prey should assess the degree of threat posed by different predators and match their behaviour according to current levels of risk."

The behaviour of long-toed salamanders (*Ambystoma macrodactylum*) presents an example in this context. When threatened, the long-toed salamander defends itself by waving its tail and secreting a white milky fluid. The excreted fluid is distasteful, toxic and adhesive, but it is also used for nutrient and energy storage during hibernation.

Hence, salamanders subjected to frequent predatory attack will be energetically compromised as they use up their energy stores.

Symbiosis

Leafhoppers (*Eurymela fenestrata*) are protected by ants (*Iridomyrmex purpureus*) in a symbiotic relationship. The ants protect the leafhoppers from predators and in return the leafhoppers feeding on plants exude honeydew from their anus that provides energy and nutrients to tending ants.

Ecological interactions can be divided into host and associate relationships. A host is any entity that harbours another that is called the associate. Host and associate relationships among species that are mutually or reciprocally beneficial are called mutualisms. If the host and associate are physically connected, the relationship is called symbiosis. Approximately 60 per cent of all plants, for example, have a symbiotic relationship with arbuscular mycorrhizal fungi. Symbiotic plants and fungi exchange carbohydrates for mineral nutrients. Symbiosis differs from indirect mutualisms where the organisms live apart. For example, tropical rainforests regulate the Earth's atmosphere. Trees living in the equatorial regions of the planet supply oxygen into the atmosphere that sustains species living in distant polar regions of the planet. This relationship is called commensalism because many other host species receive the benefits of clean air at no cost or harm to the associate tree species supplying the oxygen. The host and associate relationship is called parasitism if one species benefits while the other suffers. Competition among species or among members of the same species is defined as reciprocal antagonism, such as grasses competing for growth space.

Popular ecological study systems for mutualism include, fungus-growing ants employing agricultural symbiosis, bacteria living in the guts of insects and other organisms, the fig wasp and yucca moth pollination complex, lichens with fungi and photosynthetic algae, and corals with photosynthetic algae.

Intraspecific behaviours are notable in the social insects, slime moulds, social spiders, human society, and naked mole rats where eusocialism has evolved. Social behaviours include reciprocally beneficial behaviours among kin and nest mates. Social behaviours evolve from kin and group selection. Kin selection explains altruism through genetic relationships, whereby an altruistic behaviour leading to death is rewarded by the survival of genetic copies distributed among surviving relatives. The social insects, including ants, bees and wasps are most famously studied for this type of relationship because the male drones are clones that share the same genetic make-up as every other male in the colony. In contrast, group selectionists find examples of altruism among non-genetic relatives and explain this through selection acting on the group, whereby it becomes selectively advantageous for groups if their members express altruistic behaviours to one another. Groups that are predominantely altruists beat groups that are predominantely selfish.

A often quoted behavioural ecology hypothesis is known as Lack's brood reduction hypothesis (named after David Lack). Lack's hypothesis posits an evolutionary and ecological explanation as to why birds lay a series of eggs with an asynchronous delay leading to nestlings of mixed age and weights. According to Lack, this brood behaviour is an ecological insurance that allows the larger birds to survive in poor years and all birds to survive when food is plentiful.

Elaborate sexual displays and posturing are encountered in the behavioural ecology of animals. The birds of paradise, for example, display elaborate ornaments and song during courtship. These displays serve a dual purpose of signalling healthy or well-adapted individuals and good genes. The elaborate displays are driven by sexual selection as an advertisement of quality of traits among male suitors.

Biogeography

The word *biogeography* is an amalgamation of *biology* and *geography*. Biogeography is the comparative study of the geographic distribution of organisms and the corresponding evolution of their traits in space and time. The Journal of Biogeography was established in 1974. Biogeography and ecology share many of their disciplinary roots. For example, the theory of island biogeography, published by the mathematician Robert MacArthur and ecologist Edward O. Wilson in 1967 is considered one of the fundamentals of ecological theory.

Biogeography has a long history in the natural sciences where questions arise concerning the spatial distribution of plants and animals. Ecology and evolution provide the explanatory context for biogeographical studies. Biogeographical patterns result from ecological processes that influence range distributions, such as migration and dispersal. and from historical processes that split populations or species into different areas. The biogeographic processes that result in the natural splitting of species explains much of the modern distribution of the Earth's biota. The splitting of lineages in a species is called vicariance biogeography and it is a sub-discipline of biogeography. There are also practical applications in the field of biogeography concerning ecological systems and processes. For example, the range and distribution of biodiversity and invasive species responding to climate change is a serious concern and active area of research in context of global warming.

Molecular Ecology

The important relationship between ecology and genetic inheritance predates modern molecular analytical techniques. Molecular ecological research became more feasible with the development of genetic technologies, such as the polymerase chain reaction (PCR). The rise of molecular technologies and influx of research questions into this new ecological field resulted in the publication *Molecular Ecology* in 1992. Molecular ecology uses various analytical techniques to study genes in an evolutionary and ecological context. In 1994, professor John Avise played a leading role in this area of science with the publication of his book, *Molecular Markers, Natural History and Evolution.* Newer technologies opened a wave of genetic analysis into organisms once difficult to study from an ecological or evolutionary standpoint, such as bacteria, fungi and nematodes. Molecular ecology engendered a new research paradigm to investigate ecological questions considered otherwise intractable. Molecular ecology revealed previously obscured details in the intricacies of nature and improved resolution into probing questions about behavioural and biogeographical ecology. For example, molecular ecology revealed promiscuous sexual behaviour and multiple male partners in tree swallows previously thought to be socially monogamous. In a biogeographical context, the marriage between genetics, ecology and evolution resulted in a new sub-discipline called phylogeography.

Ecology and the Environment

"The environment of any organism is the class composed of the sum of those phenomena that enter a reaction system of the organism or otherwise directly impinge upon it to affect its mode of life at any time throughout its life cycle as ordered by the demands of the ontogeny of the organism or as ordered by any other condition of the organism that alters its environmental demands."

The environment is dynamically interlinked with ecology. Like the term ecology, environment has different conceptual meanings and to many these terms also overlap with the concept of *nature.* Environment "... includes the physical world, the social world of human relations and the built world of human creation". This section describes the physical environmental attributes or parameters that are external to the level of biological organization under investigation, including abiotic factors such as temperature, radiation, light, chemistry, climate and geology, and biotic factors, including genes, cells, organisms, members of the same species (conspecifics) and other species that share a habitat. The physical environmental connection means that the laws of thermodynamics applies to ecology. Armed with an understanding of metabolic and thermodynamic principles a complete accounting of energy and material flow can be traced through an ecosystem.

Environmental and ecological relations are studied through reference to conceptually manageable and isolated parts. However, once the effective environmental components are understood they conceptually link back together as a *holocoenotic* system. In other words, the organism and the environment form a dynamic whole (or umwelt). Change in one ecological or environmental factor can concurrently affect the dynamic state of an entire ecosystem.

Ecological studies are necessarily holistic as opposed to reductionistic. Holism has three scientific meanings or uses that identify with:

1. the mechanistic complexity of ecosystems;
2. the practical description of patterns in quantitative reductionist terms where correlations may be identified but nothing is understood about the causal relations without reference to the whole system;
3. a metaphysical hierarchy whereby the causal relations of larger systems are understood without reference to the smaller parts.

An example of the metaphysical aspect to holism is the trend of increased exterior thickness in shells of different species. The reason for a thickness increase can be understood through reference to principals of natural selection via predation without any reference to the biomolecular properties of the exterior shells.

Metabolism and the Early Atmosphere

Metabolism — the rate at which energy and material resources are taken up from the environment, transformed within an organism, and allocated to maintenance, growth and reproduction — is a fundamental physiological trait.

The Earth formed approximately 4.5 billion years ago and environmental conditions were too extreme for life to form for the first 500 million years. During this early Hadean period, the Earth started to cool allowing time for a crust and oceans to form. Environmental conditions were unsuitable for the origins of life for the first billion years after the Earth formed. The Earth's atmosphere transformed from hydrogen dominant, to one composed mostly of methane and ammonia. Over the next billion years the metabolic activity of life transformed the atmosphere to higher concentrations of carbon dioxide, nitrogen, and water vapour. These gases changed the way that light from the sun hit the Earth's surface and greenhouse effects trapped in heat. There were untapped sources of free energy within the mixture of reducing and oxidizing gasses that set the stages for primitive ecosystems to evolve and, in turn, the atmosphere also evolved.

Throughout history, the Earth's atmosphere and biogeochemical cycles has been in a dynamic equilibrium with planetary ecosystems. The history is characterized by periods of significant transformation followed by millions of years of stability.

Radiation: Heat, Temperature and Light

The biology of life operates within a certain range of temperatures. Heat is a form of energy that regulates temperature. Heat affects growth rates, activity, behaviour and primary production. Temperature is largely dependent on the incidence of solar radiation. The latitudinal and longitudinal spatial variation of temperature greatly affects climates and consequently the distribution of biodiversity and levels of primary production in different ecosystems or biomes across the planet. Heat and temperature relate importantly to metabolic activity. Poikilotherms, for example, have a body temperature that is largely regulated and dependent on the temperature of the external environment. In contrast, homeotherms regulate their internal body temperature by expending metabolic energy.

There is a relationship between light, primary production, and ecological energy budgets. Sunlight is the primary input of energy into the planet's ecosystems. Light is composed of electromagnetic energy of different wavelengths. Radiant energy from the sun generates heat, provides photons of light measured as active energy in the chemical reactions of life, and also acts as a catalyst for genetic mutation. Plants, algae, and some bacteria absorb light and assimilate the energy through photosynthesis. Organisms capable of assimilating energy by photosynthesis or through inorganic fixation of H_2S are autotrophs. Autotrophs—responsible for primary production—assimilate light energy that becomes metabolically stored as potential energy in the form of biochemical enthalpic bonds.

The rate of diffusion of carbon dioxide and oxygen is approximately 10,000 times slower in water than it is in air. When soils become flooded, they quickly lose oxygen from low-concentration (hypoxic) to an (anoxic) environment where anaerobic bacteria thrive among the roots. Water also influences the spectral properties of light that becomes more diffuse as it is reflected off the water surface and submerged particles. Aquatic plants exhibit a wide variety of morphological and physiological adaptations that allow them to survive, compete and diversify these environments. For example, the roots and stems develop large cellular air spaces to allow for the efficient transportation gases (for example, CO_2 and O_2) used in respiration and photosynthesis. In drained soil, microorganisms use oxygen during respiration. In aquatic environments, anaerobic soil microorganisms use nitrate, manganic ions, ferric ions, sulfate, carbon dioxide and some organic compounds. The activity of soil microorganisms and the chemistry of the water reduces the oxidation-reduction potentials of the water. Carbon dioxide, for example, is reduced to methane (CH_4) by methanogenic bacteria. Salt water also requires special physiological adaptations to deal with water loss. Salt water plants (or halophytes) are able to osmo-regulate their internal salt (NaCl) concentrations or develop special organs for shedding salt away. The physiology of fish is also specially adapted to deal with high levels of salt through osmoregulation. Their gills form electrochemical gradients that mediate salt excrusion in salt water and uptake in fresh water.

Gravity

The shape and energy of the land is affected to a large degree by gravitational forces. On a larger scale, the distribution of gravitational forces on the earth are uneven and influence the shape and movement of tectonic plates as well as having an influence on geomorphic processes such as orogeny and erosion. These forces govern many of the geophysical properties and distributions of ecological biomes across the Earth. On a organism scale, gravitational forces provide directional cues for plant and fungal growth (gravitropism), orientation cues for animal migrations, and influence the biomechanics and size of animals. Ecological traits, such as allocation of biomass in trees during growth are subject to mechanical failure as gravitational forces influence the position and structure of branches and leaves. The cardiovascular systems of all animals are functionally adapted to overcome pressure and gravitational forces that change according to the features of organisms (e.g., height, size, shape), their behaviour (e.g., diving, running, flying), and the habitat occupied (e.g., water, hot deserts, cold tundra).

Pressure

Climatic and osmotic pressure places physiological constraints on organisms, such as flight and respiration at high altitudes, or diving to deep ocean depths. These constraints influence vertical limits of ecosystems in the biosphere as organisms are physiologically sensitive and adapted to atmospheric and osmotic water pressure differences. Oxygen levels, for example, decrease with increasing pressure and are a limiting factor for life at higher altitudes Water transportation through trees is another important ecophysiological parameter dependent upon pressure. Water pressure in the depths of oceans requires adaptations to deal with the different living conditions. Mammals, such as whales, dolphins and seals are adapted to deal with changes in sound due to water pressure differences.

Wind and Turbulence

The architecture of inflorescence in grasses is subject to the physical pressures of wind and shaped by the forces of natural selection facilitating wind-pollination (or anemophily).

Turbulent forces in air and water have significant effects on the environment and ecosystem distribution, form and dynamics. On a planetary scale, ecosystems are affected by circulation patterns in the global trade winds. Wind power and the turbulent forces it creates can influence heat, nutrient, and biochemical profiles of ecosystems. For example, wind running over the surface of a lake creates turbulence, mixing the water column and influencing the environmental profile to create thermally layered zones, partially governing how fish, algae, and other parts of the aquatic ecology are structured Wind speed and turbulence also exert influence on rates of evapotranspiration rates and energy budgets in plants and animals Wind speed, temperature and moisture content can vary as winds travel across different landfeatures and elevations. The westerlies, for example, come into contact with the coastal and interior mountains of western North America to produce a rain shadow on the leeward side of the mountain. The air expands and moisture condenses as the winds move up in elevation which can cause precipitation; this is called orographic lift. This environmental process produces spatial divisions in biodiversity, as species adapted to wetter conditions are range-restricted to the coastal mountain valleys and unable to migrate across the xeric ecosystems of the Columbia Basin to intermix with sister lineages that are segregated to the interior mountain systems. Plants convert carbon dioxide into biomass and emit oxygen into the atmosphere. Approximately 350 million years ago (near the Devonian period) the photosynthetic process brought the concentration of atmospheric oxygen above 17 per cent, which allowed combustion to occur. Fire releases CO_2 and converts fuel into ash and tar. Fire is a significant ecological parameter that raises many issues pertaining to its control and suppression in management. While the issue of fire in relation to ecology and plants has been recognized for a long time Charles Cooper brought attention to the issue of forest fires in relation to the ecology of forest fire suppression and management in the 1960s.

Fire creates environmental mosaics and a patchiness to ecosystem age and canopy structure. Native North Americans were among the first to influence fire regimes by controlling their spread near their homes or by lighting fires to stimulate the production of herbaceous foods and basketry materials. The altered state of soil nutrient supply and cleared canopy structure also opens new ecological niches for seedling establishment. Most ecosystem are adapted to natural fire cycles. Plants, for example, are equipped with a variety of adaptations to deal with forest fires. Some species (e.g., *Pinus halepensis*) cannot germinate until after their seeds have lived through a fire. This environmental trigger for seedlings is called serotiny. Some compounds from smoke also promote seed germination.

Biogeochemistry

Ecologists study and measure nutrient budgets to understand how these materials are regulated and flow through the environment. This research has led to an understanding that there is a global feedback between ecosystems and the physical parameters of this planet including minerals, soil, pH, ions, water and atmospheric gases. There are six major elements, including H (hydrogen), C (carbon), N (nitrogen), O (oxygen), S (sulfur), and P (phosphorus) that form the constitution of all biological macromolecules and feed into the Earth's geochemical processes. From the smallest scale of biology the combined effect of billions upon billions of ecological processes amplify and ultimately regulate the biogeochemical cycles of the Earth. Understanding the relations and cycles mediated between these elements and their ecological pathways has significant bearing toward understanding global biogeochemistry.

The ecology of global carbon budgets gives one example of the linkage between biodiversity and biogeochemistry. For starters, the earth's oceans are estimated to hold 40,000 gigatonnes (Gt) carbon, vegetation and soil is estimated to hold 2070 Gt carbon, and fossil fuel emissions are estimated to emit an annual flux of 6.3 Gt carbon. At different times in the Earth's history there has been major restructuring in these global carbon budgets that was regulated to a large extent by the ecology of the land. For example, through the early-mid Eocene volcanic outgassing, the oxidation of methane stored in wetlands, and seafloor gases increased atmospheric CO_2 concentrations to levels as high as

3500 ppm. In the Oligocene, from 25 to 32 million years ago, there was another significant restructuring in the global carbon cycle as grasses evolved a special type of C4 photosynthesis and expanded their ranges. This new photosynthetic pathway evolved in response to the drop in atmospheric CO_2 concentrations below 550 ppm. Ecosystem functions such as these feedback significantly into global atmospheric models for carbon cycling. Loss in the abundance and distribution of biodiversity causes global carbon cycle feedbacks that are expected to increase rates of global warming in the next century. The effect of global warming melting large sections of permafrost creates a new mosaic of flooded areas where decomposition results in the emission of methane (CH_4). Hence, there is a relationship between global warming, decomposition and respiration in soils and wetlands producing significant climate feedbacks and altered global biogeochemical cycles. There is concern over increases in atmospheric methane in the context of the global carbon cycle, because methane is also a greenhouse gas that is 23 times more effective at absorbing long-wave radiation on a 100 year time scale.

Unlike many of the scientific disciplines, ecology has a complex and winding origin due in large part to its interdisciplinary nature. Several published books provide extensive coverage of the classics. In the early 20th century, ecology was an analytical form of natural history. The descriptive nature of natural history included examination of the interaction of organisms with both their environment and their community. Such examinations were conducted by important natural historians including James Hutton and Jean-Baptiste Lamarck contributed to the development of ecology. The term 'ecology' (German: *Oekologie*) is a more recent scientific development and was first coined by the German biologist Ernst Haeckel in his book *Generelle Morpologie der Organismen.*

By ecology we mean the body of knowledge concerning the economy of nature—the investigation of the total relations of the animal both to its inorganic and its organic environment; including, above all, its friendly and inimical relations with those animals and plants with which it comes directly or indirectly into contact-in a word, ecology is the study of all those complex interrelations referred to by Darwin as the conditions of the struggle of existence.

Opinions differ on who was the founder of modern ecological theory. Some mark Haeckel's definition as the beginning, others say it was Eugen Warming with the writing of Oecology of Plants: An Introduction to the Study of Plant Communities (1895). Ecology may also be thought to have begun with Carl Linnaeus' research principals on the economy of nature that matured in the early 18th century. He founded an early branch of ecological study he called the economy of nature. The works of Linnaeus influenced Darwin in *The Origin of Species* where he adopted the usage of Linnaeus' phrase on the *economy or polity of nature*. Linnaeus made the first to attempt to define *the balance of nature*, which had previously been held as an assumption rather than formulated as a testable hypothesis.

Haeckel, who admired Darwin's work, defined ecology in reference to the economy of nature which has lead some to question if ecology is synonymous with Linnaeus' concepts for the economy of nature. Biogeographer Alexander von Humbolt was also foundational and was among the first to recognize ecological gradients and alluded to the modern ecological law of species to area relationships.

The modern synthesis of ecology is a young science, which first attracted substantial formal attention at the end of the 19th century (around the same time as evolutionary studies) and become even more popular during the 1960s environmental movement. However, many observations, interpretations and discoveries relating to ecology extend back to much earlier studies in natural history. For example, the concept on the balance or regulation of nature can be traced back to Herodotos (died *c.* 425 BC) who described an early account of mutualism along the Nile river where crocodiles open their mouths to beneficially allow sandpipers safe access to remove leeches. In the broader contributions to the historical development of the ecological sciences, Aristotle is considered one of the earliest naturalists who had an influential role in the philosophical development of ecological sciences. One of Aristotle's students, Theophrastus, made astute ecological observations about plants and posited a philosophical stance about the autonomous relations between plants and their environment that is more in line with modern ecological thought. Both Aristotle and Theophrastus made extensive observations on plant and animal migrations, biogeography, physiology, and their habits in what might be considered a modern analog of the ecological niche.

The first American ecology book was published in 1905 by Frederic Clements. In his book, Clements forwarded the idea of plant communities as a superorganism. This publication launched a debate between ecological holism and individualism that lasted until the 1970s. The Clements superorganism concept proposed that ecosystems progress through regular and determined stages of serial development that are analogous to developmental stages of an organism whose parts function to maintain the integrity of the whole. The Clementsian paradigm was challenged by Henry Gleason. According to Gleason, ecological communities develop from the unique and coincidental association of individual organisms. This perceptual shift placed the focus back onto the life histories of individual organisms and how this relates to the development of community associations.

The Clementsian superorganism concept has not been completely rejected, but it was an overextended application of holism, which remains a significant theme in contemporary ecological studies. Holism was first introduced in 1926 by a polarizing historical figure, a South African

General named Jan Christian Smuts. Smuts was inspired by Clement's superorganism theory when he developed and published on the unifying concept of holism, which runs in stark contrast to his racial views as the father of apartheid. Around the same time, Charles Elton pioneered the concept of food chains in his classical book 'Animal Ecology'. Elton defined ecological relations using concepts of food-chains, food-cycles, food-size, and described numerical relations among different functional groups and their relative abundance. Elton's term 'food-cycle' was replaced by 'food-web' in a subsequent ecological text. Elton's book broke conceptual ground by illustrating complex ecological relations through simpler food-web diagrams.

The number of authors publishing on the topic of ecology has grown considerably since the turn of 20th century. The explosion of information available to the modern researcher of ecology makes it an impossible task for one individual to sift through the entire history. Hence, the identification of classics in the history of ecology is a difficult designation to make.

The layout of the first ecological experiment, noted by Charles Darwin in *The Origin of Species*, was studied in a grass garden at Woburn Abbey in 1817. The experiment studied the performance of different mixtures of species planted in different kinds of soils.

From Aristotle to Darwin the natural world was predominantly considered static and unchanged since its original creation. Prior to *The Origin of Species* there was little appreciation or understanding of the dynamic and reciprocal relations between organisms, their adaptations and their modifications to the environment.Ecosystems of planet Earth are coupled to human environments. Ecosystems regulate the global geophysical cycles of energy, climate, soil nutrients, and water that in turn support and grow natural capital (including the environmental, physiological, cognitive, cultural, and spiritual dimensions of life). Ultimately, every manufactured product in human environments comes from natural systems. Ecosystems are considered common-pool resources because ecosystems do not exclude beneficiaries and they can be depleted or degraded. For example, green space within communities provides common-pool health services. Research shows that people who are more engaged with regular access to natural areas have lower rates of diabetes, heart disease and psychological disorders. These ecological health services are regularly depleted through urban development projects that do not factor in the common-pool value of ecosystems.

The ecological commons delivers a diverse supply of community services that sustains the well-being of human society. The Millennium Ecosystem Assessment, an international UN initiative involving more than 1,360 experts worldwide, identifies four main ecosystem service types having 30 sub-categories stemming from natural capital. The ecological commons includes provisioning (e.g., food, raw materials, medicine, water supplies), regulating (e.g., climate, water, soil retention, flood retention), cultural (e.g., science and education, artistic, spiritual), and supporting (e.g., soil formation, nutrient cycling, water cycling) services.

Policy and human institutions should rarely assume that human enterprise is benign. A safer assumption holds that human enterprise almost always exacts an ecological toll — a debit taken from the ecological commons.

Ecology is an economic science that uses many of the same terms and methods that are used in accounting. Natural capital is the stock of materials or information stored in biodiversity that generates services that can enhance the welfare of communities.

The WWF 2008 living planet report and other researchers report that human civilization has exceeded the bio-regenerative capacity of the planet. This means that human consumption is extracting more natural resources than can be replenished by ecosystems around the world. In 1992, professor William Rees developed the concept of our ecological footprint. The ecological footprint is a way of accounting the level of impact that human development is having on the Earth's ecosystems. All indications are that the human enterprise is unsustainable as the ecological footprint of society is placing too much stress on the ecology of the planet. The mainstream growth-based economic system adopted by governments worldwide does not include a price or markets for natural capital. This type of economic system places further ecological debt onto future generations.

Human societies are increasingly being placed under stress as the ecological commons is diminished through an accounting system that has incorrectly assumed "... that nature is a fixed, indestructible capital asset.": 44 While nature is resilient and it does regenerate, there are limits to what can be extracted, but conventional monetary analyses are unable to detect the problem. Evidence of the limits in natural capital are found in the global assessments of biodiversity, which indicate that the current epoch, the Anthropocene is a sixth mass extinction. Species loss is accelerating at 100-1000 times faster than average background rates in the fossil record. The ecology of the planet has been radically transformed by human society and development causing massive loss of ecosystem services that otherwise deliver and freely sustain equitable benefits to human society through the ecological commons. The ecology of the planet is further threatened by global warming, but investments in nature conservation can provide a regulatory feedback to store and regulate carbon and other greenhouse gases. The field of conservation biology involves ecologists that are researching the nature of the biodiversity threat and searching for solutions to sustain the planet's ecosystems for future generations.

"Human activities are associated directly or indirectly with nearly every aspect of the current extinction spasm."

The current wave of threats, including massive extinction rates and concurrent loss of natural capital to the detriment of human society, is happening rapidly. This is called a biodiversity crisis, because 50 per cent of the worlds species are predicted to go extinct within the next 50 years. The world's fisheries are facing dire challenges as the threat of global collapse appears imminent, with serious ramifications for the well-being of humanity. Governments of the G8 met in 2007 and set forth 'The Economics of Ecosystems and Biodiversity' (TEEB) initiative:

In a global study we will initiate the process of analyzing the global economic benefit of biological diversity, the costs of the loss of biodiversity and the failure to take protective measures versus the costs of effective conservation.

Ecologists are teaming up with economists to measure the wealth of ecosystems and to express their value as a way of finding solutions to the biodiversity crisis. Some researchers have attempted to place a dollar figure on ecosystem services, such as the value that the Canadian boreal forest is contributing to global ecosystem services. If ecologically intact, the boreal forest has an estimated value of US$ 3.7 trillion. The boreal forest ecosystem is one of the planet's great atmospheric regulators and it stores more carbon than any other biome on the planet The annual value for ecological services of the Boreal Forest is estimated at US$ 93.2 billion, or 2.5 greater than the annual value of resource extraction. The economic value of 17 ecosystem services for the entire biosphere (calculated in 1997) has an estimated average value of US$ 33 trillion (10^{12}) per year. These ecological economic values are not currently included in calculations of national income accounts, the GDP and they have no price attributes because they exist mostly outside of the global markets. The loss of natural capital continues to accelerate and goes undetected by mainstream monetary analysis.

6 Adaptation

Adaptation is the evolutionary process whereby a population becomes better suited to its habitat. This process takes place over many generations, and is one of the basic phenomena of biology.

The term *adaptation* may also refer to a feature which is especially important for an organism's survival. For example, the adaptation of horses' teeth to the grinding of grass, or their ability to run fast and escape predators. Such adaptations are produced in a variable population by the better suited forms reproducing more successfully, that is, by natural selection.

General Principles

The significance of an adaptation can only be understood in relation to the total biology of the species. —*Julian Huxley*.

Adaptation is, first of all, a *process*, rather than a physical part of a body. The distinction may be seen in an internal parasite (such as a fluke), where the bodily structure is greatly simplified, but nevertheless the organism is highly adapted to its unusual environment. From this we see that adaptation is not just a matter of visible traits: in such parasites critical adaptations take place in the life-cycle, which is often quite complex. However, as a practical term, adaptation is often used for the *product*: those features of a species which result from the process. Many aspects of an animal or plant can be correctly called adaptations, though there are always some features whose function is in doubt. By using the term *adaptation* for the evolutionary *process*, and *adaptive trait* for the bodily part or function (the product), the two senses of the word may be distinguished.

Adaptation may be seen as one aspect of a two-stage process. First, there is speciation (species-splitting or cladogenesis), caused by geographical isolation or some other mechanism Second, there follows adaptation, driven by natural selection. Something like this must have happened with Darwin's finches, and there are many other examples. The present favourite is the evolution of cichlid fish in African lakes, where the question of reproductive isolation is much more complex.

Another great principle is that an organism must be viable at all stages of its development and at all stages of its evolution. This is obviously true, and it follows that there are *constraints* on the evolution of development, behaviour and structure of organisms. The main constraint, over which there has been much debate, is the requirement that changes in the system during evolution should be relatively small changes, because the body systems are so complex and interlinked. This is a sound principle, though there may be rare exceptions: polyploidy in plants is common, and the symbiosis of micro-organisms that formed the eukaryota is a more exotic example.

All adaptations help organisms survive in their ecological niches. These adaptative traits may be structural, behavioural or physiological. Structural adaptations are physical features of an organism (shape, body covering, defensive or offensive armament); and also the internal organization). Behavioural adaptations are composed of inherited behaviour chains and/or the ability to learn: behaviours may be inherited in detail (instincts), or a tendency for learning may be inherited (see neuropsychology). Examples: searching for food, mating, vocalizations. Physiological adaptations permit the organism to perform special functions (for instance, making venom, secreting slime, phototropism); but also more general functions such as growth and development, temperature regulation, ionic balance and other aspects of homeostasis. Adaptation, then, affects all aspects of the life of an organism.

Definitions

The following definitions are mainly due to Theodosius Dobzhansky:

1. *Adaptation* is the evolutionary process whereby an organism becomes better able to live in its habitat or habitats.
2. *Adaptedness* is the state of being adapted the degree to which an organism is able to live and reproduce in a given set of habitats.
3. An *adaptive trait* is an aspect of the developmental pattern of the organism which enables or enhances the probability of that organism surviving and reproducing.

Adaptedness and Fitness

From the above definitions, it is clear that there is a relationship between adaptedness and *fitness* (a key population genetics concept). Fitness is an estimate and a predictor of the rate of natural selection. What natural selection does is change the relative frequencies of alternative phenotypes, insofar as they are heritable. Although the two are connected, the one does not imply the other: a phenotype with high adaptedness may not have high fitness. Dobzhansky mentioned the example of the Californian redwood, which is highly adapted, but a relic species in danger of extinction. Elliott Sober commented that adaptation was a retrospective concept since it implied something about the history of a trait, whereas fitness predicts a trait's future.

1. *Fitness:* The degree of demographic difference among phenotypes. Usually a relative measure: the average contribution to a breeding population by a phenotype or a class of phenotypes. This is also known as *Darwinian fitness, relative fitness, selective coefficient,* and other terms.
2. *Adaptedness:* Usually an absolute measure: the average absolute contribution to the breeding population by a carrier of a phenotype or a class of phenotypes. Also known as *absolute fitness,* and as the Malthusian parameter when applied to species as a whole.

Brief History

Adaptation as a fact of life has been accepted by all the great thinkers who have tackled the world of living organisms. It is their explanations of how adaptation arises that separates these thinkers. A few of the most significant ideas:

> Empedocles did not believe that adaptation required a final cause (~ purpose), but "came about naturally, since such things survived" Aristotle, however, did believe in final causes.

In natural theology, adaptation was interpreted as the work of a deity, even as evidence for the existence of God. William Paley believed that organisms were perfectly adapted to the lives they lead, an argument that shadowed Leibniz, who had argued that God had brought about the best of all possible worlds. Voltaire's Dr. Pangloss is a parody of this optimistic idea, and Hume also argued against design. The *Bridgewater Treatises* are a product of natural theology, though some of the authors managed to present their work in a fairly neutral manner. The series was lampooned by Robert Knox, who held quasi-evolutionary views, as the *Bilgewater Treatises*. Darwin broke with the tradition by emphasising the flaws and limitations which occurred in the animal and plant worlds.

Lamarck

Lamarck is a proto-evolutionary theory of the inheritance of acquired traits, whose main purpose is to explain adaptations by natural means. He proposed a tendency for organisms to become more complex, moving up a ladder of progress, plus 'the influence of circumstances', usually expressed as *use and disuse*. His evolutionary ideas, and those of Geoffroy, fail because they cannot be reconciled with heredity. This was known even before Mendel by medical men interested in human races Wells, Lawrence), and especially by Weismann.

Many other students of natural history, such as Buffon, accepted adaptation, and some also accepted evolution, without voicing their opinions as to the mechanism. This illustrates the real merit of Darwin and Wallace, and secondary figures such as Bates, for pushing forward a mechanism whose significance had only been glimpsed previously. A century later, experimental field studies and breeding experiments by such as Ford and Dobzhansky produced evidence that natural selection was not only the 'engine' behind adaptation, but was a much stronger force than had previously been thought.

Changes in Habitat

Before Darwin, adaptation was seen as a fixed relationship between an organism and its habitat. It was not appreciated that as the climate changed, so did the habitat; and as the habitat changed, so did the biota. Also, habitats are subject to changes in their biota: for example, invasions of species from other areas. The relative numbers of species in a given habitat are always changing. Change is the rule, though much depends on the speed and degree of the change.

When the habitat changes, three main things may happen to a resident population: habitat tracking, genetic change or extinction. In fact, all three things may occur in sequence. Of these three effects, only genetic change brings about adaptation.

Habitat Tracking

When a habitat changes, the most common thing to happen is that the resident population moves to another locale which suits it; this is the typical response of flying insects or oceanic organisms, who have wide (though not unlimited) opportunity for movement. This common response is called *habitat tracking*. It is one explanation put forward for the periods of apparent stasis in the fossil record (the punctuated equilibrium thesis).

Genetic Change

Genetic change is what occurs in a population when natural selection acts on the genetic variability of the population. By this means, the population adapts genetically to its circumstances. Genetic changes may result in visible structures, or may adjust physiological activity in a way that suits the changed habitat.

It is now clear that habitats and biota do frequently change. Therefore, it follows that the process of adaptation is never finally complete. Over time, it may happen that the environment changes little, and the species comes to fit its surroundings better and better. On the other hand, it may happen that changes in the environment occur relatively rapidly, and then the species becomes less and less well adapted. Seen like this, adaptation is a genetic *tracking process*, which goes on all the time to some extent, but especially when the population cannot or does not move to another, less hostile area. Also, to a greater or lesser extent, the process affects every species in a particular ecosystem.

In co-evolution, where the existence of one species is tightly bound up with the life of another species, new or 'improved' adaptations which occur in one species are often followed by the appearance and spread of corresponding features in the other species. There are many examples of this; the idea emphasises that the life and death of living things is intimately connected, not just with the physical environment, but with the life of other species. These relationships are intrinsically dynamic, and may continue on a trajectory for millions of years, as has the relationship between flowering plants and insects (pollination).

The gut contents, wing structures, and mouthpart morphologies of fossilized beetles and flies suggest that they acted as early pollinators. The association between beetles and angiosperms during the early Cretaceous period led to parallel radiations of angiosperms and insects into the late Cretaceous. The evolution of nectaries in late Cretaceous flowers signals the beginning of the mutualism between hymenopterans and angiosperms.

There are some important adaptations to do with the overall coordination of the systems in the body. Such adaptations may have significant consequences. Examples, in vertebrates, would be temperature regulation, or improvements in brain function, or an effective immune system. An example in plants would be the development of the reproductive system in flowering plants. Such adaptations may make the clade (monophyletic group) more viable in a wide range of habitats. The acquisition of such major adaptations has often served as the spark for adaptive radiation, and huge success for long periods of time for a whole group of animals or plants.

Compromise and Conflict Between Adaptations

It is a profound truth that Nature does not know best; that genetical evolution ... is a story of waste, makeshift, compromise and blunder. — *Peter Medawar*

All adaptations have a downside: horse legs are great for running on grass, but they can't scratch their backs; mammals' hair helps temperature, but offers a niche for ectoparasites; the only flying penguins do is under water. Adaptations serving different functions may be mutually destructive. Compromise and make-shift occur widely, not perfection. Selection pressures pull in different directions, and the adaptation that results is some kind of compromise.

Since the phenotype as a whole is the target of selection, it is impossible to improve simultaneously all aspects of the phenotype to the same degree. — *Ernst Mayr*

Consider the antlers of the Irish elk, (often supposed to be far too large; in deer antler size has an allometric relationship to body size). Obviously antlers serve positively for defence against predators, and to score victories in the annual rut. But they are costly in terms of resource. Their size during the last glacial period presumably depended on the relative gain and loss of reproductive capacity in the population of elks during that time. Another example: camouflage to avoid detection is destroyed when vivid colours are displayed at mating time. Here the risk to life is counterbalanced by the necessity for reproduction.

Henry Walter Bates' work on Amazonian butterflies led him to develop the first scientific account of mimicry, especially the kind of mimicry which bears his name: Batesian mimicry. This is the mimicry by a palatable species of an unpalatable or noxious species. A common example seen in temperate gardens is the hover-fly, many of which — though bearing no sting — mimic the warning colouration of hymenoptera (wasps and bees). Such mimicry does not need to be perfect to improve the survival of the palatable species.

Bates, Wallace and Müller believed that Batesian and Müllerian mimicry provided evidence for the action of natural selection, a view which is now standard amongst biologists. All aspects of this situation can be, and have been, the subject of research. Field and experimental work on these ideas continues to this day; the topic connects strongly to speciation, genetics and development.

The peacock's ornamental train (grown anew in time for each mating season) is a famous adaptation. It must reduce his maneuverability and flight, and is hugely conspicuous; also, its growth costs food resources. Darwin's explanation of its advantage was in terms of sexual selection: "it depends on the advantage which certain individuals have over other individuals of the same sex and species, in exclusive relation to reproduction." The kind of sexual selection represented by the peacock is called 'mate choice', with an implication that the process selects the more fit over the less fit, and so has survival value. The recognition of sexual selection was for a long time in abeyance, but has been rehabilitated. In practice, the blue peafowl *Pavo cristatus* is a pretty successful species, with a big natural range in India, so the overall outcome of their mating system is quite viable.

The conflict between the size of the human foetal brain at birth, (which cannot be larger than about 400ccs, else it will not get through the mother's pelvis) and the size needed for an adult brain (about 1400ccs), means the brain of a newborn child is quite immature. The most vital things in human life (locomotion, speech) just have to wait while the brain grows and matures. That is the result of the birth compromise. Much of the problem comes from our upright bipedal stance, without which our pelvis could be shaped more suitably for birth. Neanderthals had a similar problem.

This occurs when a species or population has characteristics which (by chance) are suited for conditions which have not yet arisen. For example, the polyploid ricegrass *Spartina townsendii* is better adapted than either of its parent species to their own habitat of saline marsh and mud-flats. White Leghorn fowl are markedly more resistant to vitamin B deficiency than other breeds. On a plentiful diet there is no difference, but on a restricted diet this preadaptation could be decisive.

Pre-adaptation may occur because a natural population carries a huge quantity of genetic variability. In diploid eukaryotes, this is a consequence of the system of sexual reproduction, where mutant alleles get partially shielded, for example, by the selective advantage of heterozygotes. Micro-organisms, with their huge populations, also carry a great deal of genetic variability.

The first experimental evidence of the pre-adaptive nature of genetic variants in micro-organisms was provided by Salvador Luria and Max Delbrück who developed fluctuation analysis, a method to show the random fluctuation of pre-existing genetic changes that conferred resistance to phage in the bacterium *Escherichia coli.*

Co-option of Existing Traits: Exaptation

The classic example is the ear ossicles of mammals, which we know from palaeontological and embrological studies originated in the upper and lower jaws and the hyoid of their Synapsid ancestors, and further back still were part of the gill arches of early fish. We owe this esoteric knowledge to the comparative anatomists, who, a century ago, were at the cutting edge of evolutionary studies. The word *exaptation* was coined to cover these shifts in function, which are surprisingly common in evolutionary history. The origin of wings from feathers that were originally used for temperature regulation is a more recent discovery.

Non-adaptive Traits

Some traits appear to be not adaptive, that is, selectively neutral. There may be various causes: the utility of a trait is lost and does not now appear adaptive; the utility of a trait is unknown; the trait is a consequence of another trait that is adaptive (i.e. spandrels). Because genes have pleiotropic effects, not all traits may be functional. Of course, a trait may have been adaptive at some point in an organism's evolutionary history, but habitats change, leading to adaptations becoming redundant or even a hindrance (maladaptations). Such adaptations are termed vestigial. So, the utility of adaptations may ebb and flow.

Fitness Landscapes; Drift

Sewall Wright's explanation for evolutionary stasis was that organisms come to occupy *adaptive peaks*. In order to evolve to another, higher peak, the species would first have to pass through a valley of maladaptive intermediate stages. This could happen by genetic drift if the population were small enough. This was Wright's *shifting balance theory of evolution*. There has been much skepticism among evolutionary biologists as to whether these rather delicate conditions hold often in natural populations. Ronald Fisher felt that most populations in nature were too large for these effects of genetic drift to be important.

Vestigial Organs

Many organisms have vestigial organs, which are the remnants of fully functional structures in their ancestors. As a result of changes in lifestyle the organs became redundant, and are either not functional or reduced in functionality. With the loss of function goes the loss of positive selection, and the subsequent accumulation of deleterious mutations. Since any structure represents some kind of cost to the general economy of the body, an advantage may accrue from their elimination once they are not functional. Examples: wisdom teeth in humans; the loss of pigment and functional eyes in cave fauna; the loss of structure in endoparasites.

If a population cannot move or change sufficiently to preserve its long-term viability, then obviously, it will become extinct, at least in that locale. The species may or may not survive in other locales. Species extinction occurs when the death rate over the entire species (population, gene pool ...) exceeds the birth rate for a long enough period for the species to disappear. It was an observation of Van Valen that groups of species tend to have a characteristic and fairly regular rate of extinction.

Co-extinction

Just as we have co-adaptation, there is also co-extinction. Co-extinction refers to the loss of a species due to the extinction of another; for example, the extinction of parasitic insects following the loss of their hosts. Co-extinction can also occur when a flowering plant loses its pollinator, or through the disruption of a food chain "Species co-extinction is a manifestation of the interconnectedness of organisms in complex ecosystems. . . . While co-extinction may not be the most important cause of species extinctions, it is certainly an insidious one".

Flexibility, Acclimatization, Learning

Flexibility deals with the relative capacity of an organism to maintain themselves in different habitats: their degree of specialization. *Acclimatization* is a term used for automatic physiological adjustments during life; *learning* is the term used for improvement in behavioral performance during life. In biology these terms are preferred, not adaptation, for changes during life which improve the performance of individuals. These adjustments are not inherited genetically by the next generation.

Adaptation, on the other hand, occurs over many generations; it is a gradual process caused by natural selection which changes the genetic make-up of a population so the collective performs better in its niche.

Flexibility

Populations differ in their phenotypic plasticity, which is the ability of an organism with a given genotype to change its phenotype in response to changes in its habitat, or to its move to a different habitat.

To a greater or lesser extent, all living things can adjust to circumstances. The degree of flexibility is inherited, and varies to some extent between individuals. A highly specialized animal or plant lives only in a well-defined habitat, eats a specific type of food, and cannot survive if its needs are not met. Many herbivores are like this; extreme examples are koalas which depend on eucalyptus, and pandas which require bamboo. A generalist, on the other hand, eats a range of food, and can survive in many different conditions. Examples are humans, rats, crabs and many carnivores. The *tendency* to behave in a specialized or exploratory manner is inherited — it is an adaptation.

Rather different is *developmental flexibility:* "An animal or plant is developmentally flexible if when it is raised or transferred to new conditions it develops so that it is better fitted to survive in the new circumstances". Once again, there are huge differences between species, and the *capacities* to be flexible are inherited.

Acclimatization

If humans move to a higher altitude, respiration and physical exertion become a problem, but after spending time in high altitude conditions they *acclimatize* to the pressure by increasing production of red blood corpuscles. The *ability* to acclimatize is an adaptation, but not the acclimatization itself. Fecundity goes down, but deaths from some tropical diseases also goes down.

Over a longer period of time, some people will reproduce better at these high altitudes than others. They will contribute more heavily to later generations. Gradually the whole population becomes adapted to the new conditions.

This we know takes place, because the performance of long-term communities at higher altitude is significantly better than the performance of new arrivals, even when the new arrivals have had time to make physiological adjustments.

Some kinds of acclimatization happen so rapidly that they are better called reflexes. The rapid colour changes in some flatfish, cephalopods, chameleons are examples.

Learning

Social learning is supreme for humans, and is possible for quite a few mammals and birds: of course, that does not involve genetic transmission except to the extent that the capacities are inherited. Similarly, the *capacity to learn* is an inherited adaptation, but not what is learnt; the capacity for human speech is inherited, but not the details of language.

Function

To say something has a function is to say something about what it does for the organism, obviously. It also says something about its history: how it has come about. A heart pumps blood: that is its function. It also emits sound, which is just an ancillary side-effect. That is not its function. The heart has a history (which may be well or poorly understood), and that history is about how natural selection formed and maintained the heart as a pump. Every aspect of an organism that has a function has a history. Now, an adaptation must have a functional history: therefore we expect it must have undergone selection caused by relative survival in its habitat. It would be quite wrong to use the word adaptation about a trait which arose as a by-product.

It is widely regarded as unprofessional for a biologist to say something like 'A wing is for flying', although that is their normal function. A biologist would be conscious that sometime in the remote past feathers on a small dinosaur had the function of retaining heat, and that later many wings were not used for flying (e.g. penguins, ostriches). So, the biologist would rather say that the wings on a bird or an insect usually had the *function* of aiding flight. That would carry the connotation of being an adaptation with a history of evolution by natural selection.

Teleonomy

'Teleonomy' is a term invented to describe the study of goal-directed functions which are not guided by the conscious forethought of man or any supernatural entity. It is contrasted with Aristotle's teleology, which has connotations of intention, purpose and foresight. Evolution is teleonomic; adaptation hoards hindsight rather than foresight. The following is a definition for its use in biology:

"The hypothesis that adaptations arise without the existence of a prior purpose, but by the action of natural selection on genetic variability".

The term may have been suggested by Colin Pittendrigh in 1958; it grew out of cybernetics and self-organising systems. Ernst Mayr, George C. Williams and Jacques Monod picked up the term and used it in evolutionary biology.

Philosophers of science have also commented on the term. Ernest Nagel analysed the concept of goal-directedness in biology; and David Hull commented on the use of teleology and teleonomy by biologists.

Haldane can be found remarking, "Teleology is like a mistress to a biologist: he cannot live without her but he's unwilling to be seen with her in public." Today the mistress has become a lawfully wedded wife. Biologists no longer feel obligated to apologize for their use of teleological language; they flaunt it. The only concession which they make to its disreputable past is to rename it 'teleonomy'.

7 Organism

In biology, an organism is any living system (such as animal, plant, fungus, or micro-organism). In at least some form, all organisms are capable of response to stimuli, reproduction, growth and development, and maintenance of homeostasis as a stable whole. An organism may either be unicellular (single-celled) or be composed of, as in humans, many billions of cells grouped into specialized tissues and organs. The term *multicellular* (many-celled) describes any organism made up of more than one cell.

The term 'organism' *organismos*, from Ancient Greek—*organon* 'organ, instrument, tool') first appeared in the English language in 1701 and took on its current definition by 1834 (Oxford English Dictionary).

Scientific classification in biology considers organisms synonymous with life on Earth. Based on cell type, organisms may be divided into the prokaryotic and eukaryotic groups. The prokaryotes represent two separate domains, the Bacteria and Archaea. Eukaryotic organisms, with a membrane-bounded cell nucleus, also contain organelles, namely mitochondria and (in plants) plastids, generally considered to be derived from endosymbiotic bacteria. Fungi, animals and plants are examples of species that are eukaryotes.

More recently a clade, Neomura, has been proposed, which groups together the Archaea and Eukarya. Neomura is thought to have evolved from Bacteria, more specifically from Actinobacteria.

Semantics

The word '*organism*' may broadly be defined as *an assembly of molecules that function as a more or less stable whole and has the properties of life.* However, many sources propose definitions that exclude viruses and theoretically-possible man-made non-organic life forms. Viruses are dependent on the biochemical machinery of a host cell for reproduction.

Chambers Online Reference provides a broad definition: "any living structure, such as a plant, animal, fungus or bacterium, capable of growth and reproduction".

In multicellular life the word 'organism' usually describes the whole hierarchical assemblage of systems (for example circulatory, digestive, or reproductive) themselves collections of organs; these are, in turn, collections of tissues, which are themselves made of cells. In some plants and the nematode *Caenorhabditis elegans*, individual cells are totipotent.

A superorganism is an organism consisting of many individuals working together as a single functional or social unit.

Viruses

Viruses are not typically considered to be organisms because they are incapable of 'independent' or autonomous reproduction or metabolism. This controversy is problematic because some cellular organisms are also incapable of independent survival (but not of independent metabolism and procreation) and live as obligatory intracellular parasites. Although viruses have a few enzymes and molecules characteristic of living organisms, they have no metabolism of their own and cannot synthesize and organize the organic compounds that form them. Naturally, this rules out autonomous reproduction and they can only be passively replicated by the machinery of the host cell. In this sense they are similar to inanimate matter. While viruses sustain no independent metabolism, and thus are usually not accounted organisms, they do have their own genes and they do evolve by similar mechanisms by which organisms evolve.

Organizational Terminology

All organisms are classified by the science of alpha taxonomy into either taxa or clades.

Taxa are ranked groups of organisms, which run from the general (domain) to the specific (species). A broad scheme of ranks in hierarchical order is:

- Domain
- Kingdom
- Phylum
- Class
- Order
- Family
- Genus
- Species

To give an example, *Homo sapiens* is the Latin binomial equating to modern humans. All members of the species *sapiens* are, at least in theory, genetically able to interbreed. Several species may belong to a genus, but the members of different species within a genus are unable to interbreed to produce fertile offspring. Homo, however, only has one surviving species (sapiens); *Homo erectus, Homo neanderthalensis* having become extinct thousands of years ago. Several genera belong to the same family and so on up the hierarchy. Eventually, the relevant kingdom

(Animalia, in the case of humans) is placed into one of the three domains depending upon certain genetic and structural characteristics.

All living organisms known to science are given classification by this system such that the species within a particular family are more closely related and genetically similar than the species within a particular phylum.

Organisms are complex chemical systems, organized in ways that promote reproduction and some measure of sustainability or survival. The molecular phenomena of chemistry are fundamental in understanding organisms, but it is a philosophical error (reductionism) to reduce organismal biology to mere chemistry. It is generally the phenomena of entire organisms that determine their fitness to an environment and therefore the survivability of their DNA based genes.

Organisms clearly owe their origin, metabolism, and many other internal functions to chemical phenomena, especially the chemistry of large organic molecules. Organisms are complex systems of chemical compounds which, through interaction with each other and the environment, play a wide variety of roles.

Organisms are semi-closed chemical systems. Although they are individual units of life (as the definition requires) they are not closed to the environment around them. To operate they constantly take in and release energy. Autotrophs produce usable energy (in the form of organic compounds) using light from the sun or inorganic compounds while heterotrophs take in organic compounds from the environment.

The primary chemical element in these compounds is carbon. The physical properties of this element such as its great affinity for bonding with other small atoms, including other carbon atoms, and its small size makes it capable of forming multiple bonds, make it ideal as the basis of organic life. It is able to form small three-atom compounds (such as carbon dioxide), as well as large chains of many thousands of atoms that can store data (nucleic acids), hold cells together, and transmit information (protein).

Macromolecules

Compounds that make up organisms may be divided into macromolecules and other, smaller molecules. The four groups of macromolecule are nucleic acids, proteins, carbohydrates and lipids. Nucleic acids (specifically deoxyribonucleic acid, or DNA) store genetic data as a sequence of nucleotides. The particular sequence of the four different types of nucleotides (adenine, cytosine, guanine, and thymine) dictate the many characteristics that constitute the organism. The sequence is divided up into codons, each of which is a particular sequence of three nucleotides and corresponds to a particular amino acid. Thus a sequence of DNA codes for a particular protein which, due to the chemical properties of the amino acids of which it is made, folds in a particular manner and so performs a particular function.

The following functions of protein have been recognized:

- Enzymes, which catalyze all of the reactions of metabolism;
- Structural proteins, such as tubulin, or collagen;
- Regulatory proteins, such as transcription factors or cyclins that regulate the cell cycle;
- Signaling molecules or their receptors such as some hormones and their receptors.

Defensive proteins, which can include everything from antibodies of the immune system, to toxins (e.g., dendrotoxins of snakes), to proteins that include unusual amino acids like canavanine.

Lipids make up the membrane of cells that constitutes a barrier, containing everything within the cell and preventing compounds from freely passing into, and out of, the cell. In some multicellular organisms they serve to store energy and mediate communication between cells. Carbohydrates also store and transport energy in some organisms, but are more easily broken down than lipids.

Structure

All organisms consist of monomeric units called cells; some contain a single cell (unicellular) and others contain many units (multicellular). Multicellular organisms are able to specialize cells to perform specific functions, a group of such cells is tissue the four basic types of which are epithelium, nervous tissue, muscle tissue and connective tissue. Several types of tissue work together in the form of an organ to produce a particular function (such as the pumping of the blood by the heart, or as a barrier to the environment as the skin). This pattern continues to a higher level with several organs functioning as an organ system to allow for reproduction, digestion, &c. Many multicelled organisms consist of several organ systems, which coordinate to allow for life.

The Cell

The cell theory, first developed in 1839 by Schleiden and Schwann, states that all organisms are composed of one or more cells; all cells come from preexisting cells; all vital functions of an organism occur within cells, and cells contain the hereditary information necessary for regulating cell functions and for transmitting information to the next generation of cells.

There are two types of cells, eukaryotic and prokaryotic. Prokaryotic cells are usually singletons, while eukaryotic cells are usually found in multi-cellular organisms. Prokaryotic cells lack a nuclear membrane so DNA is unbound within the cell, eukaryotic cells have nuclear membranes.

All cells, whether prokaryotic or eukaryotic, have a membrane, which envelops the cell, separates its interior from its environment, regulates what moves in and out, and maintains the electric potential of the cell. Inside the membrane, a salty cytoplasm takes up most of the cell volume. All cells possess DNA, the hereditary material of genes, and RNA, containing the information necessary to build various proteins such as enzymes, the cell's primary machinery. There are also other kinds of biomolecules in cells.

All cells share several abilities:

- Reproduction by cell division (binary fission, mitosis or meiosis).
- Use of enzymes and other proteins coded for by DNA genes and made via messenger RNA intermediates and ribosomes.

Cell components, converting energy, molecules and releasing by-products. The functioning of a cell depends upon its ability to extract and use chemical energy stored in organic molecules. This energy is derived from metabolic pathways.

Response to external and internal stimuli such as changes in temperature, pH or nutrient levels.

Cell contents are contained within a cell surface membrane that contains proteins and a lipid bilayer.

Life Span

One of the basic parameters of organism is its life span. Some organisms live as short as one day, while some plants can live thousands of years. Aging is important when determining life span of most organisms, bacterium, a virus or even a prion.

Evolution

In biology, the theory of universal common descent proposes that all organisms on Earth are descended from a common ancestor or ancestral gene pool. Evidence for common descent may be found in traits shared between all living organisms. In Darwin's day, the evidence of shared traits was based solely on visible observation of morphologic similarities, such as the fact that all birds have wings, even those that do not fly.

Today, there is debate over whether or not all organisms descended from a common ancestor, or a 'last universal ancestor' (LUA), also called the 'last universal common ancestor' (LUCA). The universality of genetic coding suggests common ancestry. For example, every living cell makes use of nucleic acids as its genetic material, and uses the same twenty amino acids as the building blocks for proteins, although exceptions to the basic twenty amino acids have been found. However, throughout history groupings based on appearance or function of species have sometimes been polyphyletic due to convergent evolution.

The 'last universal ancestor' (LUA), or 'last universal common ancestor' (LUCA), is the name given to the hypothetical single cellular organism or single cell that gave rise to all life on Earth 3.5 to 3.8 billion years ago ; however, this hypothesis has since been refuted on many grounds. For example, it was once thought that the genetic code was universal (see: universal genetic code), but many variations have been discovered including various alternative mitochondrial codes. Back in the early 1970s, evolutionary biologists thought that a given piece of DNA specified the same protein subunit in every living thing, and that the genetic code was thus universal. This was interpreted as evidence that every organism had inherited its genetic code from a single common ancestor, aka, an LUCA. In 1979, however, exceptions to the code were found in mitochondria, the tiny energy factories inside cells. Researchers studying human mitochondrial genes discovered that they used an alternative code, and many slight variants have been discovered since, including various alternative mitochondrial codes, as well as small variants such as *Mycoplasma* translating the codon UGA as tryptophan. Biologists subsequently found exceptions in bacteria and in the nuclei of algae and single-celled animals. For example, certain proteins may use alternative initiation (start) codons not normally used by that species. In certain proteins, non-standard amino acids are substituted for standard stop codons, depending upon associated signal sequences in the messenger RNA: UGA can code for selenocysteine and UAG can code for pyrrolysine. Selenocysteine is now viewed as the 21st amino acid, and pyrrolysine is viewed as the 22nd. A detailed description of variations in the genetic code can be found at the NCBI web site.

It is now clear that the genetic code is not the same in all living things and this provides credence that all living things did not evolve on a firmly-rooted tree of life from a single LUCA. Further support that there is no LUCA has been provided over the years by horizontal/lateral gene transfer in both prokaryote and eukaryote single cell organisms. This is why phylogenetic trees cannot be rooted; why almost all phylogenetic trees have different branching structures, particularly near the base of the tree; and why many organisms have been found with codons and sections of their DNA sequence that are sometimes unrelated to other species.

Information about the early development of life includes input from many different fields, including geology and planetary science. These sciences provide information about the history of the Earth and the changes produced by life. However, a great deal of information about the early Earth has been destroyed by geological processes over the course of time.

The chemical evolution from self-catalytic chemical reactions to life (see Origin of life) is not a part of biological evolution, but it is unclear at which point such increasingly complex sets of reactions became what we would consider, today, to be living organisms.

Not much is known about the earliest developments in life. However, all existing organisms share certain traits, including cellular structure and genetic code. Most scientists interpret this to mean all existing organisms share a common ancestor, which had already developed the most fundamental cellular processes, but there is no scientific consensus on the relationship of the three domains of life (Archaea, Bacteria, Eukaryota) or the origin of life. Attempts to shed light on the earliest history of life generally focus on the behaviour of macromolecules, particularly RNA, and the behaviour of complex systems.

The emergence of oxygenic photosynthesis (around 3 billion years ago) and the subsequent emergence of an oxygen-rich, non-reducing atmosphere can be traced through the formation of banded iron deposits, and later red beds of iron oxides. This was a necessary prerequisite for the development of aerobic cellular respiration, believed to have emerged around 2 billion years ago.

In the last billion years, simple multicellular plants and animals began to appear in the oceans. Soon after the emergence of the first animals, the Cambrian explosion (a period of unrivaled and remarkable, but brief, organismal diversity documented in the fossils found at the Burgess Shale) saw the creation of all the major body plans, or phyla, of modern animals. This event is now believed to have been triggered by the development of the Hox genes. About 500 million years ago, plants and fungi colonized the land, and were soon followed by arthropods and other animals, leading to the development of today's land ecosystems.

The evolutionary process may be exceedingly slow. Fossil evidence indicates that the diversity and complexity of modern life has developed over much of the history of the earth. Geological evidence indicates that the Earth is approximately 4.6 billion years old. Studies on guppies by

David Reznick at the University of California, Riverside, however, have shown that the rate of evolution through natural selection can proceed 10 thousand to 10 million times faster than what is indicated in the fossil record. Such comparative studies however are invariably biased by disparities in the time scales over which evolutionary change is measured in the laboratory, field experiments, and the fossil record.

Horizontal Gene Transfer, and the History of Life

The ancestry of living organisms has traditionally been reconstructed from morphology, but is increasingly supplemented with phylogenetics - the reconstruction of phylogenies by the comparison of genetic (DNA) sequence.

"Sequence comparisons suggest recent horizontal transfer of many genes among diverse species including across the boundaries of phylogenetic 'domains'. Thus determining the phylogenetic history of a species can not be done conclusively by determining evolutionary trees for single genes."

Biologist Gogarten suggests "the original metaphor of a tree no longer fits the data from recent genome research", therefore "biologists [should] use the metaphor of a mosaic to describe the different histories combined in individual genomes and use [the] metaphor of a net to visualize the rich exchange and cooperative effects of HGT among microbes."

Future of Life (Cloning and Synthetic Organisms)

In modern terms, the category of organism cloning refers to the procedure of creating a new multicellular organism, genetically identical to another. However, cloning also has the potential of creating entirely new species of organisms. Organism cloning is the subject of much ethical debate (see Bioethics, Ethics of cloning, and Designer baby articles).

The J. Craig Venter Institute has recently assembled a synthetic yeast genome, *Mycoplasma genitalium*, by recombination of 25 overlapping DNA fragments in a single step. "The use of yeast recombination greatly simplifies the assembly of large DNA molecules from both synthetic and natural fragments." Other companies, such as Synthetic Genomics, have already been formed to take advantage of the many commercial uses of custom designed genomes.

Microorganism

A microorganism (from the Greek: 'small' a, *organismós*, 'organism'; also spelled micro organism or micro-organism) or microbe is an organism that is microscopic (usually too small to be seen by the naked human eye). The study of microorganisms is called microbiology, a subject that began with Anton van Leeuwenhoek's discovery of microorganisms in 1675, using a microscope of his own design.

Microorganisms are very diverse; they include bacteria, fungi, archaea, and protists; microscopic plants (called green algae); and animals such as plankton and the planarian. Some microbiologists also include viruses, but others consider these as non-living. Most microorganisms are unicellular (single-celled), but this is not universal, since some multicellular organisms are microscopic, while some unicellular protists and bacteria, like *Thiomargarita namibiensis*, are macroscopic and visible to the naked eye.

Microorganisms live in all parts of the biosphere where there is liquid water, including soil, hot springs, on the ocean floor, high in the atmosphere and deep inside rocks within the Earth's crust. Microorganisms are critical to nutrient recycling in ecosystems as they act as decomposers. As some microorganisms can fix nitrogen, they are a vital part of the nitrogen cycle, and recent studies indicate that airborne microbes may play a role in precipitation and weather.

Microbes are also exploited by people in biotechnology, both in traditional food and beverage preparation, and in modern technologies based on genetic engineering. However, pathogenic microbes are harmful, since they invade and grow within other organisms, causing diseases that kill millions of people, other animals, and plants.

Single-celled microorganisms were the first forms of life to develop on Earth, approximately 3-4 billion years ago. Further evolution was slow, and for about 3 billion years in the Precambrian eon, all organisms were microscopic. So, for most of the history of life on Earth the only forms of life were microorganisms. Bacteria, algae and fungi have been identified in amber that is 220 million years old, which shows that the morphology of microorganisms has changed little since the triassic period.

Most microorganisms can reproduce rapidly and microbes such as bacteria can also freely exchange genes by conjugation, transformation and transduction between widely-divergent species. This horizontal gene transfer, coupled with a high mutation rate and many other means of genetic variation, allows microorganisms to swiftly evolve (via natural selection) to survive in new environments and respond to environmental stresses. This rapid evolution is important in medicine, as it has led to the recent development of 'super-bugs' — pathogenic bacteria that are resistant to modern antibiotics.

Pre-Microbiology

The possibility that microorganisms exist was discussed for many centuries before their actual discovery in the 17th century. The earliest known idea to indicate the possibility of diseases spreading by yet unseen organisms was that of the Roman scholar Marcus Terentius Varro in a 1st century BC book titled *On Agriculture* in which he warns against locating a homestead near swamps:

"... and because there are bred certain minute creatures which cannot be seen by the eyes, which float in the air and enter the body through the mouth and nose and there cause serious diseases."

In *The Canon of Medicine* (1020), Abu Ali ibn Sina (Avicenna) stated that bodily secretion is contaminated by foul foreign earthly bodies before being infected. He also hypothesized that tuberculosis and other diseases might be contagious, *i.e.* that they were infectious diseases, and used quarantine to limit their spread.

When the Black Death bubonic plague reached Andalusia in Spain, in the 14th century, Ibn Khatima wrote that infectious diseases were caused by contagious "minute bodies" that enter the human body. Later, in 1546, Girolamo Fracastoro proposed that epidemic diseases were caused by transferable seedlike entities that could transmit infection by direct or indirect contact, or even without contact over long distances.

All these early claims about the existence of microorganisms were speculative and were not based on any data or science. Microorganisms were neither proven, observed, nor correctly and accurately described until the 17th century. The reason for this was that all these early studies lacked the microscope.

History of Microorganisms' Discovery

Anton van Leeuwenhoek was the one of the first people to observe microorganisms, using a microscope of his own design, and made one of the most important contributions to biology. Robert Hooke was the first to use a microscope to observe living things; his 1665 book *Micrographia* contained descriptions of plant cells.

Before Leeuwenhoek's discovery of microorganisms in 1675, it had been a mystery why grapes could be turned into wine, milk into cheese, or why food would spoil.

Leeuwenhoek did not make the connection between these processes and microorganisms, but using a microscope, he did establish that there were forms of life that were not visible to the naked eye. Leeuwenhoek's discovery, along with subsequent observations by Lazzaro Spallanzani and Louis Pasteur, ended the long-held belief that life spontaneously appeared from non-living substances during the process of spoilage.

Lazzaro Spallanzani found that boiling broth would sterilise it and kill any microorganisms in it. He also found that new microorganisms could only settle in a broth if the broth was exposed to the air. Louis Pasteur expanded upon Spallanzani's findings by exposing boiled broths to the air, in vessels that contained a filter to prevent all particles from passing through to the growth medium, and also in vessels with no filter at all, with air being admitted via a curved tube that would not allow dust particles to come in contact with the broth. By boiling the broth beforehand, Pasteur ensured that no microorganisms survived within the broths at the beginning of his experiment. Nothing grew in the broths in the course of Pasteur's experiment.

This meant that the living organisms that grew in such broths came from outside, as spores on dust, rather than spontaneously generated within the broth. Thus, Pasteur dealt the death blow to the theory of spontaneous generation and supported germ theory.

In 1767, Dr. J.Z. Holwell reported that Indian physicians at the time knew that microbes caused diseases: "They lay it down as a principle, that the immediate cause of the smallpox exists in the mortal part of every human and animal form; that the mediate (or second) *acting* cause, which stirs up the first, and throws it into a state of fermentation, is multitudes of imperceptible animalculae floating in the atmosphere; that these are the cause of all epidemical diseases, but more particularly of the small pox".

In 1876, Robert Koch established that microbes can cause disease. He found that the blood of cattle who were infected with anthrax always had large numbers of *Bacillus anthracis.* Koch found that he could transmit anthrax from one animal to another by taking a small sample of blood from the infected animal and injecting it into a healthy one, and this caused the healthy animal to become sick. He also found that he could grow the bacteria in a nutrient broth, then inject it into a healthy animal, and cause illness. Based on these experiments, he devised criteria for establishing a causal link between a microbe and a disease and these are now known as Koch's postulates. Although these postulates cannot be applied in all cases, they do retain historical importance to the development of scientific thought and are still being used today.

Classification and Structure

Microorganisms can be found almost anywhere in the taxonomic organization of life on the planet. Bacteria and archaea are almost always microscopic, while a number of eukaryotes are also microscopic, including most protists, some fungi, as well as some animals and plants. Viruses are generally regarded as not living and therefore are not microbes, although the field of microbiology also encompasses the study of viruses.

Prokaryotes

Prokaryotes are organisms that lack a cell nucleus and the other membrane bound organelles. They are almost always unicellular, although some species such as myxobacteria can aggregate into complex structures as part of their life cycle.

Consisting of two domains, bacteria and archaea, the prokaryotes are the most diverse and abundant group of organisms on Earth and inhabit practically all environments where some liquid water is available and the temperature is below +140 °C. They are found in sea water, soil, air, animals' gastrointestinal tracts, hot springs and even deep beneath the Earth's crust in rocks. Practically all surfaces which have not been specially sterilized are covered by prokaryotes. The number of prokaryotes on Earth is estimated to be around five million trillion trillion, or 5×10^{30}, accounting for at least half the biomass on Earth.

Bacteria are practically all invisible to the naked eye, with a few extremely rare exceptions, such as *Thiomargarita namibiensis*. They lack membrane-bound organelles, and can function and reproduce as individual cells, but often aggregate in multicellular colonies. Their genome is usually a single loop of DNA, although they can also harbor small pieces of DNA called plasmids. These plasmids can be transferred between cells through bacterial conjugation. Bacteria are surrounded by a cell wall, which provides strength and rigidity to their cells. They reproduce by binary fission or sometimes by budding, but do not undergo sexual reproduction. Some species form extraordinarily resilient spores, but for bacteria this is a mechanism for survival, not reproduction. Under optimal conditions bacteria can grow extremely rapidly and can double as quickly as every 10 minutes.

Archaea

Archaea are also single-celled organisms that lack nuclei. In the past, the differences between bacteria and archaea were not recognised and archaea were classified with bacteria as part of the kingdom Monera. However, in 1990 the microbiologist Carl Woese proposed the three-domain system that divided living things into bacteria, archaea and eukaryotes. Archaea differ from bacteria in both their genetics and biochemistry. For example, while bacterial cell membranes are made from phosphoglycerides with ester bonds, archaean membranes are made of ether lipids.

Archaea were originally described in extreme environments, such as hot springs, but have since been found in all types of habitats only now are scientists beginning to realize how common archaea are in the environment, with crenarchaeota being the most common form of life in the ocean, dominating ecosystems below 150 m in depth. These organisms are also common in soil and play a vital role in ammonia oxidation.

Most living things which are visible to the naked eye in their adult form are eukaryotes, including humans. However, a large number of eukaryotes are also microorganisms. Unlike bacteria and archaea, eukaryotes contain organelles such as the cell nucleus, the Golgi apparatus and mitochondria in their cells. The nucleus is an organelle which houses the DNA that makes up a cell's genome. DNA itself is arranged in complex chromosomes. Mitochondria are organelles vital in metabolism as they are the site of the citric acid cycle and oxidative phosphorylation. They evolved from symbiotic bacteria and retain a remnant genome. Like bacteria, plant cells have cell walls, and contain organelles such as chloroplasts in addition to the organelles in other eukaryotes. Chloroplasts produce energy from light by photosynthesis, and were also originally symbiotic bacteria.

Unicellular eukaryotes are those eukaryotic organisms that consist of a single cell throughout their life cycle. This qualification is significant since most multicellular eukaryotes consist of a single cell called a zygote at the beginning of their life cycles. Microbial eukaryotes can be either haploid or diploid, and some organisms have multiple cell nuclei (see coenocyte). However, not all microorganisms are unicellular as some microscopic eukaryotes are made from multiple cells.

Protists

Of eukaryotic groups, the protists are most commonly unicellular and microscopic. This is a highly diverse group of organisms that are not easy to classify. Several algae species are multicellular protists, and slime molds have unique life cycles that involve switching between unicellular, colonial, and multicellular forms. The number of species of protozoa is uncertain, since we may have identified only a small proportion of the diversity in this group of organisms.

Mostly animals are multicellular, but some are too small to be seen by the naked eye. Microscopic arthropods include dust mites and spider mites. Microscopic crustaceans include copepods and the cladocera, while many nematodes are too small to be seen with the naked eye. Another particularly common group of microscopic animals are the rotifers, which are filter feeders that are usually found in fresh water. Micro-animals reproduce both sexually and asexually and may reach new habitats as eggs that survive harsh environments that would kill the adult animal. However, some simple animals, such as rotifers and nematodes, can dry out completely and remain dormant for long periods of time.

Fungi

The fungi have several unicellular species, such as baker's yeast (*Saccharomyces cerevisiae*) and fission yeast (*Schizosaccharomyces pombe*). Some fungi, such as the pathogenic yeast *Candida albicans*, can undergo phenotypic switching and grow as single cells in some environments, and filamentous hyphae in others. Fungi reproduce both asexually, by budding or binary fission, as well by producing spores, which are called conidia when produced asexually, or basidiospores when produced sexually.

Plants

The green algae are a large group of photosynthetic eukaryotes that include many microscopic organisms. Although some green algae are classified as protists, others such as charophyta are classified with embryophyte plants, which are the most familiar group of land plants. Algae can grow as single cells, or in long chains of cells. The green algae include unicellular and colonial flagellates, usually but not always with two flagella per cell, as well as various colonial, coccoid, and filamentous forms. In the Charales, which are the algae most closely related to higher plants, cells differentiate into several distinct tissues within the organism. There are about 6000 species of green algae.

Habitats and Ecology

Microorganisms are found in almost every habitat present in nature. Even in hostile environments such as the poles, deserts, geysers, rocks, and the deep sea. Some types of microorganisms have adapted to the extreme conditions and sustained colonies; these organisms are known as extremophiles. Extremophiles have been isolated from rocks as much as 7 kilometres below the Earth's surface, and it has been suggested that the amount of living organisms below the Earth's surface may be comparable with the amount of life on or above the surface. Extremophiles have been known to survive for a prolonged time in a vacuum, and can be highly resistant to radiation, which may even allow them to survive in space. Many types of microorganisms have intimate symbiotic relationships with other larger organisms; some of which are mutually beneficial (mutualism), while others can be damaging to the host organism (parasitism). If microorganisms can cause disease in a host they are known as pathogens.

Hygiene

Hygiene is the avoidance of infection or food spoiling by eliminating microorganisms from the surroundings. As microorganisms, particularly bacteria, are found practically everywhere, this means in most cases the reduction of harmful microorganisms to acceptable levels. However, in some cases it is required that an object or substance be completely sterile, i.e. devoid of all living entities and viruses. A good example of this is a hypodermic needle.

In food preparation microorganisms are reduced by preservation methods (such as the addition of vinegar), clean utensils used in preparation, short storage periods or by cool temperatures. If complete sterility is needed, the two most common methods are irradiation and the use of an autoclave, which resembles a pressure cooker.

There are several methods for investigating the level of hygiene in a sample of food, drinking water, equipment etc. Water samples can be filtrated through an extremely fine filter. This filter is then placed in a nutrient medium. Microorganisms on the filter then grow to form a visible colony. Harmful microorganisms can be detected in food by placing a sample in a nutrient broth designed to enrich the organisms in question. Various methods, such as selective media or PCR, can then be used for detection. The hygiene of hard surfaces, such as cooking pots, can be tested by touching them with a solid piece of nutrient medium and then allowing the microorganisms to grow on it.

There are no conditions where all microorganisms would grow, and therefore often several different methods are needed. For example, a food sample might be analyzed on three different nutrient mediums designed to indicate the presence of "total" bacteria (conditions where many, but not all, bacteria grow), molds (conditions where the growth of bacteria is prevented by e.g. antibiotics) and coliform bacteria (these indicate a sewage contamination).

8 Endangered Species

An endangered species is a population of organisms which is at risk of becoming extinct because it is either few in numbers, or threatened by changing environmental or predation parameters. Also it could mean that due to deforestation there may be a lack of food and/or water. The International Union for Conservation of Nature (IUCN) has calculated the percentage of endangered species as 40 per cent of all organisms based on the sample of species that have been evaluated through 2006. Many nations have laws offering protection to conservation reliant species: for example, forbidding hunting, restricting land development or creating preserves. Only a few of the many species at risk of extinction actually make it to the lists and obtain legal protection. Many more species become extinct, or potentially will become extinct, without gaining public notice.

The conservation status of a species is an indicator of the likelihood of that endangered species not living. Many factors are taken into account when assessing the conservation status of a species; not simply the number remaining, but the overall increase or decrease in the population over time, breeding success rates, known threats, and so on. The IUCN Red List is the best known conservation status listing.

Internationally, 190 countries have signed an accord agreeing to create Biodiversity Action Plans to protect endangered and other threatened species. In the United States this plan is usually called a species Recovery Plan.

IUCN Red list of threatened species uses the term *endangered species* as a specific category of imperilment, rather than as a general term. Under the IUCN Categories and Criteria, *endangered species* is between *critically endangered* and *vulnerable*. Also *critically endangered* species may also be counted as *endangered species* and fill all the criteria.

The more general term used by the IUCN for species at risk of extinction is *threatened species*, which also includes the less-at-risk category of vulnerable species together with endangered and critically endangered. IUCN categories include:

- ***Extinct:*** the last remaining member of the species has died, or is presumed beyond reasonable doubt to have died. *Examples:* Thylacine, Dodo, Passenger Pigeon, Tyrannosaurus, Caribbean Monk Seal, Dimetrodon, Aurochs.
- ***Extinct in the wild:*** captive individuals survive, but there is no free-living, natural population. *Examples:* Alagoas Curassow, Guinea pig.
- ***Critically endangered:*** faces an extremely high risk of extinction in the immediate future. *Examples:* Mountain Gorilla, Arakan Forest Turtle, Ethiopian wolf, Darwin's Fox, Javan Rhino, Brazilian Merganser, Gharial, Vaquita.
- ***Endangered:*** faces a very high risk of extinction in the near future. *Examples:* Dhole, Blue Whale, Bonobo, Giant Panda, Snow Leopard, African Wild Dog Tiger,

Indian Rhinoceros, three species of Albatrosses Crowned Solitary Eagle, Markhor, Orangutan, Grevy's zebra.

- ***Vulnerable:*** faces a high risk of extinction in the medium-term. *Examples:* Cheetah Gaur, Lion, Sloth Bear, Wolverine, Manatee, Polar Bear, African Golden Cat, Komodo dragon.
- ***Conservation dependent:*** The following animals are not severely threatened, but the animal must depend on conservation programmes. *Examples:* Spotted Hyena, Blanford's fox, Leopard Shark, Black Caiman, Killer whale.
- ***Near threatened:*** may be considered threatened in the near future. *Examples:* Blue-billed Duck, Solitary Eagle, Small-clawed Otter, Maned Wolf, Tiger Shark, Okapi.
- ***Least concern:*** no immediate threat to the survival of the species. *Examples:* Nootka Cypress, Wood Pigeon, Harp Seal, White-tailed Mongoose, House Mouse.

Under the Endangered Species Act in the United States, 'endangered' is the more protected of the two categories. The Salt Creek tiger beetle (*Cicindela nevadica lincolniana*) is an example of an endangered subspecies protected under the ESA.

In the United States alone, the "known species threatened with extinction is ten times higher than the number protected under the Endangered Species Act". The US Fish and Wildlife Service as well as the National Marine Fisheries Service are held responsible for classifying and protecting endangered species, yet, adding a particular species to the list is a long, controversial process and in reality it represents only a fraction of imperiled plant and animal life.

Some endangered species laws are controversial. Typical areas of controversy include: criteria for placing a species on the endangered species list, and criteria for removing a species from the list once its population has recovered; whether restrictions on land development constitute a 'taking' of land by the government; the related question of whether private landowners should be compensated for the loss of uses of their lands; and obtaining reasonable exceptions to protection laws.

Under the Bush administration, the former policy that required federal officials to consult a wildlife expert before taking actions that could damage endangered species was lifted. Under the Obama administration, this policy has been reinstated.

Being listed as an endangered species can have negative effect since it could make a species more desirable for collectors and poachers. This effect is potentially reducible, such as in China where commercially farmed turtles may be reducing some of the pressure to poach endangered species.

Another problem with the listing species is its effect of inciting the use of the 'shoot, shovel, and shut-up' method of clearing endangered species from an area of land. Some landowners currently may perceive a diminution in value for their land after finding an endangered animal on it. They have allegedly opted to silently kill and bury the animals or destroy habitat, thus removing the problem from their land, but at the same time further reducing the population of an endangered species. The effectiveness of the Endangered Species Act, which coined the term 'endangered species', has been questioned by business advocacy groups and their publications, but is nevertheless widely recognized as an effective recovery tool by wildlife scientists who work with the species. Nineteen species have been delisted and recovered and 93 per cent of listed species in the northeastern United States have a recovering or stable population.

Currently, 1,556 known species in the world have been identified as endangered, or near extinction, and are under protection by government law. This approximation, however, does not take into consideration the number of species threatened with endangerment that are not included under the protection of such laws as the Endangered Species Act. According to NatureServe's global conservation status, approximately thirteen per cent of vertebrates (excluding marine fish), seventeen per cent of vascular plants, and six to eighteen per cent of fungi are considered imperiled. Thus, in total, between seven and eighteen percent of the United States' known animals, fungi, and plants are near extinction. This total is substantially more than the number of species protected under the Endangered Species Act in the United States, which means numerous species are inching closer and closer toward extinction.

Even in the search to learn more about these species, many ecologists do not take into consideration the impact they leave on the environment and its inhabitants. It is apparent that the "quest for ecological knowledge, which is so critical for informing efforts to understand and conserve Earth's biodiversity along with valued ecosystem goods and services, frequently raises complex ethical questions", and there is no clear way to identify and resolve these issues. Environmentalists tend to focus on the whole ecological sphere instead of the welfare of individual animals. Focussing on such a broad view tends to diminish the value of each individual creature. "Biodiversity conservation is currently a principle goal for resource management of 11.5 per cent of the world's surface area." Large portions of life occur outside these protected areas and must be taken into consideration if the conservation of endangered species is going to be effective.

Impact on Biodiversity and Endangered Species

In order to conserve the biodiversity of the planet, one must take into consideration the reasons why so many species are becoming endangered. "Habitat loss is the most widespread cause of species endangerment in the U.S., affecting 85 per cent of imperiled species". When an animal's ecosystem is not maintained, they lose their home and are either forced to adapt to new surroundings or perish. Pollution is another factor that causes many species to become endangered, especially a large proportion of aquatic life. Also, over-exploitation, disease and climate change have led to the endangerment of several species.

However, the most important factor leading to the endangerment of the majority of wildlife in the world is the human impact on the species and their environment. "As human use of resources, energy, and space intensified over the past few centuries, the diversity of life has been substantially diminished in most parts of the world". Basically, as the human impact on the environment increases, the diversity of life decreases. Humans are constantly using the resources and space of other species for themselves, negatively impacting the survival rate of many creatures.

Humans also set standards for which species they think should be saved and which species they find unimportant or undesirable. For example, the coqui frog, an invasive species in Hawaii, is so common there that its 'nocturnal singing' reduces the value of homes and prevents hotels from using rooms near forests. Hawaiians have proposed eliminating the frog, and several wildlife managers want to release a pathogen to kill the frogs. The frog has decreased the value of homes and caused a loss of business for several hotels, so the Hawaiians decided it was acceptable to get rid of the group of coqui frog living near them.

Another example where the human impact affected the welfare of a species sex in the instance of non-native mute swans establishing themselves at Arrowhead Lake in Vermont. When the population of swans grew to eight birds, the Vermont Fish and Wildlife Department decided to take action. Two swans were eventually killed, angering animal welfare organizations and people living near the lake. The case of the Arrowhead Lake swans demonstrates what one considers the natural environment based on human assumptions. Simply because the swans were not normally living there does not mean it is not part of their natural habitat, and there is certainly no reason for them to be destroyed because of human dissatisfaction.

Yet another example of the human impact in the lives of endangered species is that of the Preble's meadow jumping mouse. Research has shown that the mouse is not taxonomically different from the Bear Lodge meadow jumping mouse and the US Fish and Wildlife Service has proposed removing the Preble's mouse from the endangered species list based on this information.

A final example of the human impact on existing species is the issue of toe clipping in ecological research. While ecologists are doing research on different species to advance their knowledge of methods of conservation, they must take into consideration the impact they have on the wildlife they are studying. Toe clipping "has been reported to result in a number of adverse effects on the animals, including inflammation and infection of the feet and limbs". This example demonstrates how humans must take into consideration the well-being of the animal even before they perform research to help conserve the species. The human impact on species and their environments has many negative effects. It is important for humans to help maintain all species in the world and not deter their development.

"Diversity of life and living systems are a necessary condition for human development". Many question the importance of maintaining biodiversity in today's world, where conservation efforts prove costly and time consuming. The fact is that the preservation of all species is necessary for human survival. Species should be saved for "aesthetic and moral justifications; the importance of wild species as providers of products and services essential to human welfare; the value of particular species as indicators of environmental health or as keystone species crucial to the functioning of ecosystems; and the scientific breakthroughs that have come from the study of wild organisms". In other words, species serve as a source of art and entertainment, provide products such as medicine for human well-being, indicate the welfare of the overall environment and ecosystem, and provided research that resulted in scientific discoveries. An example of an 'aesthetic justification' in conserving endangered species is that of the introduction of the gray wolf into Yellowstone National Park. The gray wolf has brought numerous amounts of tourists to the park and added to the biodiversity in the protected region.

Another example, supporting the conservation of endangered species as providers of products for human well-being, is the scrub mint. It has been found that the scrub mint contains an anti-fungal agent and a natural insecticide. Also, the deterioration of the bald eagle and the peregrine falcon "alerted people to the potential health hazards associated with the widespread spraying of DDT and other persistent pesticides".

This serves as an example of how certain fish can serve as identifiers of environmental health and protect human life as well as other species. Finally, an example of species providing for scientific discoveries is the instance of the Pacific yew which "became the source of taxol, one of the most potent anticancer compounds ever discovered". Endangered species could prove useful to human development, maintenance of biodiversity and preservation of ecosystems.

Another approach is known as ecosystem conservation, where a focus is placed less on preserving any individual given species than on preserving the proper functioning of the ecosystem as a whole.

Helping Preserve Endangered Species

It is the goal of conservationists to create and expand upon ways to preserve endangered species and maintain biodiversity. There are several ways in which one can aid in preserving the world's species who are nearing extinction. One such way is obtaining more information on different groups of species, especially invertebrates, fungi, and marine organisms, where sufficient data is lacking.

For example, to understand the causes of population declines and extinction an experiment was conducted on the butterfly population in Finland. In this analysis, the butterflies' endangered list classification, distribution, density, larval specificity, dispersal ability, adult habitat breadth, flight period and body size were all recorded and examined to determine the threatened state of each species. It was found that the butterflies' distribution has declined by fifty-one and a half percent, and they have a severely restricted habitat. One example of specific butterflies who have a declining distribution rate are the Frigga's Fritillary and Grizzled Skipper, who have been affected by habitat loss due to extensive draining of the bogs where they live. This experiment proves that when we know the causes of endangerment, we can successfully create solutions for the management of biodiversity.

Another way to help preserve endangered species is to create a new professional society dedicated to ecological ethics. This could help ecologists make ethical decisions in their research and management of biodiversity. Also, creating more awareness on environmental ethics can help encourage species preservation. "Courses in ethics for students, and training programmes for ecologists and biodiversity managers" all could create environmental awareness and prevent violations of ethics in research and management. One final way in which one can conserve endangered species is through federal agency investments and protection enacted by the federal government. "Ecologists have proposed biological corridors, biosphere reserves, ecosystem management, and ecoregional planning as approaches to integrate biodiversity conservation and socioeconomic development at increasingly larger spatial scales".

One example of a federal mandated conservation zone is the Northwest Hawaiian Islands Marine National Monument, the largest marine protected area in the world. The monument is essential to the preservation of underwater communities and overfished regions. Only researchers working in the area are permitted to fish, no corals may be removed, and the Department of Homeland Security will enforce restrictions on vessels passing through the waters via satellite imaging. The monument will serve as a home to an estimated seven thousand species, most of which cannot be found anywhere else in the world. This environmental monument demonstrates the fact that it is possible to create a safe environment for endangered species, as well as maintaining some of the world's largest ecosystems.

Captive Breeding Programmes

Captive breeding is the process of breeding rare or endangered species in human controlled environments with restricted settings, such as wildlife preserves, zoos and other conservation facilities. Captive breeding is meant to save species from going extinct. It is supposed to stabilize the population of the species so it is no longer at risk for disappearing.

This technique has been used with success for many species for some time, with probably the oldest known such instances of captive mating being attributed to menageries of European and Asian rulers, a case in point being the Pere David's Deer. However, captive breeding techniques are usually difficult to implement for highly mobile species like some migratory birds (eg. cranes) and fishes (eg. Hilsa). Additionally, if the captive breeding population is too small, inbreeding may occur due to a reduced gene pool; this may lead to the population lacking immunity to diseases.

Legal Private Farming for Profit

Whereas poaching causes substantial reductions in endangered animal populations, legal private farming for profit has the opposite effect. Legal private farming has caused substantial increases in the populations of both the southern black rhinoceros and the southern white rhinoceros. Dr. Richard Emslie, a scientific officer at the IUCN, said of such programs, "Effective law enforcement has become much easier now that the animals are largely privately owned ... We have been able to bring local communities into the conservation programmes. There are increasingly strong economic incentives attached to looking after rhinos rather than simply poaching: from eco-tourism or selling them on for a profit. So many owners are keeping them secure. The private sector has been key to helping our work".

Conservation experts view the effect of China's turtle farming on the wild turtle populations of China and South-Eastern Asia — many of which are endangered — as 'poorly understood". While they commend the gradual replacement of wild-caught turtles with farm-raised ones gradually in the marketplace (the percentage of farm-raised individuals in the 'visible' trade growing from around 30 per cent in 2000 to around 70 per cent ca. 2007), they are concerned with the fact that a lot of wild animals are caught to provide farmers with the breeding stock. As the conservation expert Peter Paul van Dijk noted, turtle farmers often believe in the superiority of wild-caught animals as the breeding stock, which may create an incentive for turtle hunters to seek and catch the very last remaining wild specimens of some endangered turtle species.

Extinction

In biology and ecology, extinction is the end of an organism or group of taxa. The moment of extinction is generally considered to be the death of the last individual of that species (although the capacity to breed and recover may have been lost before this point). Because a species' potential range may be very large, determining this moment is difficult, and is usually done retrospectively. This difficulty leads to phenomena such as Lazarus taxa, where a species presumed extinct abruptly 're-appears' (typically in the fossil record) after a period of apparent absence.

Through evolution, new species arise through the process of speciation–where new varieties of organisms arise and thrive when they are able to find and exploit an ecological niche–and species become extinct when they are no longer able to survive in changing conditions or against superior competition. A typical species becomes extinct within 10 million years of its first appearance, although some species, called living fossils, survive virtually unchanged for hundreds of millions of years. Extinction, though, is usually a natural phenomenon; it is estimated that 99.9 per cent of all species that have ever lived are now extinct.

Mass extinctions are relatively rare events, however, isolated extinctions are quite common. Several extinctions during the Holocene extinction have been attributed to the rise of human activity; however, there is no clear consensus among the scientific community on the effect of human activity on extinctions. Only recently have extinctions been recorded and scientists have become alarmed at the high rates of recent extinctions. It is estimated most species that go extinct have never been documented by scientists. Some scientists estimate that up to half of presently existing species may become extinct by 2100.

A species becomes extinct when the last existing member of that species dies. Extinction therefore becomes a certainty when there are no surviving individuals that are able to reproduce and create a new generation. A species may become functionally extinct when only a handful of individuals survive, which are unable to reproduce due to poor health, age, sparse distribution over a large range, a lack of individuals of both sexes (in sexually reproducing species), or other reasons.

Pinpointing the extinction (or pseudoextinction) of a species requires a clear definition of that species. If it is to be declared extinct, the species in question must be uniquely identifiable from any ancestor or daughter species, or from other closely related species. Extinction of a species (or replacement by a daughter species) plays a key role in the punctuated equilibrium hypothesis of Stephen Jay Gould and Niles Eldredge.

In ecology, *extinction* is often used informally to refer to local extinction, in which a species ceases to exist in the chosen area of study, but still exists elsewhere. This phenomenon is also known as extirpation. Local extinctions may be followed by a replacement of the species taken from other locations; wolf reintroduction is an example of this. Species which are not extinct are termed extant. Those that are extant but threatened by extinction are referred to as threatened or endangered species.

An important aspect of extinction at the present time are human attempts to preserve critically endangered species, which is reflected by the creation of the conservation status 'Extinct in the Wild' (EW). Species listed under this status by the World Conservation Union (IUCN) are not known to have any living specimens in the wild, and are maintained only in zoos or other artificial environments. Some of these species are functionally extinct, as they are no longer part of their natural habitat and it is unlikely the species will ever be restored to the wild. When possible, modern zoological institutions attempt to maintain a viable population for species preservation and possible future reintroduction to the wild through use of carefully planned breeding programmes.

The extinction of one species' wild population can have knock-on effects, causing further extinctions. These are also called "chains of extinction". This is especially common with extinction of keystone species.

Descendants may or may not exist for extinct species. Daughter species that evolve from a parent species carry on most of the parent species' genetic information, and even though the parent species may become extinct, the daughter species lives on. In other cases, species have produced no new variants, or none that are able to survive the parent species' extinction. Extinction of a parent species where daughter species or subspecies are still alive is also called *pseudoextinction.*

Pseudoextinction is difficult to demonstrate unless one has a strong chain of evidence linking a living species to members of a pre-existing species. For example, it is sometimes claimed that the extinct *Hyracotherium*, which was an early horse that shares a common ancestor with the modern horse, is pseudoextinct, rather than extinct, because there are several extant species of *Equus*, including zebra and donkeys. However, as fossil species typically leave no genetic material behind, it is not possible to say whether *Hyracotherium* actually evolved into more modern horse species or simply evolved from a common ancestor with modern horses. Pseudoextinction is much easier to demonstrate for larger taxonomic groups.

Extinction Causes

There are a variety of causes that can contribute directly or indirectly to the extinction of a species or group of species. 'Just as each species is unique', write Beverly and Stephen Stearns, "so is each extinction ... the causes for each are varied–some subtle and complex, others obvious and simple". Most simply, any species that is unable to survive or reproduce in its environment, and unable to move to a new environment where it can do so, dies out and becomes extinct. Extinction of a species may come suddenly when an otherwise healthy species is wiped out completely, as when toxic pollution renders its entire habitat unlivable; or may occur gradually over thousands or millions of years, such as when a species gradually loses out in competition for food to better adapted competitors.

Assessing the relative importance of genetic factors compared to environmental ones as the causes of extinction has been compared to the nature-nurture debate. The question of whether more extinctions in the fossil record have been caused by evolution or by catastrophe is a subject of discussion; Mark Newman, the author of *Modelling Extinction* argues for a mathematical model that falls between the two positions. By contrast, conservation biology uses the extinction vortex model to classify extinctions by cause. When concerns about human extinction have been raised, for example in Sir Martin Rees' 2003 book *Our Final Hour*, those concerns lie with the effects of climate change or technological disaster.

Currently, environmental groups and some governments are concerned with the extinction of species caused by humanity, and are attempting to combat further extinctions through a variety of conservation programmes. Humans can cause extinction of a species through overharvesting, pollution, habitat destruction, introduction of new predators and food competitors, overhunting, and other influences. According to the World Conservation Union (WCU, also known as IUCN), 784 extinctions have been recorded since the year 1500 (to the year 2004), the arbitrary date selected to define 'modern' extinctions, with many more likely to have gone unnoticed (several species have also been listed as extinct since the 2004 date).

Genetics and Demographic Phenomena

Population genetics and demographic phenomena affect the evolution, and therefore the risk of extinction, of species. Limited geographic range is the most important determinant of genus extinction at background rates but becomes increasingly irrelevant as mass extinction arises.

Natural selection acts to propagate beneficial genetic traits and eliminate weaknesses. It is nevertheless possible for a deleterious mutation to be spread throughout a population through the effect of genetic drift.

A diverse or deep gene pool gives a population a higher chance of surviving an adverse change in conditions. Effects that cause or reward a loss in genetic diversity can increase the chances of extinction of a species. Population bottlenecks can dramatically reduce genetic diversity by severely limiting the number of reproducing individuals and make inbreeding more frequent. The founder effect can cause rapid, individual-based speciation and is the most dramatic example of a population bottleneck.

Genetic Pollution

Purebred, naturally evolved, region specific wild species can be threatened with extinction in a big way through the process of genetic pollution – i.e., uncontrolled hybridization, introgression genetic swamping which leads to homogenization or replacement of local genotypes as a result of a numerical and/or fitness advantage of the introduced plant or animal. Nonnative species can bring about a form of extinction of native plants and animals by hybridization and introgression, either through purposeful introduction by humans or through habitat modification, bringing previously isolated species into contact. These phenomena can be especially detrimental for rare species coming into contact with more abundant ones, where the abundant ones can interbreed with them, swamping the entire rarer gene pool and creating hybrids, thus driving the entire original purebred native stock to complete extinction. Such extinctions are not always apparent from morphological (outward appearance) observations alone. Some degree of gene flow may be a normal, evolutionarily constructive process, and all constellations of genes and genotypes cannot be preserved however, hybridization with or without introgression may, nevertheless, threaten a rare species' existence.

Widespread genetic pollution also leads to weakening of the naturally evolved (wild) region specific gene pool leading to weaker hybrid animals and plants which are not able to cope with natural environs over the long run and fast tracks them towards final extinction.

The gene pool of a species or a population is the complete set of unique alleles that would be found by inspecting the genetic material of every living member of that species or population. A large gene pool indicates extensive genetic diversity, which is associated with robust populations that can survive bouts of intense selection. Meanwhile, low genetic diversity can cause reduced biological fitness and an increased chance of extinction amongst the reducing population of purebred individuals from a species.

The degradation of a species' habitat may alter the fitness landscape to such an extent that the species is no longer able to survive and becomes extinct. This may occur by direct effects, such as the environment becoming toxic, or indirectly, by limiting a species' ability to compete effectively for diminished resources or against new competitor species.

Habitat degradation through toxicity can kill off a species very rapidly, by killing all living members through contamination or sterilizing them. It can also occur over longer periods at lower toxicity levels by affecting life span, reproductive capacity, or competitiveness.

Habitat degradation can also take the form of a physical destruction of niche habitats. The widespread destruction of tropical rainforests and replacement with open pastureland is widely cited as an example of this;

elimination of the dense forest eliminated the infrastructure needed by many species to survive. For example, a fern that depends on dense shade for protection from direct sunlight can no longer survive without forest to shelter it. Another example is the destruction of ocean floors by bottom trawling.

Diminished resources or introduction of new competitor species also often accompany habitat degradation. Global warming has allowed some species to expand their range, bringing unwelcome competition to other species that previously occupied that area. Sometimes these new competitors are predators and directly affect prey species, while at other times they may merely outcompete vulnerable species for limited resources. Vital resources including water and food can also be limited during habitat degradation, leading to extinction.

Predation, Competition, and Disease

Humans have been transporting animals and plants from one part of the world to another for thousands of years, sometimes deliberately (e.g., livestock released by sailors onto islands as a source of food) and sometimes accidentally (e.g., rats escaping from boats). In most cases, such introductions are unsuccessful, but when they do become established as an invasive alien species, the consequences can be catastrophic. Invasive alien species can affect native species directly by eating them, competing with them, and introducing pathogens or parasites that sicken or kill them or, indirectly, by destroying or degrading their habitat. Human populations may themselves act as invasive predators. According to the 'overkill hypothesis', the swift extinction of the megafauna in areas such as New Zealand, Australia, Madagascar and Hawaii resulted from the sudden introduction of human beings to environments full of animals that had never seen them before, and were therefore completely unadapted to their predation techniques.

Coextinction

Coextinction refers to the loss of a species due to the extinction of another; for example, the extinction of parasitic insects following the loss of their hosts. Coextinction can also occur when a species loses its pollinator, or to predators in a food chain who lose their prey. "Species coextinction is a manifestation of the interconnectedness of organisms in complex ecosystems. ... While coextinction may not be the most important cause of species extinctions, it is certainly an insidious one". Coextinction is especially common when a keystone species goes extinct.

Global Warming

There is also discussion about the long term affects of global warming on the extinction process. Currently, studies have concluded that global warming may drive one quarter of all land animals and plants to extinction by 2050. The absolute worst case scenario that we are facing is 1/3 to 1/2 of all plant and animal species facing extinction. The ecologically rich hot spots where potentially most damage would be done include places like South Africa's Cape Floristic Region, and the Caribbean Basin. These areas include a doubling of present carbon dioxide levels and rising temperatures that could eliminate 56,000 plant and 3,700 animal species in these hot spot regions.

The white form of the lemuroid possum, only found in the mountain forests of northern Queensland, was once named as the first mammal species sub-form to be driven extinct by global warming. However since then one possum have been found. Also a more common brown form of the lemuroid possum is only considered 'near threatened' and is not at risk of extinction.

Mass Extinctions

There have been at least five mass extinctions in the history of life on earth, and four in the last 3.5 billion years in which many species have disappeared in a relatively short period of geological time. The most recent of these, the Cretaceous–Tertiary extinction event 65 million years ago at the end of the Cretaceous period, is best known for having wiped out the non-avian dinosaurs, among many other species.

According to a 1998 survey of 400 biologists conducted by New York's American Museum of Natural History, nearly 70 percent believed that they were currently in the early stages of a human-caused extinction, known as the Holocene extinction. In that survey, the same proportion of respondents agreed with the prediction that up to 20 per cent of all living populations could become extinct within 30 years (by 2028). Biologist E. O. Wilson estimated in 2002 that if current rates of human destruction of the biosphere continue, one-half of all species of life on earth will be extinct in 100 years. More significantly the rate of species extinctions at present is estimated at 100 to 1000 times 'background' or average extinction rates in the evolutionary time scale of planet Earth.

In the 1800s when extinction was first described, the idea of extinction was threatening to those who held a belief in the Great Chain of Being, a theological position that did not allow for 'missing links'.

The possibility of extinction was not widely accepted before the 1800s. The devoted naturalist Carl Linnaeus, could 'hardly entertain' the idea that humans could cause the extinction of a species. When parts of the world had not been thoroughly examined and charted, scientists could not rule out that animals found only in the fossil record were not simply 'hiding' in unexplored regions of the Earth. Georges Cuvier is credited with establishing extinction as a fact in a 1796 lecture to the French Institute. Cuvier's observations of fossil bones convinced him that they did not originate in extant animals. This discovery was critical for the spread of uniformitarianism, and lead to the first book publicizing the idea of evolution though Cuvier himself strongly opposed the theories of evolution advanced by Lamarck and others.

Biologist Bruce Walsh of the University of Arizona states three reasons for scientific interest in the preservation of species; genetic resources, ecosystem stability, and ethics; and today the scientific community 'stress[es] the importance' of maintaining biodiversity.

In modern times, commercial and industrial interests often have to contend with the effects of production on plant and animal life. However, some technologies with minimal, or no, proven harmful effects on *Homo sapiens* can be devastating to wildlife (for example, DDT). Biogeographer Jared Diamond notes that while big business may label environmental concerns as 'exaggerated', and often cause 'devastating damage', some corporations find it in their interest to adopt good conservation practices, and even engage in preservation efforts that surpass those taken by national parks.

Governments sometimes see the loss of native species as a loss to ecotourism, and can enact laws with severe punishment against the trade in native species in an effort to prevent extinction in the wild. Nature preserves are created by governments as a means to provide continuing habitats to species crowded by human expansion. The 1992 Convention on Biological Diversity has resulted in international Biodiversity Action Plan programmes, which attempt to provide comprehensive guidelines for government biodiversity conservation. Advocacy groups, such as The Wildlands Project and the Alliance for Zero Extinctions, work to educate the public and pressure governments into action.

People who live close to nature can be dependent on the survival of all the species in their environment, leaving them highly exposed to extinction risks. However, people prioritize day-to-day survival over species conservation; with human overpopulation in tropical developing countries, there has been enormous pressure on forests due to subsistence agriculture, including slash-and-burn agricultural techniques that can reduce endangered species's habitats.

Human Attitudes and Interests

Extinction is an important research topic in the field of zoology, and biology in general, and has also become an area of concern outside the scientific community. A number of organizations, such as the Worldwide Fund for Nature, have been created with the goal of preserving species from extinction. Governments have attempted, through enacting laws, to avoid habitat destruction, agricultural over-harvesting, and pollution. While many human-caused extinctions have been accidental, humans have also engaged in the deliberate destruction of some species, such as dangerous viruses, and the total destruction of other problematic species has been suggested. Other species were deliberately driven to extinction, or nearly so, due to poaching or because they were 'undesirable', or to push for other human agendas. One example was the near extinction of the American bison, which was nearly wiped out by mass hunts sanctioned by the United States government, in order to force the removal of Native Americans, many of whom relied on the bison for food.

Humans have aggressively worked toward the extinction of many species of viruses and bacteria in the cause of disease eradication. For example, the smallpox virus is now extinct in the wild — although samples are retained in laboratory settings, and the polio virus is now confined to small parts of the world as a result of human efforts to prevent the disease it causes.

Olivia Judson is one of six modern scientists to have advocated the deliberate extinction of specific species. Her September 25, 2003 *New York Times* article, 'A Bug's Death', advocates 'specicide' of thirty mosquito species through the introduction of a genetic element, capable of inserting itself into another crucial gene, to create recessive 'knockout genes'. Her arguments for doing so are that the *Anopheles* mosquitoes (which spread malaria) and *Aedes* mosquitoes (which spread dengue fever, yellow fever, elephantiasis, and other diseases) represent only 30 species; eradicating these would save at least one million human lives per annum at a cost of reducing the genetic diversity of the family Culicidae by only one per cent. She further argues that since species become extinct 'all the time' the disappearance of a few more will not destroy the ecosystem: "We're not left with a wasteland every time a species vanishes. Removing one species sometimes causes shifts in the populations of other species — but different need not mean worse." In addition, anti-malarial and mosquito control programmes offer little realistic hope to the 300 million people in developing nations who will be infected with acute illnesses this year. Although trials are ongoing, she writes that if they fail: "We should consider the ultimate swatting."

Recent technological advances have encouraged the hypothesis that by using DNA from the remains of an extinct species, through the process of cloning, the species may be 'brought back to life'. Proposed targets for cloning include the dinosaurs, the mammoth, thylacine, and the Pyrenean Ibex. In order for such a programme to succeed, a sufficient number of individuals would have to be cloned, from the DNA of different individuals (in the case of sexually reproducing organisms) to create a viable population. Though bioethical and philosophical objections have been raised, the cloning of extinct creatures seems a viable outcome of the continuing advancements in our science and technology.

In 2003, scientists attempted to clone the extinct Pyrenean Ibex (C. p. pyrenaica). This initial attempt failed; of the 285 embryos reconstructed, 54 were transferred to

12 mountain goats and mountain goat-domesticated goat hybrids, but only two survived the initial two months of gestation before they too died.

In 2009, a second attempt was made to clone the Pyrenean Ibex; one clone was born alive, but died seven minutes later, due to physical defects in the lungs.

The concept of cloning extinct species was thought to be popularized by the successful novel and movie Jurassic Park, though it may have been first used in John Brosnan's 1984 novel Carnosaur, and later in Piers Anthony's Balook novel, which resurrected a Baluchitherium.

Natural History

Natural history is the scientific research of plants or animals, leaning more towards the observational than experimental methods of study, and encompasses more research that is published in magazines than in academic journals. Grouped among the natural sciences, *Natural history* is the systematic study of any category of natural objects or organisms. That is a very broad designation in a world filled with many narrowly focused disciplines, so while modern natural history dates historically from studies in the ancient Greco-Roman world and then the medieval Arabic world through to the scattered European Renaissance scientists working in near isolation, today's field is more of a cross discipline umbrella of many specialty sciences that like geobiology have a strong multi-disciplinary nature combining scientists and scientific knowledge of many specialty sciences.

A person who studies natural history is known as a naturalist or 'natural historian'. Natural history is categorized among the natural sciences. As a published topic, it originated from studies in the ancient Greco-Roman world. The modern topic comprises many specialty sciences such as geobiology.

The English term 'natural history' is a translation of the Latin *naturalis historia*. Its meaning has narrowed considerably over time. In antiquity, it covered more-or-less anything which is connected with nature or which uses materials drawn from nature; see for example the contents of Pliny's encyclopedia of this title, published circa AD 77-79.

Until well into the nineteenth century, knowledge was considered by Europeans to have two main divisions: the humanities (including theology), and studies of nature. Studies of nature could in turn be divided, with natural history being the descriptive counterpart to natural philosophy which was the analytical study of nature. In modern terms, natural philosophy roughly corresponded to modern physics and chemistry, while natural history included the biological and geological sciences. The two were strongly associated. During the heyday of the gentleman scientists, many figures contributed to both fields, and early papers in both were commonly read at professional science society meetings such as the Royal Society and the French Academy of Sciences — both founded during the seventeenth century.

The growth of many separate scientific disciplines in the twentieth century altered the way in which the term 'natural history' was used. Since it encompasses research that is now normally published within distinct disciplines, it may be considered an archaic or popular term.

Although terminology was and remains somewhat vague, a number of increasingly restricted uses can be distinguished. The less restricted uses are 'umbrella terms' for distinct modern scientific disciplines. Modern uses exclude chemistry and almost all of physics (astronomy is sometimes included).

As used in the titles of institutions such as the American Museum of Natural History or the British Natural History Museum, the term covers most of modern biology and geology.

A more restricted use excludes those areas of geology not concerned with living organisms. In this sense, natural history includes all of biology (the study of living organisms such as plants, animals, fungi, bacteria, etc. and their relationships in natural systems) and paleobiology (the study of extinct life), but only some life-related areas of geology, such as stratigraphy and petrology.

Applied only within biology, it is used for the study of particular organisms. Thus the 'natural history of primates' involves describing the relevant structures, operations and circumstances of primates, such as their diet, reproduction, social grouping, and interactions with other species.

The term may be used to denote the less strictly organized study, description, and classification of natural objects, such as animals, plants, minerals, which emphasise fieldwork as opposed to more systematic scientific investigation such as experimental or laboratory work.

Modern definitions of the term include:

- Natural history is "the scientific study of plants or animals (more observational than experimental) usually published in popular magazines rather than in academic journals"
- "Natural history is the scientific research of plants and animals in their natural environments. It is concerned with degrees of organization from individual organisms to an entire ecosystem, and emphasizes identification, life history, distribution, abundance, and inter-relationships. It may include an aesthetic component."

History

Natural history begins with Aristotle and other ancient philosophers who analyzed the diversity of the natural world. From the ancient Greeks until the work of Carolus Linnaeus (also known as Carl Linnaeus, or Carl von Linné) and other 18th century naturalists, the main concept of natural history was the *scala naturae* or Great Chain of Being, a conceptual arrangement of minerals, vegetables, more primitive forms of animals, and more complex life forms on a linear scale of increasing 'perfection', culminating in our species.

While natural history was basically static in medieval Europe, it continued to be developed by Arabic scholars during the Arab Agricultural Revolution. Al-Jahiz described early evolutionary ideas such as the struggle for existence. He also introduced the idea of a food chain, and was an early adherent of environmental determinism. Al-Dinawari is considered the founder of Arabic botany for his *Book of Plants*, in which he described at least 637 plants and discussed plant development from germination (sprouting) to death, describing the phases of plant growth and the production of flowers and fruit. Abu al-Abbas al-Nabati developed an early scientific method for botany, introducing empirical and experimental techniques in the testing, description and identification of numerous materia medica, and separating unverified reports from those supported by actual tests and observations. His student Ibn al-Baitar wrote a pharmaceutical encyclopedia describing 1,400 plants, foods, and drugs, 300 of which were his own original discoveries. A Latin translation of his work was useful to European biologists and pharmacists in the 18th and 19th centuries. Earth sciences such as geology were also studied extensively by Arabic geologists.

From the 13th century, the work of Aristotle was adapted rather rigidly into Christian philosophy, particularly by Thomas Aquinas, forming the basis for natural theology. During the Renaissance, scholars (herbalists and humanists, particularly) returned to direct observation of plants and animals for natural history, and many began to accumulate large collections of exotic specimens and unusual monsters. In Victorian Scotland it was believed that the study of natural history contributed to good mental health. The rapid increase in the number of known organisms prompted many attempts at classifying and organizing species into taxonomic groups, culminating in the system of the Swedish naturalist Carl Linnaeus.

In modern Europe, professional disciplines such as physiology, botany, zoology, geology, and palaeontology were formed. *Natural history*, formerly the main subject taught by college science professors, was increasingly scorned by scientists of a more specialized manner and relegated to an 'amateur' activity, rather than a part of science proper. Particularly in Britain and the United States, this grew into specialist hobbies such as the study of birds, butterflies, seashells (malacology/conchology), beetles and wild flowers; meanwhile, scientists tried to define a unified discipline of biology (though with only partial success, at least until the modern evolutionary synthesis). Still, the traditions of natural history continue to play a part in the study of biology, especially ecology (the study of natural systems involving living organisms and the inorganic components of the Earth's biosphere that support them), ethology (the scientific study of animal behaviour), and evolutionary biology (the study of the relationships between life-forms over very long periods of time), and re-emerges today as integrative organismal biology.

Amateur collectors and natural history entrepreneurs played an important role in building the large natural history collections of the nineteenth and early twentieth centuries, such as the Smithsonian Institution's National Museum of Natural History.

Museums

Natural history museums, which evolved from cabinets of curiosities, played an important role in the emergence of professional biological disciplines and research programs. Particularly in the 19th century, scientists began to use their natural history collections as teaching tools for advanced students and the basis for their own morphological research.

The term 'natural history' alone, or sometimes together with archeology, forms the name of many national, regional and local natural history societies that maintain records for birds (ornithology), mammals (mammalogy), insects (entomology), fungi (mycology) and plants (botany). They may also have microscopical and geological sections.

Examples of these societies in Britain include the Natural History Society of Northumbria founded in 1829, British Entomological and Natural History Society founded in 1872, Birmingham Natural History Society, Glasgow Natural History Society, London Natural History Society founded in 1858, Manchester Microscopical and Natural History Society established in 1880, Scarborough Field Naturalists' Society and the Sorby Natural History Society, Sheffield, founded in 1918. The growth of natural history societies was also spurred due to the growth of British colonies in tropical regions with numerous new species to be discovered. Many civil servants took an interest in their new surroundings, sending specimens back to museums in Britain.

9 Deforestation

Deforestation is the clearance of naturally occurring forests by logging and burning.

Deforestation occurs for many reasons: trees or derived charcoal are used as, or sold, for fuel or as a commodity, while cleared land is used as pasture for livestock, plantations of commodities, and settlements. The removal of trees without sufficient reforestation has resulted in damage to habitat, biodiversity loss and aridity. It has adverse impacts on biosequestration of atmospheric carbon dioxide. Deforested regions typically incur significant adverse soil erosion and frequently degrade into wasteland.

Disregard or ignorance of intrinsic value, lack of ascribed value, lax forest management and deficient environmental law are some of the factors that allow deforestation to occur on a large scale. In many countries, deforestation is an ongoing issue that is causing extinction, changes to climatic conditions, desertification, and displacement of indigenous people.

Among countries with a per capita GDP of at least US$ 4,600, net deforestation rates have ceased to increase.

There are many root causes of contemporary deforestation, including corruption of government institutions the inequitable distribution of wealth and power, population growth nd overpopulation, and urbanization. Globalization is often viewed as another root cause of deforestation, though there are cases in which the impacts of globalization (new flows of labour, capital, commodities, and ideas) have promoted localized forest recovery.

In 2000 the United Nations Food and Agriculture Organization (FAO) found that "the role of population dynamics in a local setting may vary from decisive to negligible," and that deforestation can result from "a combination of population pressure and stagnating economic, social and technological conditions."

Jungle burned for agriculture in southern Mexico

According to the United Nations Framework Convention on Climate Change (UNFCCC) secretariat, the overwhelming direct cause of deforestation is agriculture. Subsistence farming is responsible for 48 per cent of deforestation; commercial agriculture is responsible for 32 per cent of deforestation; logging is responsible for 14 per cent of deforestation and fuel wood removals make up 5 per cent of deforestation.

The degradation of forest ecosystems has also been traced to economic incentives that make forest conversion appear more profitable than forest conservation. Many important forest functions have no markets, and hence, no economic value that is readily apparent to the forests' owners or the communities that rely on forests for their well-being. From the perspective of the developing world, the benefits of forest as carbon sinks or biodiversity reserves go primarily to richer developed nations and there is insufficient compensation for these services. Developing countries feel that some countries in the developed world, such as the United States of America, cut down their forests centuries ago and benefited greatly from this deforestation, and that it is hypocritical to deny developing countries the same opportunities: that the poor shouldn't have to bear the cost of preservation when the rich created the problem.

Experts do not agree on whether industrial logging is an important contributor to global deforestation Similarly, there is no consensus on whether poverty is important in deforestation. Some argue that poor people are more likely to clear forest because they have no alternatives, others that the poor lack the ability to pay for the materials and labour needed to clear forest. Claims that population growth drives deforestation have been disputed; one study found that population increases due to high fertility rates were a primary driver of tropical deforestation in only 8 per cent of cases.

Some commentators have noted a shift in the drivers of deforestation over the past 30 years. Whereas deforestation was primarily driven by subsistence activities and government-sponsored development projects like transmigration in countries like Indonesia and colonization in Latin America, India, Java etc during late 19th century and the earlier half of the 20th century. By the 1990s the majority of deforestation was caused by industrial factors, including extractive industries, large-scale cattle ranching, and extensive agriculture.

Atmospheric

Deforestation is ongoing and is shaping climate and geography.

Deforestation is a contributor to global warming, and is often cited as one of the major causes of the enhanced greenhouse effect. Tropical deforestation is responsible for approximately 20 per cent of world greenhouse gas emissions According to the Intergovernmental Panel on Climate Change deforestation, mainly in tropical areas, could account for up to one-third of total anthropogenic carbon dioxide emissions. But recent calculations suggest that carbon dioxide emissions from deforestation and forest degradation (excluding peatland emissions) contribute about 12 per cent of total anthropogenic carbon dioxide emissions with a range from 6 to 17 per cent. Trees and other plants remove carbon (in the form of carbon dioxide) from the atmosphere during the process of photosynthesis and release oxygen back into the atmosphere during normal respiration. Only when actively growing can a tree or forest remove carbon over an annual or longer timeframe. Both the decay and burning of wood releases much of this stored carbon back to the atmosphere. In order for forests to take up carbon, the wood must be harvested and turned into long-lived products and trees must be re-planted. Deforestation may cause carbon stores held in soil to be released. Forests are stores of carbon and can be either sinks or sources depending upon environmental circumstances. Mature forests alternate between being net sinks and net sources of carbon dioxide (see carbon dioxide sink and carbon cycle).

Reducing emissions from the tropical deforestation and forest degradation (REDD) in developing countries has emerged as new potential to complement ongoing climate policies. The idea consists in providing financial compensations for the reduction of greenhouse gas (GHG) emissions from deforestation and forest degradation".

Rainforests are widely believed by laymen to contribute a significant amount of world's oxygen, although it is now accepted by scientists that rainforests contribute little net oxygen to the atmosphere and deforestation will have no effect on atmospheric oxygen levels. However, the incineration and burning of forest plants to clear land releases large amounts of CO_2, which contributes to global warming.

Forests are also able to extract carbon dioxide and pollutants from the air, thus contributing to biosphere stability.

The water cycle is also affected by deforestation. Trees extract groundwater through their roots and release it into the atmosphere. When part of a forest is removed, the trees no longer evaporate away this water, resulting in a much drier climate. Deforestation reduces the content of water in the soil and groundwater as well as atmospheric moisture. Deforestation reduces soil cohesion, so that erosion, flooding and landslides ensue. Forests enhance the recharge of aquifers in some locales, however, forests are a major source of aquifer depletion on most locales.

Shrinking forest cover lessens the landscape's capacity to intercept, retain and transpire precipitation. Instead of trapping precipitation, which then percolates to groundwater systems, deforested areas become sources of surface water runoff, which moves much faster than subsurface flows. That quicker transport of surface water can translate into flash flooding and more localized floods than would occur with the forest cover. Deforestation also contributes to decreased evapotranspiration, which lessens atmospheric moisture which in some cases affects precipitation levels down wind from the deforested area, as water is not recycled to downwind forests, but is lost in runoff and returns directly to the oceans. According to one preliminary study, in deforested north and northwest China, the average annual precipitation decreased by one third between the 1950s and the 1980s.

Trees, and plants in general, affect the water cycle significantly:

- their canopies intercept a proportion of precipitation, which is then evaporated back to the atmosphere canopy interception);
- their litter, stems and trunks slow down surface runoff;
- their roots create macropores — large conduits — in the soil that increase infiltration of water;
- they contribute to terrestrial evaporation and reduce soil moisture via transpiration;
- their litter and other organic residue change soil properties that affect the capacity of soil to store water;
- their leaves control the humidity of the atmosphere by transpiring. 99 per cent of the water absorbed by the roots moves up to the leaves and is transpired.

As a result, the presence or absence of trees can change the quantity of water on the surface, in the soil or groundwater, or in the atmosphere. This in turn changes erosion rates and the availability of water for either ecosystem functions or human services.

The forest may have little impact on flooding in the case of large rainfall events, which overwhelm the storage capacity of forest soil if the soils are at or close to saturation.

Undisturbed forest has very low rates of soil loss, approximately 2 metric tons per square kilometer (6 short tons per square mile). Deforestation generally increases rates of soil erosion, by increasing the amount of runoff and reducing the protection of the soil from tree litter. This can be an advantage in excessively leached tropical rain forest soils. Forestry operations themselves also increase erosion through the development of roads and the use of mechanized equipment.

China's Loess Plateau was cleared of forest millennia ago. Since then it has been eroding, creating dramatic incised valleys, and providing the sediment that gives the Yellow River its yellow color and that causes the flooding of the river in the lower reaches (hence the river's nickname 'China's sorrow').

Removal of trees does not always increase erosion rates. In certain regions of southwest US, shrubs and trees have been encroaching on grassland. The trees themselves enhance the loss of grass between tree canopies. The bare intercanopy areas become highly erodible. The US Forest Service, in Bandelier National Monument for example, is studying how to restore the former ecosystem, and reduce erosion, by removing the trees.

Tree roots bind soil together, and if the soil is sufficiently shallow they act to keep the soil in place by also binding with underlying bedrock. Tree removal on steep slopes with shallow soil thus increases the risk of landslides, which can threaten people living nearby. However most deforestation only affects the trunks of trees, allowing for the roots to stay rooted, negating the landslide.

Deforestation results in declines in biodiversity. The removal or destruction of areas of forest cover has resulted in a degraded environment with reduced biodiversity Forests support biodiversity, providing habitat for wildlife; moreover, forests foster medicinal conservation. With forest biotopes being irreplaceable source of new drugs (such as taxol), deforestation can destroy genetic variations (such as crop resistance) irretrievably.

Since the tropical rainforests are the most diverse ecosystems on Earth and about 80 per cent of the world's known biodiversity could be found in tropical rainforests, removal or destruction of significant areas of forest cover has resulted in a degraded environment with reduced biodiversity.

Scientific understanding of the process of extinction is insufficient to accurately make predictions about the impact of deforestation on biodiversity. Most predictions of forestry related biodiversity loss are based on species-area models, with an underlying assumption that as forest are declines species diversity will decline similarly. However, many such models have been proven to be wrong and loss of habitat does not necessarily lead to large scale loss of species. Species-area models are known to overpredict the number of species known to be threatened in areas where actual deforestation is ongoing, and greatly overpredict the number of threatened species that are widespread.

It has been estimated that we are losing 137 plant, animal and insect species every single day due to rainforest deforestation, which equates to 50,000 species a year. Others state that tropical rainforest deforestation is contributing to the ongoing Holocene mass extinction. The known extinction rates from deforestation rates are very low, approximately one species per year from mammals and birds which extrapolates to approximately 23,000 species per year for all species. Predictions have been made that more than 40 per cent of the animal and plant species in Southeast Asia could be wiped out in the 21st century. Such predictions were called into question by 1995 data that show that within regions of Southeast Asia much of the original forest has been converted to monospecific plantations, but that potentially endangered species are few and tree flora remains widespread and stable.

Damage to forests and other aspects of nature could halve living standards for the world's poor and reduce global GDP by about seven per cent by 2050, a major report concluded at the Convention on Biological Diversity (CBD) meeting in Bonn. Historically utilization of forest products, including timber and fuel wood, have played a key role in human societies, comparable to the roles of water and cultivable land. Today, developed countries continue to utilize timber for building houses, and wood pulp for paper. In developing countries almost three billion people rely on wood for heating and cooking.

The forest products industry is a large part of the economy in both developed and developing countries. Short-term economic gains made by conversion of forest to agriculture, or over-exploitation of wood products, typically leads to loss of long-term income and long term biological productivity (hence reduction in nature's services). West Africa, Madagascar, Southeast Asia and many other regions have experienced lower revenue because of declining timber harvests. Illegal logging causes billions of dollars of losses to national economies annually.

The new procedures to get amounts of wood are causing more harm to the economy and overpowers the amount of money spent by people employed in logging. According to a study, "in most areas studied, the various ventures that prompted deforestation rarely generated more than US$5 for every ton of carbon they released and frequently returned far less than US$ 1". The price on the European market for an offset tied to a one-ton reduction in carbon is 23 euro (about US$35).

Small scale deforestation was practiced by some societies for tens of thousands of years before the beginnings of civilization. The first evidence of deforestation appears in the Mesolithic period. It was probably used to convert closed forests into more open ecosystems favourable to game animals. With the advent of agriculture, larger areas began to be deforested, and fire became the prime tool to clear land for crops. In Europe there is little solid evidence before 7000 BC. Mesolithic foragers used fire to create openings for red deer and wild boar. In Great Britain, shade-tolerant species such as oak and ash are replaced in the pollen record by hazels, brambles, grasses and nettles. Removal of the forests led to decreased transpiration, resulting in the formation of upland peat bogs. Widespread decrease in elm pollen across Europe between 8400-8300 BC and 7200-7000 BC, starting in southern Europe and gradually moving north to Great Britain, may represent land clearing by fire at the onset of Neolithic agriculture.

The Neolithic period saw extensive deforestation for farming land. Stone axes were being made from about 3000 BC not just from flint, but from a wide variety of hard rocks from across Britain and North America as well. They include the noted Langdale axe industry in the English Lake District, quarries developed at Penmaenmawr in North Wales and numerous other locations. Rough-outs were made locally near the quarries, and some were polished locally to give a fine finish. This step not only increased the mechanical strength of the axe, but also made penetration of wood easier. Flint was still used from sources such as Grimes Graves but from many other mines across Europe.

Evidence of deforestation has been found in Minoan Crete; for example the environs of the Palace of Knossos were severely deforested in the Bronze Age.

Throughout most of history, humans were hunter gatherers who hunted within forests. In most areas, such as the Amazon, the tropics, Central America, and the Caribbean, only after shortages of wood and other forest products occur are policies implemented to ensure forest resources are used in a sustainable manner.

In ancient Greece, Tjeered van Andel and co-writers summarized three regional studies of historic erosion and alluviation and found that, wherever adequate evidence exists, a major phase of erosion follows, by about 500-1,000 years the introduction of farming in the various regions of Greece, ranging from the later Neolithic to the Early Bronze Age. The thousand years following the mid-first millennium BCE saw serious, intermittent pulses of soil erosion in numerous places. The historic silting of ports along the southern coasts of Asia Minor (*e.g.* Clarus, and the examples of Ephesus, Priene and Miletus, where harbors had to be abandoned because of the silt deposited by the Meander) and in coastal Syria during the last centuries BC.

Easter Island has suffered from heavy soil erosion in recent centuries, aggravated by agriculture and deforestation Jared Diamond gives an extensive look into the collapse of the ancient Easter Islanders in his book *Collapse.* The disappearance of the island's trees seems to coincide with a decline of its civilization around the 17th and 18th century. He attributed the collapse to deforestation and over-exploitation of all resources.

The famous silting up of the harbour for Bruges, which moved port commerce to Antwerp, also followed a period of increased settlement growth (and apparently of deforestation) in the upper river basins. In early medieval Riez in upper Provence, alluvial silt from two small rivers raised the riverbeds and widened the floodplain, which slowly buried the Roman settlement in alluvium and gradually moved new construction to higher ground; concurrently the headwater valleys above Riez were being opened to pasturage. From William B. Greeley's, The Relation of Geography to Timber Supply, Economic Geography, 1925, vol. 1, p. 1-11. Source of 'Today' map: compiled by George Draffan from roadless area map in The Big Outside: A Descriptive Inventory of the Big Wilderness Areas of the United States, by Dave Foreman and Howie Wolke. These maps represent only virgin forest lost. Some regrowth has occurred but not to the age, size or extent of 1620 due to population increases and food cultivation.

A typical progress trap was that cities were often built in a forested area, which would provide wood for some industry (e.g. construction, shipbuilding, pottery). When deforestation occurs without proper replanting, however; local wood supplies become difficult to obtain near enough to remain competitive, leading to the city's abandonment, as happened repeatedly in Ancient Asia Minor.

With most of the population remaining active in (or indirectly dependent on) the agricultural sector, the main pressure in most areas remained land clearing for crop and cattle farming. Enough wild green was usually left standing (and partially used, e.g. to collect firewood, timber and fruits, or to graze pigs) for wildlife to remain viable. The elite's (nobility and higher clergy)protection of their own hunting privileges and game often protected significant woodlands.

Major parts in the spread (and thus more durable growth) of the population were played by monastical 'pioneering' (especially by the Benedictine and Commercial orders) and some feudal lords' recruiting farmers to settle (and become tax payers) by offering relatively good legal and fiscal conditions. Even when speculators sought to encourage towns, settlers needed an agricultural belt around or sometimes within defensive walls. When populations were quickly decreased by causes such as the Black Death or devastating warfare (e.g. Genghis Khan's Mongol hordes in eastern and central Europe, Thirty Years' War in Germany), this could lead to settlements being abandoned. The land was reclaimed by nature, but the secondary forests usually lacked the original biodiversity.

From 1100 to 1500 AD, significant deforestation took place in Western Europe as a result of the expanding human population. The large-scale building of wooden sailing ships by European (coastal) naval owners since the 15th century for exploration, colonisation, slave trade–and other trade on the high seas consumed many forest resources. Piracy also contributed to the over harvesting of forests, as in Spain. This led to a weakening of the domestic economy after Columbus' discovery of America, as the economy became dependent on colonial activities (plundering, mining, cattle, plantations, trade, etc.)

In *Changes in the Land* (1983), William Cronon analyzed and documented 17th-century English colonists' reports of increased seasonal flooding in New England during the period when new settlers initially cleared the forests for agriculture. They believed flooding was linked to widespread forest clearing upstream.

The massive use of charcoal on an industrial scale in Early Modern Europe was a new type of consumption of western forests; even in Stuart England, the relatively primitive production of charcoal has already reached an impressive level. Stuart England was so widely deforested that it depended on the Baltic trade for ship timbers, and looked to the untapped forests of New England to supply the need. Each of Nelson's Royal Navy war ships at Trafalgar (1805) required 6,000 mature oaks for its construction. In France, Colbert planted oak forests to supply the French navy in the future. When the oak plantations matured in the mid-nineteenth century, the masts were no longer required because shipping had changed.

Norman F. Cantor's summary of the effects of late medieval deforestation applies equally well to Early Modern Europe.

Europeans had lived in the midst of vast forests throughout the earlier medieval centuries. After 1250 they became so skilled at deforestation that by 1500 they were running short of wood for heating and cooking. They were faced with a nutritional decline because of the elimination of the generous supply of wild game that had inhabited the now-disappearing forests, which throughout medieval times had provided the staple of their carnivorous high-protein diet. By 1500 Europe was on the edge of a fuel and nutritional disaster [from] which it was saved in the sixteenth century only by the burning of soft coal and the cultivation of potatoes and maize.

Industrial Era

In the 19th century, introduction of steamboats in the United States was the cause of deforestation of banks of major rivers, such as the Mississippi River, with increased and more severe flooding one of the environmental results. The steamboat crews cut wood every day from the riverbanks to fuel the steam engines. Between St. Louis and the confluence with the Ohio River to the south, the Mississippi became more wide and shallow, and changed its channel laterally. Attempts to improve navigation by the use of snagpullers often resulted in crews' clearing large trees 100 to 200 feet back from the banks. Several French colonial towns of the Illinois Country, such as Kaskaskia, Cahokia and St. Philippe, Illinois were flooded and abandoned in the late 19th century, with a loss to the cultural record of their archeology.

Specific parallels are seen in the twentieth-century deforestation occurring in many developing nations.

Rates of Deforestation

Global deforestation sharply accelerated around 1852. It has been estimated that about half of the Earth's mature tropical forests — between 7.5 million and 8 million km^2 (2.9 million to 3 million sq mi) of the original 15 million to 16 million km^2 (5.8 million to 6.2 million sq mi) that until 1947 covered the planet — have now been cleared. Some scientists have predicted that unless significant measures (such as seeking out and protecting old growth forests that have not been disturbed) are taken on a worldwide basis, by 2030 there will only be ten per cent remaining, with another ten per cent in a degraded condition 80 per cent will have been lost, and with them hundreds of thousands of irreplaceable species.

The difficulties of estimating deforestation rates are nowhere more apparent than in the widely varying estimates of rates of rainforest deforestation. Some environmental groups argue that one fifth of the world's tropical rainforest was destroyed between 1960 and 1990, that rainforests 50 years ago covered 14 per cent of the world's land surface and have been reduced to 6 per cent, and that all tropical forests will be gone by 2090. Meanwhile, Alan Grainger of Leeds University argues that there is no credible evidence of any long-term decline in rainforest area. Bjørn Lomborg, author of *The Skeptical Environmentalist*, claims that global forest cover has remained approximately stable since the middle of the twentieth century. Along similar lines, some have claimed that for every acre of rain forest cut down each year, more than 50 acres (20 ha) of new forest are growing in the tropics.

These divergent viewpoints are the result of the uncertainties in the extent of tropical deforestation. For tropical countries, deforestation estimates are very uncertain and could be in error by as much as +/- 50 per cent, while a 2002 analysis of satellite imagery suggested that the rate of deforestation in the humid tropics (approximately 5.8 million hectares per year) was roughly 23 per cent lower than the most commonly quoted rates. Conversely, a new analysis of satellite images reveals that deforestation of the Amazon rainforest is twice as fast as scientists previously estimated.

Some have argued that deforestation trends may follow a Kuznets curve, which if true would nonetheless fail to eliminate the risk of irreversible loss of non-economic forest values (e.g., the extinction of species).

A 2005 report by the United Nations Food and Agriculture Organization (FAO) estimates that although the Earth's total forest area continues to decrease at about 13 million hectares per year, the global rate of deforestation has recently been slowing. Still others claim that rainforests are being destroyed at an ever-quickening pace. The London-based Rainforest Foundation notes that "the UN figure is based on a definition of forest as being an area with as little as 10 per cent actual tree cover, which would therefore include areas that are actually savannah-like ecosystems and badly damaged forests." Other critics of the FAO data point out that they do not distinguish between forest types, and that they are based largely on reporting from forestry departments of individual countries, which do not take into account unofficial activities like illegal logging.

Despite these uncertainties, there is agreement that destruction of rainforests remains a significant environmental problem. Up to 90 per cent of West Africa's coastal rainforests have disappeared since 1900. In South Asia, about 88 per cent of the rainforests have been lost. Much of what remains of the world's rainforests is in the Amazon basin, where the Amazon Rainforest covers approximately 4 million square kilometres. The regions with the highest tropical deforestation rate between 2000 and 2005 were Central America–which lost 1.3 per cent of its forests each year–and tropical Asia. In Central America, two-thirds of lowland tropical forests have been turned into pasture since 1950 and 40 per cent of all the rainforests have been lost in the last 40 years. Brazil has lost 90-95 per cent of its Mata Atlântica forest. Madagascar has lost 90 per cent of its eastern rainforests. As of 2007, less than one per cent of Haiti's forests remained Mexico, India, the Philippines, Indonesia, Thailand, Myanmar, Malaysia, Bangladesh, China, Sri Lanka, Laos, Nigeria, the Democratic Republic of the Congo, Liberia, Guinea, Ghana and the Côte d'Ivoire, have lost large areas of their rainforest. Several countries, notably Brazil, have declared their deforestation a national emergency.

Major international organizations, including the United Nations and the World Bank, have begun to develop programmes aimed at curbing deforestation. The blanket term Reducing Emissions from Deforestation and Forest Degradation (REDD) describes these sorts of programmes, which use direct monetary or other incentives to encourage developing countries to limit and/or roll back deforestation. Funding has been an issue, but at the UN Framework Convention on Climate Change (UNFCCC) Conference of the Parties-15 (COP-15) in Copenhagen in December 2009, an accord was reached with a collective commitment by developed countries for new and additional resources, including forestry and investments through international institutions, that will approach USD 30 billion for the period

2010 - 2012. Significant work is underway on tools for use in monitoring developing country adherence to their agreed REDD targets. These tools, which rely on remote forest monitoring using satellite imagery and other data sources, include the Center for Global Development's FORMA (Forest Monitoring for Action) initiative and the Group on Earth Observations' Forest Carbon Tracking Portal. Methodological guidance for forest monitoring was also emphasized at COP-15.

Farming

New methods are being developed to farm more intensively, such as high-yield hybrid crops, greenhouse, autonomous building gardens, and hydroponics. These methods are often dependent on chemical inputs to maintain necessary yields. In cyclic agriculture, cattle are grazed on farm land that is resting and rejuvenating. Cyclic agriculture actually increases the fertility of the soil. Intensive farming can also decrease soil nutrients by consuming at an accelerated rate the trace minerals needed for crop growth.

Forest Management

Efforts to stop or slow deforestation have been attempted for many centuries because it has long been known that deforestation can cause environmental damage sufficient in some cases to cause societies to collapse. In Tonga, paramount rulers developed policies designed to prevent conflicts between short-term gains from converting forest to farmland and long-term problems forest loss would cause, while during the seventeenth and eighteenth centuries in Tokugawa, Japan, the shoguns developed a highly sophisticated system of long-term planning to stop and even reverse deforestation of the preceding centuries through substituting timber by other products and more efficient use of land that had been farmed for many centuries. In sixteenth century Germany landowners also developed silviculture to deal with the problem of deforestation. However, these policies tend to be limited to environments with *good rainfall*, *no dry season* and *very young soils* (through volcanism or glaciation). This is because on older and less fertile soils trees grow too slowly for silviculture to be economic, whilst in areas with a strong dry season there is always a risk of forest fires destroying a tree crop before it matures.

In the areas where 'slash-and-burn' is practiced, switching to 'slash-and-char' would prevent the rapid deforestation and subsequent degradation of soils. The biochar thus created, given back to the soil, is not only a durable carbon sequestration method, but it also is an extremely beneficial amendment to the soil. Mixed with biomass it brings the creation of terra preta, one of the richest soils on the planet and the only one known to regenerate itself.

Certification of Sustainable Forest Management Practices

Certification, as provided by global certification systems such as PEFC and FSC, contributes to tackling deforestation by creating market demand for timber from sustainably managed forests. According to the United Nations Food and Agriculture Organization (FAO), "A major condition for the adoption of sustainable forest management is a demand for products that are produced sustainably and consumer willingness to pay for the higher costs entailed. Certification represents a shift from regulatory approaches to market incentives to promote sustainable forest management. By promoting the positive attributes of forest products from sustainably managed forests, certification focuses on the demand side of environmental conservation."

Reforestation

In many parts of the world, especially in East Asian countries, reforestation and afforestation are increasing the area of forested lands. The amount of woodland has increased in 22 of the world's 50 most forested nations. Asia as a whole gained 1 million hectares of forest between 2000 and 2005. Tropical forest in El Salvador expanded more than 20 per cent between 1992 and 2001. Based on these trends, one study projects that global forest will increase by 10 per cent—an area the size of India—by 2050.

In the People's Republic of China, where large scale destruction of forests has occurred, the government has in the past required that every able-bodied citizen between the ages of 11 and 60 plant three to five trees per year or do the equivalent amount of work in other forest services. The government claims that at least 1 billion trees have been planted in China every year since 1982. This is no longer required today, but March 12 of every year in China is the Planting Holiday. Also, it has introduced the Green Wall of China project, which aims to halt the expansion of the Gobi desert through the planting of trees. However, due to the large percentage of trees dying off after planting (up to 75%), the project is not very successful. There has been a 47-million-hectare increase in forest area in China since the 1970s. The total number of trees amounted to be about 35 billion and 4.55 per cent of China's land mass increased in forest coverage. The forest coverage was 12 per cent two decades ago and now is 16.55 per cent.

An ambitious proposal for China is the Aerially Delivered Re-forestation and Erosion Control System and the Proposed Sahara forest project coupled with the Seawater Greenhouse.

In Western countries, increasing consumer demand for wood products that have been produced and harvested in a sustainable manner is causing forest landowners and forest industries to become increasingly accountable for their forest management and timber harvesting practices.

The Arbor Day Foundation's Rain Forest Rescue programme is a charity that helps to prevent deforestation. The charity uses donated money to buy up and preserve rainforest land before the lumber companies can buy it. The Arbor Day Foundation then protects the land from deforestation. This also locks in the way of life of the primitive tribes living on the forest land. Organizations such as Community Forestry International, Cool Earth, The Nature Conservancy, World Wide Fund for Nature, Conservation International, African Conservation Foundation and Greenpeace also focus on preserving forest habitats. Greenpeace in particular has also mapped out the forests that are still intact and published this information on the internet HowStuffWorks in turn has made a simpler thematic map showing the amount of forests present just before the age of man (8000 years ago) and the current (reduced) levels of forest.

Forest Plantations

To meet the world's demand for wood, it has been suggested by forestry writers Botkins and Sedjo that high-yielding forest plantations are suitable. It has been calculated that plantations yielding 10 cubic meters per hectare annually could supply all the timber required for international trade on 5 per cent of the world's existing forestland. By contrast, natural forests produce about 1-2 cubic meters per hectare; therefore, 5 to 10 times more forestland would be required to meet demand. Forester Chad Oliver has suggested a forest mosaic with high-yield forest lands interpersed with conservation land.

One analysis of FAO data suggests that afforestation and reforestation projects "could reverse the global decline in woodlands within 30 years."

Reforestation through tree planting could take advantage of changing precipitation patterns due to climate change. This would be done by studying where precipitation is projected to increase and setting up reforestation projects in these locations. Areas such as Niger, Sierra Leone and Liberia are especially important candidates because they also suffer from an expanding desert (the Sahara) and decreasing biodiversity (while being important biodiversity hotspots).

While the preponderance of deforestation is due to demands for agricultural and urban use for the human population, there are some examples of military causes. One example of deliberate deforestation is that which took place in the U.S. zone of occupation in Germany after World War II. Before the onset of the Cold War defeated Germany was still considered a potential future threat rather than potential future ally. To address this threat, attempts were made to lower German industrial potential, of which forests were deemed an element. Sources in the U.S. government admitted that the purpose of this was the "ultimate destruction of the war potential of German forests." As a consequence of the practice of clear-felling, deforestation resulted which could "be replaced only by long forestry development over perhaps a century."

War can also be a cause of deforestation, either deliberately such as through the use of Agent Orange during the Vietnam War where, together with bombs and bulldozers, it contributed to the destruction of 44 per cent of the forest cover, or inadvertently such as in the 1945 Battle of Okinawa where bombardment and other combat operations reduced the lush tropical landscape into "a vast field of mud, lead, decay and maggots".

10 Biosequestration

Biosequestration is the capture and storage of the atmospheric greenhouse gas carbon dioxide by biological processes.

This may be by increased photosynthesis (through practices such as reforestation/preventing deforestation and genetic engineering); by enhanced soil carbon trapping in agriculture; or by the use of algal bio sequestration to absorb the carbon dioxide emissions from coal, oil or gas-fired electricity generation.

Biosequestration as a natural process has occurred in the past, and was responsible for the formation of the extensive coal and oil deposists which we are now burning. It is a key policy concept in the climate change mitigation debate. It does not generally refer to the sequestering of carbon dioxide in oceans (see carbon sequestration) or rock formations, depleted oil or gas reservoirs, deep saline aquifers, or deep coal seams (for all see geo-sequestration) or through the use of industrial chemical carbon dioxide scrubbing.

After water vapour (concentrations of which humans have limited capacity to influence) carbon dioxide is the most abundant and stable greenhouse gas in the atmosphere (methane rapidly reacts to form water vapour and carbon dioxide). Atmospheric carbon dioxide has increased from about 280 ppm in 1750 to 383 ppm in 2007 and is increasing at an average rate of 2 ppm pr year. The world's oceans have previously played an important role in sequestering atmospheric carbon dioxide through solubility and the action of phytoplankton. This, and the likely adverse consequences for humans and the biosphere of associated global warming, increases the significance of investigating policy mechanisms for encouraging *biosequestration.*

The Intergovernmental Panel on Climate Change (IPCC) estimates that the cutting down of forests is now contributing close to 20 per cent of the overall greenhouse gases entering the atmosphere. Candell and Raupach argue that there are four primary ways in which reforestation and reducing deforestation can increase *biosequestration.* First, by increasing the volume of existing forest. Second, by increasing the carbon density of existing forests at a stand and landscape scale. Third, by expanding the use of forest products that will sustainably replace fossil-fuel emissions. Fourth, by reducing carbon emissions that are caused from deforestation and degradation. A recent report by the Australian CSIRO found that forestry and forest-related options are the most significant and most easily achieved carbon sink making up 105 Mt per year CO_2-e or about 75 per cent of the total figure attainable for the Australian state of Queensland from 2010-2050. Among the forestry options, the CSIRO report announced, forestry with the primary aim of carbon storage (called carbon forestry) clearly has the highest attainable carbon storage capacity (77 Mt CO_2-e/yr) and is one of the easiest options to implement compared with biodiversity plantings, pre-1990 eucalypts, post 1990 plantations and managed regrowth. Legal strategies to encourage this form of biosequestration include permanent protection of forests in National Parks or on the World

Heritage List, properly funded management and bans on use of rainforest timbers and inefficient uses such as woodchipping old growth forest.

As a result of lobbying by the developing country caucus in the United Nations (associated with the United Nations Conference on Environment and Development (UNCED) in Rio de Janeiro, the non-legally binding Forest Principles were established in 1992. These linked the problem of deforestation to third world debt and inadequate technology transfer and stated that the "agreed full incremental cost of achieving benefits associated with forest conservation ... should be equitably shared by the international community" (para1(b)). Subsequently the Group of 77 argued in the 1995 *Intergovernmental Panel on Forests* (IPF) and then the 2001 *Intergovernmental Forum on Forests* (IFF), for affordable access to environmentally sound technologies without the stringency of intellectual property rights; while developed states there rejected demands for a forests fund. The expert group crated under the United Nations Forum on Forests (UNFF) reported in 2004, but in 2007 developed nations again vetoed language in the principles of the final text which might confirm their legal responsibility under international law to supply finance and environmentally sound technologies to the developing world.

In December 2007, after a two year debate on a proposal from Papua New Guinea and Costa Rica, state parties to the United Nations Framework Convention on Climate Change (FCCC) agreed to explore ways of reducing emissions from deforestation and to enhance forest carbon stocks in developing nations. The underlying idea is that developing nations should be financially compensated if they succeed in reducing their levels of deforestation (through valuing the carbon that is stored in forests); a concept termed 'avoided deforestaion (AD) or, REDD if broadened to include reducing forest degradation (see Reducing emissions from deforestation and forest degradation). Under the free market model advocated by the countries who have formed the *Coalition of Rainforest Nations*, developing nations with rainforests would sell carbon sink credits under a free market system to Kyoto Protocol Annex I states who have exceeded their emissions allowance Brazil (the state with the largest area of tropical rainforest) however, opposes including avoided deforestation in a carbon trading mechanism and instead favors creation of a multilateral development assistance fund created from donations by developed states. For REDD to be successful science and regulatory infrastructure related to forests will need to increase so nations may inventory all their forest carbon, show that they can control land use at the local level and prove that their emissions are declining.

The United Nations Framework Convention on Climate Change (UNFCCC) Article 4(1)(a) requires all Parties to "develop, periodically update, publish and make available to the Conference of the Parties" as well as "national inventories of anthropogenic emissions by sources" "removals by sinks of all greenhouse gases not controlled by the Montreal Protocol." Under the UNFCCC reporting guidelines, human-induced greenhouse emissions must be reported in six sectors: energy (including stationary energy and transport); industrial processes; solvent and other product use; agriculture; waste; and *land use, land use change and forestry* (LULUCF). The rules governing accounting and reporting of greenhouse gas emissions from LULUCF under the Kyoto Protocol are contained in several decisions of the Conference of Parties under the UNFCCC and LULUCF has been the subject of two major reports by the Intergovernmental Panel on Climate Change (IPCC). The Kyoto Protocol article 3.3 thus requires mandatory LULUCF accounting for afforestation (no forest for last 50 years), reforestation (no forest on 31 December 1989) and deforestation, as well as (in the first commitment period) under article 3.4 voluntary accounting for cropland management, grazing land management, revegetation and forest management (if not already accounted under article 3.3).

As an example, the *Australian National Greenhouse Gas Inventory* (NGGI) prepared in compliance with these requirements indicates that the energy sector accounts for 69 per cent of Australia's emissions, agriculture 16 per cent and LULUCF six per cent. Since 1990, however, emissions from the energy sector have increased 35 per cent (stationary energy up 43 per cent and transport up 23%). By comparison, emissions from LULUCF have fallen by 73 per cent . However, questions have been raised by Andrew Macintosh about the veracity of the estimates of emissions from the LULUCF sector because of discrepancies between the Australian Federal and Queensland Governments' land clearing data. Data published by the *Statewide Landcover and Trees Study* (SLATS) in Queensland, for example, show that the total amount of land clearing in Queensland identified under SLATS between 1989/90 and 2000/01 is approximately 50 per cent higher than the amount estimated by the Australian Federal Government's *National Carbon Accounting System* (NCAS) between 1990 and 2001. Satellite imaging has become crucial in obtaining data on levels of deforestation and reforestation. Landsat satellite data, for example, has been used to map tropical deforestation as part of NASA's Landsat *Pathfinder Humid Tropical Deforestation Project*, a collaborative effort among scientists from the University of Maryland, the University of New Hampshire, and NASA's Goddard Space Flight Center. The project yielded deforestation maps for the Amazon Basin, Central Africa, and Southeast Asia for three periods in the 1970s, 1980s, and 1990s.

Biosequestration may be enhanced by improving photosynthetic efficiency by modifying RuBisCO genes in plants to increase the catalytic and/or oxygenation activity of that enzyme.

One such research area involves increasing the Earth's proportion of C_4 carbon fixation photosynthetic plants. C_4 plants represent about 5 per cent of Earth's plant biomass and 1 per cent of its known plant species, but account for around 30 per cent of terrestrial carbon fixation. In leaves of C_3 plants, captured photons of solar energy undergo photosynthesis which assimilates carbon into carbohydrates (triosephosphates) in the chloroplasts of the mesophyll cells. The primary CO_2 fixation step is catalysed by ribulose-1,5-bisphosphate carboxylase/oxygenase (Rubisco) which reacts with O_2 leading to photorespiration that protects photosynthesis from photoinhibition but wastes 50 per cent of potentially fixed carbon. The C_4 photosynthetic pathway, however, concentrates CO_2 at the site of the reaction of Rubisco, thereby reducing the *biosequestration*-inhibiting photorespiration. A new frontier in crop science consists of attempts to genetically engineer C_3 staple food crops (such as wheat, barley, soybeans, potatoes and rice) with the 'turbo-charged' photosynthetic apparatus of C_4 plants.

Biochar (charcoal created by pyrolysis of biomass) is a potent form of longterm (thousands of years) *biosequestration* of atmosphereic CO_2 derived from investigation of the extremely fertile Terra preta soils of the Amazon Basin. Placing biochar in soils also improves water quality, increases soil fertility, raises agricultural productivity and reduce pressure on old growth forests. As a method of generating bio-energy with carbon storage Rob Flanagan and the EPRIDA biochar company have developed low-tech cooking stoves for developing nations that can burn agricultural wastes such as rice husks and produce 15 per cent by weight of biochar; while BEST Energies in NSW Australia have spent a decade developing an Agrichar technology that can combust96 tonnes of dry biomass each day, generating 30-40 tonnes of biochar. A parametric study of *biosequestration* by Malcolm Fowles at the Open University, indicated that to mitigate global warming, policies should encourage displacement of coal with biomass as a power source for baseload electricity generation if the latter's conversion efficiency rose over 30 per cent, otherwise *biosequestering* carbon from biomass as a cheaper mitigation option than geosequestration by CO_2 capture and storage.

Improved Agricultural and Farming Practices

Zero-till farming practices occur where there is much mulching but ploughing is not used, so that the carbon-rich organic matter in soil is not exposed to atmospheric oxygen, or to the leaching and erosion effects of rainfall. Over grazing is reduced by moving cattle and sheep away from grazed areas for several months. Ceasing ploughing has been alleged to encourage more ants to become predators of wood-eating (and CO_2 generating) termites, allows weeds to regenerate soils and helps slow water flows over the land. Dedicated biofuel and biosequestration crops, such as switchgrass (panicum virgatum), are also being developed. It requires from 0.97 to 1.34 GJ fossil energy to produce 1 tonne of switchgrass, compared with 1.99 to 2.66 GJ to produce 1 tonne of corn. Given that switchgrass contains approximately 18.8 GJ/ODT of biomass, the energy output-to-input ratio for the crop can be up to 20:1.

Biosequestration can also be enhanced by farmers choosing crops species that produce large numbers of phytoliths. Phytoliths are microscopic spherical shells of silicon that can store carbon for thousands of years.

Industries with large amounts of CO_2 emissions (such as the coal industry) are interested in *biosequestration* as a means of offsetting their greenhouse gas production. In Australia, university researchers are engineering algae to produce biofuels (hydrogen and biodiesel oils) and investigating whether this process can be used to *biosequester* carbon. Algae naturally capture sunlight and use its energy to split water into hydrogen, oxygen and oil which can be extracted. Such clean energy production also can be coupled with desalination using salt-tolerant marine algae to generate fresh water and electricity. Many new bioenergy (biofuel) technologies, including cellulosic ethanol biorefineries (using stems and branches of most plants including crop residues such as corn stalks, wheat straw and rice straw) are being promoted because they have the added advantage of *biosequestration* of CO_2. The Garnaut Climate Change Review recommends that a carbon price in a carbon emission trading scheme could include a financial incentive for *biosequestration* processes.

Garnaut recommends the use of algal biosequestration (see algae bioreactor) to absorb the constant stream of carbon dioxide emissions from coal-fired electricity generation and metal smelting until renewable forms of energy, such as solar and wind power, become more established contributors to the grid. Garnaut, for example, states: "Some algal biosequestration processes could absorb emissions from coal-fired electricity generation and metals smelting." The United Nations Collaborative Programme on Reducing Emissions from Deforestation and Forest Degradation in Developing Countries (UN-REDD Programme) is a collaboration between FAO, UNDP and UNEP under which a trust fund established in July 2008 allows donors to pool resources to generate the requisite transfer flow of resources to significantly reduce global emissions from deforestation and forest degradation .The UK government's Stern Review on the economics of climate change argued that curbing deforestation was a "highly cost-effective way of reducing greenhouse gas emissions".

James E. Hansen argues that, "An effective way to achieve drawdown [of carbon dioxide] would be to burn biofuels in power plants and capture the CO_2, with the biofuels derived from agricultural or urban wastes or grown on degraded lands using little or no fossil fuel inputs."

Under a 2009 agreement, Loy Yang Power and MBD Energy Ltd will build a pilot Fossil fuel power plant at the

Latrobe Valley power station in Australia using *biosequestration* technology in the form of an algal synthesiser system. Captured CO_2 from the waste exhaust flue gases will be injected into circulating waste water to grow oil-rich algae where sunlight and nutrients will produce heavy oil-laden slurry that can make high grade oil for energy, or stock feed. Other commercial demonstration projects involving *biosequestration* of CO_2 at point of emission have begun in Australia.

Philosophical Basis of Biosequestration

The arguments for *biosequestration* are often shaped in terms of economic theory, yet there is a well-recognised quality of life dimension to this debate. *Biosequestration* assists human beings to increase their collective and individual contributions to the essential resources of the biosphere. The policy case for *biosequestration* overlaps with principles of ecology, sustainability and sustainable development, as well as biosphere, biodiversity and ecosystem protection, environmental ethics, climate ethics and natural conservation.

The Garnaut Climate Change Review notes many barriers to increased global *biosequestration*. "There must be changes in the accounting regimes for greenhouse gases. Investments are required in research, development and commercialisation of superior approaches to *biosequestration*. Adjustments are required in the regulation of land use. New institutions will need to be developed to coordinate the interests in utilisation of *biosequestration* opportunities across small business in rural communities. Special efforts will be required to unlock potential in rural communities in developing countries." Saddler and King have argued that *biosequestration* and agricultural greenhouse gas emissions should not be handled within a global emissions trading scheme because of difficulties with measuring such emissions, problems in controlling them and the burden that would be placed on numerous small-scale farming operations. Collett likewise maintains that REDD credits (post-facto payments to developing countries for reducing their deforestation rates below an historical or projected reference rate), simply create a complex market approach to this global public health problem that reduces transparency and accountability when targets are not met and will not be as effective as developed nations voluntarily funding countries to keep their rainforests.

The World Rainforest Movement has argued that poor developing countries could be pressured to accept reforestation projects under the Kyoto Protocol's Clean Development Mechanism in order to earn foreign exchange simply to pay off the interest on debt to the World Bank. Tensions also exist over forest management between the sovereignty claims of nations states, arguments about common heritage of mankind and the rights of indigenous peoples and local communities; the Forest Peoples Programme (FPP) arguing the anti-deforestation programmes could merely allow financial benefits to flow to national treasuries, privilege would-be corporate forest degraders who manipulate the system by periodically threatening forests, rather than local communities who conserve them. The success of such projects will also depend on the accuracy of the baseline data and the number of countries involved. Further, it has been argued that if *biosequestration* is to play a significant role in mitigating anthropogenic climate change then coordinated policies should set a goal of achieving global forest cover to its extent prior to the industrial revolution in the 1800s.

It has also been argued that the United Nations mechanism for Reducing Emissions from Deforestation and Forest Degradation (REDD) may increase pressure to convert or modify other ecosystems, especially savannahs and wetlands, for food or biofuel, even though those ecosystems also have high carbon sequestration potential. Globally, for example, peatlands cover only 3 per cent of the land surface but store twice the amount of carbon as all the world's forests, whilst mangrove forests and saltmarshes are examples of relatively low-biomass ecosystems with high levels of productivity and carbon sequestration. Other researchers have argued that REDD is a critical component of an effective global biosequestration strategy that could provide significant benefits, such as the conservation of biodiversity, particularly if it moves away from focussing on protecting forests that are most cost-effective for reducing carbon emissions (such as those in Brazil where agricultural opportunity costs are relatively low, unlike Asia, which has sizeable revenues from oil palm, rubber, rice, and maize). They argue REDD could be varied to allow funding of programmes to slow peat degradation in Indonesia and target protection of biodiversity in 'hot spot'–areas with high species richness and relatively little remaining forest. Some purchasers, they maintain, of REDD carbon credits, such as multinational corporations or nations, might pay a premium to save imperiled eco-systems or areas with high-profile species.

11 Conservation Biology of Parasites

A large proportion of living species on Earth live a parasitic way of life. Parasites have traditionally been seen as targets of eradication efforts, and they have often been overlooked in conservation efforts. In the case of parasites living in the wild — and thus harmless to humans and domesticated animals — this view is changing.

Endangered Parasite Species

A note published in 1990 pointed out that the captive breeding and reintroduction programme to save the black-footed ferret would cause the loss of its specific parasites and demanded '*equal rights for parasites!*'. Then a paper in 1992 has warned that not only the loss of certain host species from the wild, but even host population bottlenecks or the fragmentation of host populations would predictably lead to the extinction of several host specific parasite species. It also noted that parasites are not only components of biodiversity by definition, but they also exert selective pressures upon their host populations that increase host genetic diversity. Firstly, this view met with open scepticism. Soon after, it became clear that the co-extinction of hosts and their specific parasites is likely to increase the current estimates of extinction rates significantly. A decade later, a study focusing on some highly host-specific groups (such as fig wasps, parasites, butterflies, and myrmecophil butterflies) estimated the number of co-endagered species (i.e. endagered by the endagered status of the host) at about 6300. Other authors argued that host specific parasite faunae have an unexpected advantage for conservation scientists. Their genealogies and population genetic patterns may help to illuminate their hosts' evolutionary and demographic history. Recently, scientists suggested that rich parasite faunae are inevitably needed for healthy ecosystem functioning and also that parasites and mutualists are the most endangered species on Earth.

Example: Extinct Avian Lice

- *Acutifrons caracarensis* parasite of the extinct Guadalupe Caracara *(Caracara lutosa)*, Guadelupe Island, Mexico;
- *Longimenopon dominicanum* parasite of the extinct Guadalupe Storm-petrel, *Oceanodroma macrodactyla*, Guadelupe Island, Mexico;
- *Campanulotes defectus* parasite of the extinct Passenger Pigeon *(Ectopistes migratorius)*, North-America;
- (*Columbicola extinctus* another parasite of the extinct Passenger Pigeon (*Ectopistes migratorius*). Interestingly, recent taxonomic studies show that it was conspecific with the lice living on Band-tailed Pigeon *(Columba fasciata)*, thus it is not extinct as a species);
- *Rallicola piageti* parasite of the extinct New Caledonian Rail *(Gallirallus lafresnayanus)*, New-Caledonia;
- *Halipeurus raphanus* parasite of the extinct Guadalupe Storm-petrel *(Oceanodroma macrodactyla)*, Guadelupe Island, Mexico;
- *Puffinoecus jamaicensis* parasite of the extinct Jamaica Petrel *(Pterodroma caribbaea)*, Jamaica;

- *Nitzschiella hemiphagae* parasite of the extinct Norfolk Island Pigeon (*Hemiphaga novaeseelandiae spadicea*), Norfolk Island, New-Zealand;
- *Patellinirmus restinctus* parasite of the extinct Norfolk Island Pigeon (*Hemiphaga novaeseelandiae spadicea*), Norfolk Island, New-Zealand;
- *Rallicola extinctus* parasite of the extinct Huia *(Heteralocha acutirostris)*, New-Zealand;
- *Philopteroides xenicus* parasite of the extinct Bushwren *(Xenicus longipes)*, New-Zealand;
- *Psittacobrosus bechsteini* parasite of the extinct Cuban Red Macaw *(Ara tricolor)*, Cuba;
- *Colpocephalum californici*, parasite of the California Condor *(Gymnogyps californianus)*. The host have been saved by captive breeding and repatriation programmes, however, the parasite have been lost, either spontaneously or perhaps exterminated by wildlife vets.

Naturally, medical (and veterinary) science and practice aim to exterminate parasites and pathogens living in humans (and in domesticated animals). In case of the few highly host-specific pathogens, this equals the extinction of the pathogen species. Throughout human history, however, only a single one species, i.e. smallpox virus, was eradicated from the Globe. The last cases of smallpox occurred 1978. However, secured stocks still exist in the United States and Russia for defensive purposes such as developing new vaccines, antiviral drugs, and diagnostic tests. It is not known whether or not these superpowers have shared their stocks with some of their allies during the Cold War.

A second candidate for purposeful extermination is the Guinea Worm *(Dracunculus medinensis)*. Once widespread across some 20 nations of Africa and Asia, the parasite nowadays is much withdrown occurring only in a few countries of Sub-Saharan Africa. Prevalent civil wars in the region, such as the War in Darfur have ensured the survival of this species up to the present.

Captive Breeding

Captive breeding is the process of breeding animals in human controlled environments with restricted settings, such as wildlife preserves, zoos and other conservation facilities; sometimes the process is construed to include release of individual organisms to the wild, when there is sufficient natural habitat to support new individuals or when the threat to the species in the wild is lessened.

This technique has been used with success for some species for some time, with probably the oldest known instances of captive breeding being attributed to menageries of European and Asian rulers, a case in point being the Pere David's Deer. The idea was popularized among modern conservationists independently by Peter Scott and Gerald Durrell in the 1950s and 1960s, founders of the Wildfowl and Wetlands Trust and Jersey Zoo — who demonstrated success with a wide variety of life forms in the 1970s ranging from birds (e.g. Pink Pigeon), mammals (e.g. Pygmy Hog), reptiles (e.g. Round Island Boa) and amphibians (e.g. Poison arrow frogs). Their ideas were independently validated by the success of Operation Oryx (under the auspices of the Fauna and Flora Preservation Society), which captive bred the Arabian Oryx starting in 1963 for eventual reintroduction to the wild. The Przewalski's horse has recently been re-introduced to the wild in Mongolia, its native habitat.

Such techniques are usually difficult to implement for highly mobile species like some migratory birds (e.g. cranes) and fishes.

If the captive breeding population is too small, inbreeding may occur due to reduced gene pool, which may lead to the population lacking immunity to diseases and other problems. Over sufficient number of generations, inbred populations can regain 'normal' genetic diversity.

The breeding of endangered species is coordinated by cooperative breeding programmes containing international studbooks and coordinators, who evaluate the roles of individual animals and institutions from a global or regional perspective. There are regional programmes for the conservation of endangered species:

- ***America:*** Species Survival Plan SSP (Association of Zoos and Aquariums AZA, Canadian Association of Zoos and Aquariums CAZA)
- ***Europe:*** European Endangered Species Programme EEP (European Association of Zoos and Aquaria EAZA)
- ***Australasia:*** Australasian Species Management Programme ASMP (Australasian Regional Association of Zoological Parks and Aquaria ARAZPA)
- ***Africa:*** African Preservation Programme APP (African Association of Zoological Gardens and Aquaria PAAZAB)
- ***Japan:*** Conservation activities of Japanese Association of Zoos and Aquariums JAZA
- ***South Asia:*** Conservation activities of South Asian Zoo Association for Regional Cooperation SAZARC
- ***South East Asia:*** Conservation activities of South East Asian Zoo Association SEAZA

Problems

Impacts of captive breeding include behavioural problems in released animals and lack of conservation of habitats being destroyed while a species is being bred. Behavioural problems include not being able to hunt or forage for food leading to starvation. Released animals do not avoid predators and are not able to find ample shelter for themselves so they die as a result. When a species is born in captivity and released into the wild they are not able to survive because they lack these skills. Golden Lion Tamarin mothers often die in the wild before having offspring because they do not have the climbing and foraging skills they need to survive. This results in populations continuing to decline despite reintroduction because the species does not produce viable offspring.

Another problem with captive breeding is the habitat loss that occurs while they are in captivity. This makes release of the species unviable because there is no habitat left to support larger populations. Since release is the ultimate goal of captive breeding, habitat loss defeats the purpose. Funds being used for captive breeding could be used for preserving wild populations and their habitat. The Sumatran Rhino will not survive purely in captivity and loss of habitat is a major factor to their extinction. If their habitat disappears, captive populations as well as wild ones will disappear along with it.

Environmentalism

Environmentalism is a broad philosophy and social movement regarding concerns for environmental conservation and improvement of the state of the environment. Environmentalism and environmental concerns are often represented by the colour green.

Environmentalism as a Social Movement

Environmentalism can also be defined as a social movement that seeks to influence the political process by lobbying, activism, and education in order to protect natural resources and ecosystems. In recognition of humanity as a participant in ecosystems, the environmental movement is centered on ecology, health, and human rights.

An environmentalist is a person who may advocate stewardship of the natural environment and the sustainable management of its resources through changes in public policy or individual behaviour by supporting practices such as recycling. In various ways (for example, grassroots activism and protests), environmentalists and environmental organizations seek to give the natural world a stronger voice in human affairs.

In recent years environmentalism has frequently been called, or compared to, a religion by its detractors. This is usually done at the same time as pointing out what are perceived as extremist viewpoints or actions of self-identified environmentalists or groups.

A concern for environmental protection has recurred in diverse forms, in different parts of the world, throughout history. For example, in the Middle East, the earliest known writings concerned with environmental pollution were Arabic medical treatises written during the 'Arab Agricultural Revolution', by writers such as Alkindus, Costa ben Luca, Rhazes, Ibn Al-Jazzar, al-Tamimi, al-Masihi, Avicenna, Ali ibn Ridwan, Isaac Israeli ben Solomon, Abd-el-latif, and Ibn al-Nafis. They were concerned with air contamination, water contamination, soil contamination, solid waste mishandling, and environmental assessments of certain localities.

In Europe, King Edward I of England banned the burning of sea-coal by proclamation in London in 1272, after its smoke had become a problem. The fuel was so common in England that this earliest of names for it was acquired because it could be carted away from some shores by the wheelbarrow. Air pollution would continue to be a problem in England, especially later during the Industrial Revolution, and extending into the recent past with the Great Smog of 1952.

In Europe, the Industrial Revolution gave rise to modern environmental pollution as it is generally understood today. The emergence of great factories and consumption of immense quantities of coal and other fossil fuels gave rise to unprecedented air pollution and the large volume of industrial chemical discharges added to the growing load of untreated human waste. The first large-scale, modern environmental laws came in the form of the British Alkali Acts, passed in 1863, to regulate the deleterious air pollution (gaseous hydrochloric acid) given off by the Leblanc process, used to produce soda ash. Environmentalism grew out of the amenity movement, which was a reaction to industrialization, the growth of cities, and worsening air and water pollution. In Victorian Britain, an early 'Back-to-Nature' movement that anticipated modern environmentalism was advocated by intellectuals such as John Ruskin, William Morris and Edward Carpenter, who were all against consumerism, pollution and other activities that were harmful to the natural world. Their ideas also inspired various proto-environmental groups in the UK, such as the Commons Preservation Society, the Kyrle Society, the Royal Society for the Protection of Birds and the Garden city movement, as well as encouraging the Socialist League and The Clarion movement to advocate measures of nature conservation.

In the United States, the beginnings of an environmental movement can be traced as far back as 1739, though it was not called environmentalism and was still considered conservation until the 1950's. Benjamin Franklin and other Philadelphia residents, citing "public rights," petitioned the Pennsylvania Assembly to stop waste dumping and remove tanneries from Philadelphia's commercial district. The US movement expanded in the 1800s, out of concerns for protecting the natural resources of the West, with individuals such as John Muir and Henry David Thoreau making key philosophical contributions. Thoreau was interested in peoples' relationship with nature and studied this by living close to nature in a simple life. He published his experiences in the book *Walden,* which argues that people should become intimately close with nature. Muir came to believe in nature's inherent right, especially after spending time hiking in Yosemite Valley and studying both the ecology and geology. He successfully lobbied congress to form Yosemite National Park and went on to set up the Sierra Club. The conservationist principles as well as the belief in an inherent right of nature were to become the bedrock of modern environmentalism.

In the 20th century, environmental ideas continued to grow in popularity and recognition. Efforts were starting to be made to save some wildlife, particularly the American Bison. The death of the last Passenger Pigeon as well as the endangerment of the American Bison helped to focus the minds of conservationists and popularize their concerns. In 1916 the National Park Service was founded by US President Woodrow Wilson.

In 1949, *A Sand County Almanac* by Aldo Leopold was published. It explained Leopold's belief that humankind should have moral respect for the environment and that it is unethical to harm it. The book is sometimes called the most influential book on conservation.

Throughout the 1950s, 1960s, 1970s and beyond, photography was used to enhance public awareness of the need for protecting land and recruiting members to environmental organizations. David Brower, Ansel Adams and Nancy Newhall created the Sierra Club Exhibit Format Series, which helped raise public environmental awareness and brought a rapidly increasing flood of new members to the Sierra Club and to the environmental movement in general. 'This Is Dinosaur' edited by Wallace Stegner with photographs by Martin Litton and Philip Hyde prevented the building of dams within Dinosaur National Monument by becoming part of a new kind of activism called environmentalism that combined the conservationist ideals of Thoreau, Leopold and Muir with hard-hitting advertising, lobbying, book distribution, letter writing campaigns, and more. The powerful use of photography in addition to the written word for conservation dated back to the creation of Yosemite National Park, when photographs convinced Abraham Lincoln to preserve the beautiful glacier carved landscape for all time. The Sierra Club Exhibit Format Series galvanized public opposition to building dams in the Grand Canyon and protected many other national treasures. The Sierra Club often led a coalition of many environmental groups including the Wilderness Society and many others. After a focus on preserving wilderness in the 1950s and 1960s, the Sierra Club and other groups broadened their focus to include such issues as air and water pollution, population control, and curbing the exploitation of natural resources.

In 1962 *Silent Spring* by American biologist Rachel Carson was published. The book cataloged the environmental impacts of the indiscriminate spraying of DDT in the US and questioned the logic of releasing large amounts of chemicals into the environment without fully understanding their effects on ecology or human health. The book suggested that DDT and other pesticides may cause cancer and that their agricultural use was a threat to wildlife, particularly birds. The resulting public concern led to the creation of the United States Environmental Protection Agency in 1970 which subsequently banned the agricultural use of DDT in the US in 1972. The limited use of DDT in disease vector control continues to this day in certain parts of the world and remains controversial. The book's legacy was to produce a far greater awareness of environmental issues and interest into how people affect the environment. With this new interest in environment came interest in problems such as air pollution and petroleum spills, and environmental interest grew. New pressure groups formed, notably Greenpeace and Friends of the Earth.

In the 1970s, the Chipko movement was formed in India; influenced by Mohandas Gandhi, they set up peaceful resistance to deforestation by literally hugging trees (leading to the term 'tree huggers'). Their peaceful methods of protest and slogan 'ecology is permanent economy' were very influential.

By the mid-1970s, many felt that people were on the edge of environmental catastrophe. The Back-to-the-land movement started to form and ideas of environmental ethics joined with anti-Vietnam War sentiments and other political issues. These individuals lived outside normal society and started to take on some of the more radical environmental theories such as deep ecology. Around this time more mainstream environmentalism was starting to show force with the signing of the Endangered Species Act in 1973 and the formation of CITES in 1975.

In 1979, James Lovelock, a former NASA scientist, published *Gaia: A new look at life on Earth*, which put forth the Gaia Hypothesis; it proposes that life on Earth can be understood as a single organism. This became an important part of the Deep Green ideology. Throughout the rest of the history of environmentalism there has been debate and argument between more radical followers of this Deep Green ideology and more mainstream environmentalists.

Environmentalism has also changed to deal with new issues such as global warming and genetic engineering.

Environmental Movement

The environmental movement (a term that sometimes includes the conservation and green movements) is a diverse scientific, social, and political movement. In general terms, environmentalists advocate the sustainable management of resources, and the protection (and restoration, when necessary) of the natural environment through changes in public policy and individual behaviour. In its recognition of humanity as a participant in ecosystems, the movement is centered around ecology, health, and human rights. Additionally, throughout history, the movement has been incorporated into religion. The movement is represented by a range of organizations, but has a younger demographic than is common in other social movements (see green seniors). Because of its large membership, varying and strong beliefs, the movement is not entirely united. Some argue that an environmental ethic of at least some sort is so urgently needed in all quarters and that the broader the movement is the better. Conversely, others assert that disunity can be a weakness in the face of strong opposition from unsympathetic political and industrial forces.

Free market environmentalism is a theory that argues that the free market, property rights, and tort law provide the best tools to preserve the health and sustainability of the environment. It considers environmental stewardship to be natural, as well as the expulsion of polluters and other aggressors through individual and class action.

CRITICISM

Preservation and Conservation

Environmental preservation in the United States is viewed as the setting aside of natural resources to prevent damage caused by contact with humans or by certain human activities, such as logging, mining, hunting, and fishing, only to replace them with new human activities such as tourism and recreation. Regulations and laws may be enacted for the preservation of natural resources.

Environmental Organizations and Conferences

Environmental organizations can be global, regional, national or local; they can be government-run or private (NGO). Despite a tendency to see environmentalism as an American or Western-centered pursuit, almost every country has its share of environmental activism. Moreover, groups dedicated to community development and social justice may also attend to environmental concerns.

There are some volunteer organizations. For example Ecoworld, which is about the environment and is based in team work and volunteer work. Some US environmental organizations, among them the Natural Resources Defence Council and the Environmental Defence Fund, specialize in bringing lawsuits (a tactic seen as particularly useful in that country). Other groups, such as the US-based National Wildlife Federation, the Nature Conservancy, and The Wilderness Society, and global groups like the World Wide Fund for Nature and Friends of the Earth,disseminate information, participate in public hearings, lobby, stage demonstrations, and may purchase land for preservation. Smaller groups, including Wildlife Conservation International, conduct research on endangered species and ecosystems. More radical organizations, such as Greenpeace, Earth First!, and the Earth Liberation Front, have more directly opposed actions they regard as environmentally harmful. While Greenpeace is devoted to nonviolent confrontation as a means of bearing witness to environmental wrongs and bringing issues into the public realm for debate, the underground Earth Liberation Front engages in the clandestine destruction of property, the release of caged or penned animals, and other criminal acts. Such tactics are regarded as unusual within the movement, however.

On an international level, concern for the environment was the subject of a UN conference in Stockholm in 1972, attended by 114 nations. Out of this meeting developed UNEP (United Nations Environment Programme) and the follow-up United Nations Conference on Environment and Development in 1992. Other international organizations in support of environmental policies development include the Commission for Environmental Cooperation (NAFTA), the European Environment Agency (EEA), and the Intergovernmental Panel on Climate Change.

12 Wildlife Management

'Wildlife management' is a general term for the process of keeping wild species at desirable levels which are determined by the wildlife managers. Wildlife management can include game keeping, wildlife conservation and pest control. Wildlife management has become an integrated science using disciplines such as mathematics, chemistry, biology, ecology, climatology and geography to gain the best results.

Wildlife conservation aims to halt the loss in the earths biodiversity by taking into consideration ecological principles such as carrying capacity, disturbance and succession and environmental conditions such as physical geography, pedology and hydrology with the aim of balancing the needs of wildlife with the needs of people ... Most wildlife is concerned with the preservation and improvement of habitats though increasingly reinstatement is being used. Techniques can include reforestation, pest control, nitrification and denitrification, irrigation, coppicing and hedge laying.

Game keeping is the management or control of wildlife for the wellbeing of game birds may include killing other animals which share the same niche or predators to maintain a high population of the more profitable species, such as pheasants introduced into woodland. In his 1933 book *Game Management*, Aldo Leopold, one of the pioneers of wildlife management as a science, defined it as "the art of making land produce sustained annual crops of wild game for recreational use".

Pest control is the control of real or perceived pests and can be for the benefit of wildlife, farmers, game keepers or safety reasons. In the United States, wildlife management practices are often implemented by a governmental agency to uphold a law, such as the Endangered Species Act of 1973. Many wildlife managers are employed by the U.S. Fish and Wildlife Service and by state governments.

In the United Kingdom, wildlife management undertaken by several organizations including government bodies such as the Forestry Commission, Charities such as the RSPB and The Wildlife Trusts and privately hired gamekeepers and contractors. Legislation has also been passed to protect wildlife such as the Wildlife and Countryside Act 1981. The UK government also give farmers subsidies through the Countryside Stewardship Scheme to improve the conservation value of there farms.

The profession of wildlife management was established in the United States in the interwar period (1920s-1930s) by Aldo Leopold and others who sought to transcend the purely restrictive policies of the previous generation of conservationists, such as anti-hunting activist William T. Hornaday. Leopold and his close associate Herbert Stoddard, who had both been trained in scientific forestry, argued that modern science and technology could be used to restore and improve wildlife habitat and thus produce abundant 'crops' of ducks, deer, and other valued wild animals.

The institutional foundations of the profession of wildlife management were established in the 1930s, when Leopold was granted the first university professorship in wildlife management (1933, University of Wisconsin, Madison), when Leopold's textbook 'Game Management' was published (1933), when The Wildlife Society was founded, when the Journal of Wildlife Management began publishing, and when the first Cooperative Wildlife Research Units were established. Conservationist planned many projects throughout the 1940s. Some of which included the harvesting of female mammals such as deer to decrease rising populations. Others included waterfowl and wetland research. The Fish and Wildlife Management Act was put in place to urge farmers to plant food for wildlife and to provide cover for them.

Wildlife management grew after World War II with the help of the GI Bill and a postwar boom in recreational hunting. An important step in wildlife management in the United States national parks occurred after several years of public controversy regarding the forced reduction of the elk population in Yellowstone National Park. In 1963, United States Secretary of the Interior Stewart Udall appointed an advisory board to collect scientific data to inform future wildlife management. In a paper known as the Leopold Report, the committee observed that culling programmes at other national parks had been ineffective, and recommended active management of Yellowstone's elk population.

Since the tumultuous 1970s, when animal rights activists and environmentalists began to challenge some aspects of wildlife management, the profession has been overshadowed by the rise of conservation biology. Although wildlife managers remain central to the implementation of the ESA and other wildlife conservation policies, Conservation biologists have shifted the focus of conservation away from wildlife management's concern with the protection and restoration of single species and toward the maintenance of ecosystems and biodiversity.

Types of Wildlife Management

There are two general types of wildlife management:

1. ***Manipulative management*** acts on a population, either changing its numbers by direct means or influencing numbers by the indirect means of altering food supply, habitat, density of predators, or prevalence of disease. This is appropriate when a population is to be harvested, or when it slides to an unacceptably low density or increases to an unacceptably high level. Such densities are inevitably the subjective view of the land owner, and may be disputed by animal welfare interests.
2. ***Custodial management*** is preventive or protective. The aim is to minimize external influences on the population and its habitat. It is appropriate in a national park where one of the stated goals is to protect ecological processes. It is also appropriate for conservation of a threatened species where the threat is of external origin rather than being intrinsic to the system.

Opposition

The control of wildlife through culling and hunting has been criticized by animal rights and animal welfare activists. Critics object to the real or perceived cruelty involved in some forms of wildlife management.

Environmentalists have also opposed hunting where they believe it is unnecessary or will negatively affect biodiversity. Critics of game keeping note that habitat manipulation and predator control are often used to maintain artificially inflated populations of valuable game animals (including introduced exotics) without regard to the ecological integrity of the habitat.

Game keepers in the UK claim to be a necessary for wildlife conservation as the amount of countryside they look after exceeds by a factor of nine the amount in nature reserves and national parks.

Management of Hunting Seasons

Wildlife management studies, research and lobbying by interest groups help designate times of the year when certain wildlife species can be legally hunted, allowing for surplus animals to be removed. In the United States, hunting season and bag limits are determined by guidelines set by the US Department of Interior, Fish and Wildlife Service (USFWS) for migratory game such as waterfowl and other migratory gamebirds. The hunting season and bag limits for state regulated game species such as deer are usually determined by State game Commissions, which are made up of representatives from various interest groups, wildlife biologists, and researchers.

Open Season

Open season is when wildlife is allowed to be hunted by law and is usually not during the breeding season. Hunters may be restricted by sex, age or class of animal, for instance there may be an open season for any male deer with 4 points or better on at least one side.

Limited Entry

Where the number of animals taken is to be tightly controlled, managers may have a type of lottery system called limited. Many apply, few are chosen. These hunts may still have age, sex or class restrictions.

Closed Season

Closed season is when wildlife is protected from hunting and is usually during its breeding season. Closed season is enforced by law, any hunting during closed season is punishable by law and termed as illegal hunting or poaching.

Hunting

Hunting is the practice of pursuing living animals (usually wildlife) for food, recreation, or trade. In present-day use, the term refers to lawful hunting, as distinguished from poaching, which is the killing, trapping or capture of the hunted species contrary to applicable law. The species which are hunted are referred to as game and are usually mammals and migratory or non-migratory gamebirds.

Hunting can also involve the elimination of vermin, as a means of pest control to prevent diseases caused by overpopulation. Hunting advocates state that hunting can be a necessary component of modern wildlife management, for example to help maintain a population of healthy animals within an environment's ecological carrying capacity when natural checks such as predators are absent. In the United States, wildlife managers are frequently part of hunting regulatory and licensing bodies, where they help to set rules on the number, manner and conditions in which game may be hunted.

The pursuit, capture and release, or capture for food of fish is called fishing, which is not commonly categorized as a form of hunting. Trapping is also usually considered a separate activity. Neither is it considered hunting to pursue animals without intent to kill them, as in wildlife photography or birdwatching. The practice of *hunting* for plants or mushrooms is a colloquial term for foraging or gathering.

The aspects of skillful tracking and acquisition of an elusive target in the pursuit of game have caused the word hunting to be used the vernacular as a metaphor (such as 'bargain hunting') sometimes with the killing aspect also implied (such as 'hunting down corruption and waste')

Hunting has a long history and may well pre-date the rise of species *Homo sapiens*. While our earliest Hominid ancestors were probably frugivore or omnivore, there is evidence that early Homo, and possibly already Australopithecine species have used larger animals for subsistence, and that hunting may have been one of the multiple environmental factors leading to replacement of holocene megafauna by smaller herbivores.

Of the closest surviving relatives of the human species, *Pan*, the Common Chimpanzee has an omnivorous diet including troop hunting behaviour based on beta males led by an alpha male, while Bonobos, on the other hand have a mostly frugivorous diet.

While it is undisputed that early humans were hunters, the importance of this fact for the final steps in the emergence of the *Homo* genus out of earlier Australopithecines, with its bipedalism and production of stone tools, and eventually also control of fire, are emphasized in the 'hunting hypothesis', and de-emphasized in scenarios that stress the omnivore status of humans as their recipe for success, and social interaction, including mating behaviour as essential in the emergence of behavioural modernity.

With the establishment of language, culture and religion, hunting became a theme of stories and myths, besides rituals such as dance and animal sacrifice. Hunting was a crucial component of hunter-gatherer societies before the domestication of livestock and the dawn of agriculture, beginning about 11,000 years ago. By the Mesolithic, hunting strategies had diversified with the developent of the bow (by 18,000 years ago) and the domestication of the dog (about 15,000 years ago).

There is fossil evidence for spear use in Asian hunting dating from approximately 16,200 years ago. The North American megafauna extinction was coincidental with the Younger Dryas impact event, making hunting a less critical factor in prehistoric species loss than had been previously thought.

Many species of animals have been hunted and caribou/wild reindeer "may well be the species of single greatest importance in the entire anthropological literature on hunting".

Hunter-gathering lifestyles remained prevalent in the New World and Sub-Saharan Africa (with the notable exception of Aztec and Incan agriculture) until the European Age of Discovery, and they persist in some tribal societies, albeit in rapid decline. Peoples that preserved paleolithic hunting-gathering until the recent past include some indigenous peoples of the Amazonas (Aché), some Central and Southern African Bushmen (Hadza people, Khoisan), some peoples of New Guinea (Fayu), the Mlabri of Thailand and Laos, the Vedda people of Sri Lanka and a handful of uncontacted peoples.

Even as animal domestication became relatively widespread, hunting was usually a significant contributor to the human food supply, even after the development of agriculture. The supplementary meat and materials from hunting included protein, bone for implements, sinew for cordage, fur, feathers, rawhide and leather used in clothing. The earliest hunting tools would have included rocks, spears, the atlatl, bow and arrows.

On ancient reliefs, especially from Mesopotamia, kings are often depicted as hunters of big game such as lions, especially from a war chariot. The cultural and psychological importance of hunting in ancient societies is represented by deities such as the horned god Cernunnos, or lunar goddesses of classical antiquity, Greek Artemis or Roman Diana. Taboos are often related to hunting, and mythological association of prey species with a divinity could be reflected in hunting restrictions such as a 'reserve' surrounding a temple. Euripides' tale of Artemis and Acteon, for example, may be seen as a caution against disrespect of prey or impudent boasting.

Hunting is still vital in marginal climates, especially those unsuited for pastoral uses or agriculture. Inuit peoples in the Arctic trap and hunt animals for clothing. From the skins of sea mammals, they may make kayaks, clothing, and footwear.

With domestication of the dog, birds of prey and the ferret, various forms of animal-aided hunting developed including venery (scent hound hunting, such as fox hunting), coursing (sight hound hunting), falconry and ferreting. These are all associated with medieval hunting; in time various dog breeds were selected for very precise tasks during the hunt, reflected in such names as pointer and setter.

Even as agriculture and animal husbandry became more prevalent, hunting often remained as a part of human culture where the environment and social conditions allowed. Hunting may be used to kill animals which prey upon domestic animals or to attempt to extirpate animals seen by humans as competition for resources such as water or forage.

As hunting moved from a subsistence activity to a social one, two trends emerged. One was that of the specialist hunter with special training and equipment. The other was the emergence of hunting as a sport for those of an upper social class. The meaning of the word 'game' in middle English evolved to include an animal which is hunted.

As game became more of a luxury than a necessity, the stylized pursuit of it also became a luxury. Dangerous hunting, as for lions or wild boars, usually on horseback (or from a chariot) had a function similar to tournaments and manly sports. Hunting was considered to be an honourable, somewhat competitive pastime to help the aristocracy practice skills of war in times of peace.

In most parts of medieval Europe, the upper class obtained the sole rights to hunt in certain areas of a feudal territory. Game in these areas was certainly used as a source of food and furs, often provided via professional huntsmen; but it was also expected to provide a form of recreation for the aristocracy. The importance of this proprietary view of game can be seen in the Robin Hood legends, in which one of the primary charges against the outlaws is that they 'hunt the King's deer'.

Hunting with Dogs

Although various animals have been used to aid the hunter, none has been as important as the dog. The domestication of the dog has led to a symbiotic relationship in which the dog has lost its evolutionary independence from humans in exchange for support.

Dogs today are used to find, chase and retrieve game and sometimes to kill it. Hunting dogs allow humans to pursue and kill prey that would otherwise be very difficult or dangerous to hunt.

Modern Sport Hunting

In time, hunting came to be seen as a sporting activity. Ultimately, the rising middle class or bourgeoisie adopted the practice and retained its image.

Although recreational hunters may choose to be selective hunters, many people hunt to enjoy the outdoors. Others enjoy game as an alternative to store bought meat. Some recreational hunters contributed to the modern environmental conservation movement. Aldo Leopold, John Muir, and Teddy Roosevelt, who spent some of their outdoor recreation time hunting, became the founding fathers of the modern Conservation movement.

Hunting and Religion

Many prehistoric (often zoomorph) deities are either predators or prey of humans, perhaps alluding to the importance of hunting for most Paleolithic cultures. In many pagan religions, specific rituals are conducted before or after a hunt; the rituals done may vary according to the species hunted or the season the hunt is taking place.

Often a hunting ground, or the hunt for one or more species, was reserved or prohibited in the context of a temple cult.

Indian and Eastern Religions

Hindu Scriptures describe hunting as an acceptable occupation as well as a sport of the kingly. Even figures considered godly are described to have engaged in hunting. One of the names of the god Shiva is '*Mrigavyadha*', the deer hunter ('*mriga*' means deer, '*vyadha*' means hunter). In the epic Ramayana, Dasharatha, the father of Ram, is said to have the ability to hunt in the dark. During one of his hunting expedition he accidentally killed Shravana, mistaking him for game. During Ram's exile in the forest, Ravana kidnapped his wife Sita from their hut while Ram was hunting a golden deer, and his brother Lakshman went after him. According to the Mahabharat, Pandu, the father of the Pandavas, accidentally killed the sage Kindama and his wife with an arrow mistaking them for a deer. Krishna is said to have died after being accidentally wounded by an arrow of a hunter.

Jainism teaches to have tremendous respect for all of life. Prohibitions for hunting and meat eating are the fundamental conditions for being a Jain.

The first Precept of Buddhism is the respect for all sentient life. The general approach by all Buddhists is to avoid killing any living animals. The Buddha explained the issue by saying "all fear death; comparing others with oneself, one should neither kill nor cause to kill".

From early Christian times, hunting has been forbidden to Roman Catholic Church clerics. Thus the 'Corpus Juris Canonici' (C. ii, X, De cleric. venat.) says "We forbid to all servants of God hunting and expeditions through the woods with hounds; and we also forbid them to keep hawks or falcons." The Fourth Council of the Lateran, held under Pope Innocent III, decreed (canon xv): "We interdict hunting or hawking to all clerics." The decree of the Council of Trent is worded more mildly: 'Let clerics abstain from illicit hunting and hawking' (Sess. XXIV, De reform., c. xii), which seems to imply that not all hunting is illicit, and canonists generally make a distinction declaring noisy (*clamorosa*) hunting unlawful but not quiet (*quieta*) hunting.

Ferraris (s.v. 'Clericus', art. 6) gives it as the general sense of canonists that hunting is allowed to clerics if it be indulged in rarely and for sufficient cause, as necessity, utility or "honest" recreation, and with that moderation which is becoming to the ecclesiastical state. Ziegler, however (De episc., l. IV, c. xix), thinks that the interpretation of the canonists is not in accordance with the letter or spirit of the laws of the Church.

Nevertheless, although a distinction between lawful and unlawful hunting is undoubtedly permissible, it is certain that a bishop can absolutely prohibit all hunting to the clerics of his diocese, as was done by synods at Milan, Avignon, Liège, Cologne and elsewhere. Benedict XIV (De synodo diœces., l. II, c. x) declared that such synodal decrees are not too severe, as an absolute prohibition of hunting is more conformable to the ecclesiastical law. In practice, therefore, the synodal statutes of various localities must be consulted to discover whether they allow quiet hunting or prohibit it altogether.

It is important to note that the Bible places no such restrictions on any Christian, as most do not observe Kosher dietary laws. Hence Protestant clerics, Catholic lay parishioners, and Protestants have no religious restrictions on hunting. This is in accord with what is found in the Bible book of Acts.

Jewish hunting law, based on the Torah, is similar, permitting hunting of non-preying animals that are additionally considered Kosher for food, although hunting preying animals for food is strictly prohibited under Rabbinic law. Hence birds of prey are specifically prohibited and non-Kosher. Hunting for sport, and not for food is also forbidden in Rabbinical Law.New Zealand has a strong hunting culture. The islands making up New Zealand originally had no land mammals apart from bats. However, once Europeans arrived game animals were introduced by acclimatisation societies to provide New Zealanders with sport and a hunting resource. Deer, pigs, goats, rabbits, Tahr and Chamois all adapted well to the New Zealand terrain and with no natural predators their population exploded. Government agencies view the animals as pests due to their effects on the natural environment and on agricultural production, but hunters view them as a resource.

Shikar (India)

During the feudal and colonial epoch on the Indian continent, hunting was a true 'regal sport' in the numerous princely states, as many (Maha)rajas, Nawabs, as well as British officers maintained a whole corps of *shikaris*, who were native professional hunters. They would be headed by a master of the hunt, who might be styled *Mir-shikar*. Often these were recruited from the normally low-ranking local tribes because of their traditional knowledge of environment and hunting techniques. Big game, such as Bengal tigers, might be hunted from the back of an elephant.

Indian social norms are generally antagonistic to hunting, while a few sects like the Bishnoi lay special emphasis on the conservation of particular species like the antelope. India's Wildlife Protection Act of 1972 bans the killing of all wild animals. However, the Chief Wildlife Warden may, if he is satisfied that any wild animal from a specified list has become dangerous to human life or is so disabled or diseased as to be beyond recovery, permit any person to hunt such animal. In such a case, the body of any wild animal killed or wounded becomes government property.

'Safari' as a distinctive way of hunting was popularized by US author Ernest Hemingway and president Theodore Roosevelt. A safari may consist of several days or even weeks-long journey and camping in the bush or jungle, while pursuing big game. Nowadays, it's often used to describe tours through African national parks to watch or hunt wildlife.

Hunters are usually tourists, accompanied by (licensed and highly regulated) professional hunters ('PH'), local guides, skinners and porters in more difficult terrains. A special safari type is the *solo-safari* where all the license acquiring, stalking, preparation and outfitting is done by the hunter himself.

Photo-safaris were popular even before the advent of ecotourism. The synonym *bloodless hunt* for hunting with the use of film and a still photo camera was first used by the Polish photographer Wlodzimierz Puchalski.

United Kingdom

Fox hunting is the type of hunting most closely associated with the United Kingdom. Originally a form of vermin control to protect livestock, it became a popular social activity for newly wealthy upper classes in Victorian times, and a traditional rural activity for riders and foot followers alike. Similar to fox hunting in many ways is the chasing of hare with hounds. Sight hounds such as greyhounds may be used to run down hare in coursing with scent hounds such as beagles. Other sorts of foxhounds may also be used for hunting deer or mink. Hunting deer on foot using stealth without hounds or horses is called deer stalking.

These forms of hunting have been controversial in the UK. Animal welfare supporters believe that hunting causes unnecessary suffering to foxes, horses and hounds. Proponents argue that it is culturally and perhaps economically important. Using dogs to chase wild mammals was made illegal in February 2005 by the Hunting Act 2004. The issues involved are addressed in the article 'fox hunting legislation'.

The shooting of game birds, especially pheasants still exists in the UK, with the British Association for Shooting and Conservation saying that over a million people per year participate in shooting, although this figure includes game shooting, clay pigeon shooting and target shooting. Shooting, as opposed to traditional hunting, requires little questing for game - around 35 million birds are released onto shooting estates every year, some having been factory farmed. Shoots can be elaborate affairs with guns placed in assigned positions with assistants to help load shotguns. When in position, 'beaters' move through the areas of cover swinging sticks or flags to drive the game out. Such events are often called 'drives'. The open season for grouse in the UK begins on August 12, the so-called *Glorious Twelfth*. The definition of game in the United Kingdom is governed by the Game Act 1831.

United States

North American hunting predates the United States by thousands of years, and was an important part of many pre-Columbian Native American cultures. Native Americans retain some hunting rights and are exempt from some laws as part of Indian treaties and otherwise under federal law– examples include eagle feather laws and exemptions in the Marine Mammal Protection Act. This is considered particularly important in Alaska Native communities.

Regulation of hunting is primarily regulated by state law; additional regulations are imposed through United States environmental law in the case of migratory birds and endangered species.

Regulations vary widely from state to state, and govern the areas, time periods, techniques and methods by which specific game animals may be hunted. Some states make a distinction between protected species and unprotected species (often vermin or varmints) for which there are no hunting regulations. Hunters of protected species require a hunting license in all states, for which completion of a hunting safety course is sometimes a prerequisite.

Hunting big game typically requires a 'tag' for each animal harvested. Tags must be purchased in addition to the hunting license, and the number of tags issued to an individual is typically limited. In cases where there are more prospective hunters than the quota for that species, tags are usually assigned by lottery. Tags may be further restricted to a specific area or 'wildlife management unit'. Hunting migratory waterfowl requires a 'duck stamp' from the Fish and Wildlife Service.

Harvest of animals other than big game is typically restricted by a 'bag limit' and a 'possession limit'. A bag limit is a maximum number of a specific animal species that an individual can harvest in a single day. A possession limit is a maximum number of a specific animal species that can be in an individual's possession at any time.

Guns usage in hunting is also typically regulated by game category, area within the state, and time period. Regulations for big game hunting often specify a minimum caliber or muzzle energy for firearms. The use of rifles is often banned for safety reasons in areas with high population density or limited topographic relief. Regulations may also limit or ban the use of lead in ammunition because of environmental concerns. Specific seasons for bow hunting or muzzle-loading black powder guns are often established to limit competition with hunters using more effective weapons. Hunting in the United States is not associated with any particular class or culture. In fact, 78 per cent of Americans support legal hunting, but relatively few Americans actually hunt. At the beginning of the 21st century, 6 per cent of Americans hunted. Southerners in states along the eastern seaboard hunted at a rate slightly below the national average (5%), and while hunting was more common in other parts of the South (9%), these rates did not surpass those of the Plains states, where 12 per cent of Midwesterners hunted. Hunting in other areas of the country fell below the national average. Overall in the 1996-2006 period, the number of hunters over the age of 16 declined by 10 per cent, a drop attributable to a number of factors including habitat loss and changes in recreation habits.

Regulation of hunting within the United States dates from the 19th century. Some modern hunters see themselves as conservationists and sportsmen in the mode of Theodore Roosevelt and the Boone and Crockett Club. Local hunting clubs and national organizations provide hunter education and help protect the future of the sport by buying land for future hunting use. Some groups represent a specific hunting interest, such as Ducks Unlimited, Pheasants Forever or Delta Waterfowl Foundation. Many hunting groups also participate in lobbying the federal government and state government.

Each year, nearly $200 million in hunters' federal excise taxes are distributed to state agencies to support wildlife management programmes, the purchase of lands open to hunters, and hunter education and safety classes. Since 1934 the sale of Federal Duck Stamps, a required purchase for migratory waterfowl hunters over 16 years old, has raised over $700 million to help purchase more than 5.2 million acres (8,100 sq mi/20,000 km^2) of habitat for the National Wildlife Refuge System lands that support waterfowl and many other wildlife species, and are often open to hunting. States also collect monies from hunting licenses to assist with management of game animals, as designated by law. A key task of Federal and state park rangers and game wardens is to enforce laws and regulations related to hunting, including species protection, hunting seasons, and hunting bans.

Varmint hunting is an American phrase for the selective killing of non-game animals seen as pests. While not always an efficient form of pest control, varmint hunting achieves selective control of pests while providing recreation and is much less regulated. Varmint species are often responsible for detrimental effects on crops, livestock, landscaping, infrastructure, and pets. Some animals (such as wild rabbits or squirrels) may be utilized for fur or meat, but often no use is made of the carcass. Which species are "varmints" depends on the circumstance and area. Common varmints may include various rodents, coyotes, crows, foxes, feral cats, and feral hogs. Some animals once considered varmints are now protected, such as wolves. In the US state of Louisiana, a non-native rodent known as a nutria have become so destructive to the local ecosystem that the state has initiated a bounty program to help control the population. Feral dogs and cats, rats, starlings, English sparrows, and pigeons may be hunted without a hunting licence in the United States.

The principles of the *Fair Chase* have been a part of the American hunting tradition for over 100 years. The role of the hunter-conservationist, popularized by Theodore Roosevelt, has been central to the development of the modern Fair Chase tradition. When internet hunting was introduced in 2005, allowing people to hunt over the internet using remotely controlled guns, the practice was widely criticized by hunters as violating the principles of fair chase. As a representative of the NRA explained, "the NRA has always maintained that fair chase, being in the field with your firearm or bow, is an important element of hunting tradition. Sitting at your desk in front of your computer, clicking at a mouse, has nothing to do with hunting."

Hunting Ranches

Indian Blackbuck, Nilgai, exotic deer antelope, Greater Kudu and Barasingha can now be found on hunting ranches in Texas, USA where they are shot for sport hunting. Hunters can pay upwards of $4000 as fees for hunting a Barasingha.

Russia

The Russian imperial hunts evolved from hunting traditions of early Russian rulers (Grand Princes and Tsars), under the influence of hunting customs of European royal courts. The imperial hunts were organized mainly in Peterhof, Tsarskoye Selo and Gatchina.

Wildlife Management

Hunting gives resource managers an important tool in managing populations that might exceed the carrying capacity of their habitat and threaten the well-being of other species or, in some instances, damage human health or safety. Hunting reduces intraspecific competition for food and shelter, reducing mortality among the remaining animals. Some environmentalists assert that (re)introducing predators would achieve the same end with greater efficiency and less negative effect such as introducing significant amounts of free lead into the environment and food chain.

Hunters often disagree, arguing that hunting is more selective, removing fewer old, sick, or young animals than natural predation. Aldo Leopold, an early environmentalist and hunter, also believed hunting could be used to manage animal populations.

Management agencies sometimes rely on hunting to control specific animal populations, as has been the case with deer in North America. These hunts may sometimes be carried out by professional shooters although others may include amateur hunters. Many U.S. city and local governments hire professional and amateur hunters each year to reduce populations of animals that are becoming hazardous, like deer, in a restricted area, such as neighborhood parks and metropolitan open spaces.

A large part of managing populations involves managing the number and, sometimes, the size or age of animals harvested so as to ensure the sustainability of the population. Tools which are frequently used to control harvest are bag limits and season closures, although gear restrictions such as archery-only seasons are becoming increasingly popular in an effort to reduce hunter success rates.

Bag Limits

Bag limits are provisions under the law which control how many animals of a given species or group of species can be killed although there are often species for which bag limits do not apply. There are also jurisdictions where bag limits are not applied at all or are not applied under certain circumstances. Where bag limits are used, however, there can be daily or seasonal bag limits. For example, ducks can often be harvested at a rate of six per hunter per day. Big game, like moose, most often have a seasonal bag limit of one animal per hunter. Bag limits may also regulate the size, sex or age of animal that a hunter can kill. In many cases, bag limits are designed to more equitably allocate harvest among the hunting population rather than to protect animal populations. The phrase 'bag limits' comes from the custom among hunters of small game to carry successful kills in a small bag, similar to a fishing kreel.

Closed Season

A closed season is a 'hunting' term used to describe a time during which hunting an animal of a given species is contrary to law. Typically, closed seasons are designed to protect a species when they are most vulnerable or, sometimes, to protect them during their breeding season . By extension, the period that is not the closed season is known as the open season.

Illegal Hunting

Illegal hunting and harvesting of wild species contrary to local and international conservation and wildlife management laws is termed as 'Poaching'. Violations of hunting laws and regulations are normally punishable by law and, collectively, such violations are known as poaching.

Historical, subsistence and sport hunting techniques can differ radically, with modern hunting regulations often addressing issues of where, when and how hunts are conducted. Techniques may vary depending on government regulations, a hunter's personal ethics, local custom, hunting-equipment and the animal being hunted. Often a hunter will use a combination of more than one technique. Laws may forbid sport hunters from using some methods used primarily in poaching and wildlife management.

- *Baiting* is the use of decoys, lures, scent
- *Battue* involves beating animals into a killing-zone or ambush
- *Beagling* is the use of beagles in hunting rabbits and sometimes in hunting foxes
- *Beating* uses beaters to flush out game and/or drive it into position
- *Blind* or *stand hunting* is waiting for animals from a concealed or elevated position
- *Calling* is the use of animal noises to attract or drive animals
- *Camouflage* is the use of visual concealment (or scent) to blend with the environment
- *Dogs* may be used to course or to help flush, herd, drive, track, point at, pursue or retrieve prey
- *Driving* is the herding of animals in a particular direction, usually toward another hunter in the group
- *Flushing* is the practice of scaring animals from concealed areas

- *Glassing* is the use of optics (such as binoculars) to more easily locate animals
- *Glue* is an indiscriminate passive form to kill birds
- *Internet hunting* is a method of hunting over the internet using webcams and remotely controlled guns
- *Netting,* including active netting with the use of cannon nets and rocket nets
- *Persistence hunting* is the use of running and tracking to pursue the prey to exhaustion.
- *Scouting* includes a variety of tasks and techniques for finding animals to hunt
- *Spotlighting or shining* is the use of artificial light to find or blind animals before killing
- *Stalking* or *still hunting* is the practice of walking quietly, in search of animals or in pursuit of an individual animal
- *Tracking* is the practice of reading physical evidence in pursuing animals
- *Trapping* is the use of devices (snares, pits, deadfalls) to capture or kill an animal

Trophy hunting is the selective seeking of wild game. It may also include the controversial hunting of captive or semi-captive animals expressly bred and raised under controlled or semi-controlled conditions so as to attain trophy characteristics (canned hunts).

History

In the 19th century, southern and central European sport hunters often pursued game only for a trophy, usually the head or pelt of an animal, which was then displayed as a sign of prowess. The rest of the animal was typically discarded. Some cultures, however, disapprove of such waste. In Nordic countries, hunting for trophies was–and still is–frowned upon. Hunting in North America in the 19th century was done primarily as a way to supplement food supplies, although it is now undertaken mainly for sport. The safari method of hunting was a development of sport hunting that saw elaborate travel in Africa, India and other places in pursuit of trophies. In modern times, trophy hunting persists and is a significant industry in some areas.

Controversy

Trophy hunting is most often criticized when it involves rare or endangered animals. Opponents may also see trophy hunting as an issue of morality or animal cruelty, criticising the killing of living creatures for recreation. Victorian era dramatist W.S. Gilbert remarked, "Deer-stalking would be a very fine sport if only the deer had guns."

There is also debate about the extent to which trophy hunting benefits the local economy. Hunters argue that fees paid contribute to the local economy and provide value to animals that would otherwise be seen as competition for grazing, livestock, and crops. This analysis is disputed by opponents of trophy hunting. Some argue that the animals are worth more to the community for ecotourism, than hunting.

Legislation Lobbied by Hunters

Hunters have worked closely with local and federal governments to enact legislation to protect wildlife habitats. The following examples represent hunter-advocated legislation enacted to generate funds for preserving and establishing habitats.

The Ontario Federation of Anglers and Hunters successfully lobbied to prevent cuts in funding for the Community Fisheries and Wildlife Involvement Program by 50 per cent.

Pittman-Robertson Wildlife Restoration Act of 1937

In 1937, hunters successfully lobbied Congress to pass the Pittman-Robertson Wildlife Restoration Act, which placed an 11 per cent tax on all hunting equipment. This self-imposed tax now generates over $700 million each year and is used exclusively to establish, restore and protect wildlife habitats. It is named for Nevada Senator Key Pittman and Virginia Congressman Absalom Willis Robertson.

Federal Duck Stamp Programme

On March 16, 1934 President Roosevelt signed the Migratory Bird Hunting Stamp Act, which requires an annual stamp purchase by all hunters over the age of sixteen. The stamps are created on behalf of the programme by the U.S. Postal Service and depict wildlife artwork chosen through an annual contest. They play an important role in habitat conservation because 98 per cent of all funds generated by their sale go directly toward the purchase or lease of wetland habitat for protection in the National Wildlife Refuge System. In addition to waterfowl, it is estimated that one third of the nation's endangered species seek food and shelter in areas protected using Duck Stamp funds. Since 1934, the sale of Federal Duck Stamps has generated $670M and helped to purchase or lease 5.2 million acres (21,000 km^2) of habitat. The stamps serve as a licence to hunt migratory birds, an entrance pass for all National Wildlife Refuge areas and are also considered collectors items often purchased for aesthetic reasons outside of the hunting and birding communities. Although non-hunters buy a significant number of Duck Stamps, 87 per cent of their sales are contributed to hunters. Distribution of funds is managed by The Migratory Bird Conservation Commission (MBCC).

Conservation Organizations Founded by Hunters

There are a number of organizations founded by hunters and by those interested in preserving wildlife populations and habitats. One of the oldest and most well-known organizations is Ducks Unlimited. Another internationally recognized hunters' conservation organization is Safari Club International.

13 Reforestation

'Reforestation' is the restocking of existing forests and woodlands which have been depleted. Reforestation can be used to improve the quality of human life by soaking up pollution and dust from the air, rebuild natural habitats and ecosystems, mitigate global warming since forests facilitate biosequestration of atmospheric carbon dioxide, and harvest for resources, particularly timber.

The term reforestation is similar to afforestation, the process of restoring and recreating areas of woodlands or forest that may have existed long ago but were deforested or otherwise removed at some point in the past.

Reforestation of large areas can be done through the use of measuring rope (for accurate plant spacing) and dibbers, (or wheeled augers for planting the larger trees) for making the hole in which a seedling or plant can be inserted. Indigenous soil inoculants (e.g., Laccaria bicolour) can optionally be used to increase survival rates in hardy environments.

A debatable issue in managed reforestation is whether or not the succeeding forest will have the same biodiversity as the original forest. If the forest is replaced with only one species of tree and all other vegetation is prevented from growing back, a monoculture forest similar to agricultural crops would be the result. However, most reforestation involves the planting of different seedlots of seedlings taken from the area often of multiple species. Another important factor is the natural regeneration of a wide variety of plant and animal species that can occur on a clearcut. In some areas the suppression of forest fires for hundreds of years has resulted in large single aged and single specied forest stands. The logging of small clearcuts and or prescribed burning, actually increases the biodiversity in these areas by creating a greater variety of treestand ages and species.

Reforestation need not be only used for recovery of accidentally destroyed forests. In some countries, such as Finland, the forests are *managed* by the wood products and pulp and paper industry. In such an arrangement, like other crops, trees are replanted wherever they are cut. In such circumstances, the industry can cut the trees in a way to allow easier reforestation. In Canada, the wood product and pulp and paper industry systematically replaces many of the trees it cuts, employing large numbers of summer workers for treeplanting work.

In just 20 years, a teak plantation in Costa Rica can produce up to about 400 m^3 of wood per hectare. As the natural teak forests of Asia become more scarce or difficult to obtain, the prices commanded by plantation-grown teak grow higher every year. Other species such as mahogany grow slower than teak in Tropical America but are also extremely valuable. Faster growers include pine, eucalyptus, and gmelina.

Reforestation, if several native species are used, can provide other benefits in addition to financial returns, including restoration of the soil, rejuvenation of local flora and fauna, and the capturing and sequestering of 38 tons of carbon dioxide per hectare per year.

The reestablishment of forests is not just simple tree planting. Forests are made up of a diversity of species and they build dead organic matter into soils over time. A major tree-planting programme in a place like this would enhance the local climate and reduce the demands of burning large amounts of fossil fuels for cooling in the summer. Forests absorb carbon dioxide through their photosynthesis cycle, and by using this idea, increasing forests with reforestation and discouraging deforestation will help mitigate global warming. Forest ecosystems are especially important to the global carbon cycle in two ways. First, they are responsible for moving around three billion tons of anthropogenic carbon every year. This amounts to about 30 per cent of all carbon dioxide emissions from fossil fuels. Second, forest ecosystems are terrestrial carbon sinks in that they store large amounts of carbon which accounts for as much as double the amount of carbon in the atmosphere.

Biodiversity on a 15-year-old reforested plot of land

Canadell and Raupach (2008) believe that there are four major strategies available to mitigate carbon emissions through forestry activities: increase the amount of forested land through a reforestation process; increase the carbon density of existing forests at a stand and landscape scale; expand the use of forest products that will sustainably replace fossil-fuel emissions; and reduce carbon emissions that are caused from deforestation and degradation.

However, achieving the first strategy requires great effort of land transformation. For example, China has used 24 million ha of new forest plantation and natural forest regrowth to offset 21 per cent of Chinese fossil fuel emissions in 2000. In theory, any tree would cover more forest area and absorb more carbon dioxide from the atmosphere. On the other hand, a genetically modified tree specimen might grow much faster than any other regular tree. Some of these trees are already being developed in the lumber and biofuel industries. These fast-growing trees would not only be planted for those industries but they can also be planted to help absorb carbon dioxide faster than regular trees.

Mitigating the rate of deforestation has huge potential toward a cost-effective contribution to protect the atmosphere's climate. At this point, there are 13 million ha of tropical regions that are deforested every year. These regions can reduce rates of deforestation by 50 per cent by 2050.

A study from the National Center for Atmospheric Research in Boulder, Colorado, USA, found that, unlike previous belief that forests in higher latitudes soak up a vast amount of carbon dioxide, more carbon dioxide is absorbed in tropical climates. Trees in temperate latitudes have a net warming effect on the climate. The heat that dark leaves absorb outweighs the carbon they soak up, therefore, tropical trees absorb carbon dioxide as well as being able to cool the planet by up to 0.7 °C.

Trees in tropical climates have, on average, larger, brighter, and more abundant leaves than non-tropical climates. The advantage of planting trees in a tropical setting is the quicker growth rate due to the longer rainy seasons. There is no need for the trees to hibernate and can therefore grow year-round.

An incredible portion of the Earth's biodiversity is situated in tropical areas. The lack of reforestation in tropical climates is putting a larger portion of species at risk of becoming endangered.

A study of the girth of 70,000 trees across Africa has shown that tropical forests are soaking up more carbon dioxide pollution than previously realized. The research suggests almost one fifth of fossil fuel emissions are absorbed by forests across Africa, Amazonia and Asia.

Simon Lewis, a climate expert at the University of Leeds, who led the study, said: "Tropical forest trees are absorbing about 18 per cent of the carbon dioxide added to the atmosphere each year from burning fossil fuels, substantially buffering the rate of change."

Extensive forest resources placed anywhere in the world will not always have a positive impact. For example, large reforestation programmes in boreal regions have a limited impact on climate mitigation. This is because it substitutes a bright snow-dominated region that reflects the sunlight with dark forest canopies. On the other hand, a positive example would be reforestation projects in tropical regions, which would lead to a positive biophysical change such as the formation of clouds. These clouds would then reflect the sunlight, creating a positive impact on climate mitigation.

Incentives for Reforestation

Some incentives can be as a simple as a financial compensation. Streck and Scholz (2006) explain how a group of scientists from various institutions have developed a compensated reduction of deforestation approach which would reward developing countries that disrupt any further act of deforestation. Countries that participate and take the option to reduce their emissions from deforestation during a committed period of time would receive financial compensation for the carbon dioxide emissions that they avoided. To raise the payments, the host country would issue government bonds or negotiate some kind of loan with a financial institution that would want to take part in the compensation promised to the other country. The funds received by the country could be invested to help find alternatives to the extensive cutdown of forests. This whole process of cutting emissions would be voluntary, but once the country has agreed to lower they emissions they would be obligated to reduce their emissions. However, if a country was not able to meet their obligation, their target would get added to their next commitment period. The authors of these proposals see this as a solely government-to-government agreement; private entities would not participate in the compensation trades.

Reforestation competes with other land uses such as food production, livestock grazing, and living space for further economic growth.

There is also the risk that through a forest fire or insect outbreak all the stored carbon in a reforested area could make its way back to the atmosphere. Reduced harvesting rates and fire suppression have caused an increase in the forest biomass in the western United States over the past century. This causes an increase of about a factor of four in the frequency of fires due to longer and hotter dry seasons.

Forestry

'Forestry' is the art and science of managing forests, tree plantations, and related natural resources. The main goal of forestry is to create and implement systems that allow forests to continue a sustainable continuation of environmental supplies and services. The challenge of forestry is to create systems that are socially accepted while sustaining the resource and any other resourses that might be affected.

Silviculture, a related science, involves the growing and tending of trees and forests. Modern forestry generally concerns itself with: assisting forests to provide timber as raw material for wood products; wildlife habitat; natural water quality management; recreation; landscape and community protection; employment; aesthetically appealing landscapes; biodiversity management; watershed management; erosion control; and a 'sink' for atmospheric carbon dioxide. A practitioner of forestry is known as a forester.

Forest ecosystems have come to be seen as the most important component of the biosphere, and forestry has emerged as a vital field of science, applied art, and technology.

The use and management of forest resources has a long history in China, dating from the Han Dynasty and taking place under the landowning gentry. It was also later written of by the Ming Dynasty Chinese scholar Xu Guangqi (1562-1633). In the Western world, formal forestry practices developed during the Middle Ages, when land was largely under the control of kings. Control of the land included hunting rights, and though peasants in many places were permitted to gather firewood and building timber and to graze animals, hunting rights were retained by the members of the nobility. Systematic management of forests for a sustainable yield of timber is said to have begun in the 16th century in both the German states and Japan. Typically, a forest was divided into specific sections and mapped; the harvest of timber was planned with an eye to regeneration.

The practice of establishing tree plantations was promoted by John Evelyn; it had already acquired some popularity in the British Isles. Louis XIV's minister Jean-Baptiste Colbert's oak forest at Tronçais, planted for the future use of the French navy, matured as expected in the mid-19th century: "Colbert had thought of everything except the steamship," Fernand Braudel observed. Schools of forestry were established after 1825; most of these schools were in Germany and France. During the nineteenth and early twentieth centuries, forest preservation programmes were established in the United States, Europe, and British India. Many foresters were either from continental Europe (like Sir Dietrich Brandis), or educated there (like Gifford Pinchot).

The enactment and evolution of forestry laws and binding regulations occurred in most Western nations in the 20th century in response to growing conservation concerns and the increasing technological capacity of logging companies.

Tropical forestry is a separate branch of forestry which deals mainly with equatorial forests that yield woods such as teak and mahogany. Sir Dietrich Brandis is considered the father of tropical forestry.

Today a strong body of research exists regarding the management of forest ecosystems and genetic improvement of tree species and varieties. Forestry also includes the development of better methods for the planting, protecting, thinning, controlled burning, felling, extracting, and processing of timber. One of the applications of modern forestry is reforestation, in which trees are planted and tended in a given area.

In many regions the forest industry is of major ecological, economic, and social importance. Third-party certification systems that provide independent verification of sound forest stewardship and sustainable forestry have become commonplace in many areas since the 1990s. These certification systems were developed as a response to criticism of some forestry practices, particularly deforestation in less developed regions along with concerns over resource management in the developed world. Some certification systems are criticised for primarily acting as marketing tools and lacking in their claimed independence.

In topographically severe forested terrain, proper forestry is important for the prevention or minimization of serious soil erosion or even landslides. In areas with a high potential for landslides, forests can stabilize soils and prevent property damage or loss, human injury, or loss of life.

Public perception of forest management has become controversial, with growing public concern over perceived mismanagement of the forest and increasing demands that forest land be managed for uses other than pure timber production, for example, indigenous rights, recreation, watershed management, and preservation of wilderness, waterways and wildlife habitat. Sharp disagreements over the role of forest fires, logging, motorized recreation and others drives debate while the public demand for wood products continues to increase.

Foresters work for the timber industry, government agencies, conservation groups, local authorities, urban parks boards, citizens' associations, and private landowners. The forestry profession includes a wide diversity of jobs, with educational requirements ranging from college bachelor's degrees to PhDs for highly specialized work. Industrial foresters plan forest regeneration starting with careful harvesting. Urban foresters manage trees in urban green spaces. Foresters work in tree nurseries growing seedlings for woodland creation or regeneration projects. Foresters improve tree genetics. Forest engineers develop new building systems. Professional foresters measure and model the growth of forests with tools like geographic information systems. Foresters may combat insect infestation, disease, forest and grassland wildfire, but increasingly allow these natural aspects of forest ecosystems to run their course when the likelihood of epidemics or risk of life or property are low. Increasingly, foresters participate in wildlife conservation planning and watershed protection. Foresters have been mainly concerned with timber management, especially reforestation, maintaining forests at prime conditions, and fire control.

Foresters develop and implement forest management plans relying on tree inventories showing an area's topographical features as well as its distribution of trees (by species) and other plant cover. Plans also include roads, culverts, proximity to human habitation, hydrological conditions, and soil reports. Forest management plans include the projected use of the land and a timetable for that use. Traditional forest management plans focus on providing logs used for timber, veneer, plywood, paper, wood fuel or other industries. Hence, considerations of product quality and quantity, employment, and profit have been of central, though not always exclusive, importance. Foresters frequently develop post-harvest site plans for reforestation, weed control, fertilization, or thinning. The objectives of landowners and leaseholder influence plans for harvest and subsequent site treatment. In Britain, plans featuring 'good forestry practice' must always consider the needs of other stakeholders such as nearby communities or rural residents living within or adjacent to woodland areas. Foresters consider tree felling and environmental legislation when developing plans. Plans instruct the sustainable harvesting and replacement of trees. They indicate whether road building or other forest engineering operations are required.

Agriculture and forest leaders are also trying to understand how the climate change legislation will affect what they do. The information gathered will provide the data that will determine the role of agriculture and forestry in a new climate change regulatory system.

14 Population Genetics

'Population genetics' is the study of the allele frequency distribution and change under the influence of the four evolutionary processes: natural selection, genetic drift, mutation and gene flow. It also takes account of population subdivision and population structure in space. It attempts to explain such phenomena as adaptation and speciation.

Population genetics was a vital ingredient in the modern evolutionary synthesis. Its primary founders were Sewall Wright, J.B.S. Haldane and R.A. Fisher, who also laid the foundations for the related discipline of quantitative genetics.

Population genetics concerns the genetic constitution of populations and how this constitution changes with time. A population is a set of organisms in which any pair of members can breed together. This implies that all members belong to the same species and live near each other.

For example, all of the moths of the same species living in an isolated forest are a population. A gene in this population may have several alternate forms, which account for variations between the phenotypes of the organisms. An example might be a gene for coloration in moths that has two alleles: black and white. A gene pool is the complete set of alleles for a gene in a single population; the allele frequency for an allele is the fraction of the genes in the pool that is composed of that allele (for example, what fraction of moth coloration genes are the black allele). Evolution occurs when there are changes in the frequencies of alleles within a population of interbreeding organisms; for example, the allele for black color in a population of moths becoming more common.

To understand the mechanisms that cause a population to evolve, it is useful to consider what conditions are required for a population not to evolve. The *Hardy-Weinberg principle* states that the frequencies of alleles (variations in a gene) in a sufficiently large population will remain constant if the only forces acting on that population are the random reshuffling of alleles during the formation of the sperm or egg, and the random combination of the alleles in these sex cells during fertilization. Such a population is said to be in *Hardy-Weinberg equilibrium*; it is not evolving.

Natural selection is the process by which heritable traits that make it more likely for an organism to survive and successfully reproduce become more common in a population over successive generations.

The natural genetic variation within a population of organisms means that some individuals will survive more successfully than others in their current environment. Factors which affect reproductive success are also important, an issue which Charles Darwin developed in his ideas on sexual selection.

Natural selection acts on the phenotype, or the observable characteristics of an organism, but the genetic (heritable) basis of any phenotype which gives a reproductive advantage will become more common in a population. Over time, this process can result in adaptations that specialize organisms for particular ecological niches and may eventually result in the emergence of new species.

Natural selection is one of the cornerstones of modern biology. The term was introduced by Darwin in his groundbreaking 1859 book *On the Origin of Species*, in which natural selection was described by analogy to artificial selection, a process by which animals and plants with traits considered desirable by human breeders are systematically favored for reproduction. The concept of natural selection was originally developed in the absence of a valid theory of heredity; at the time of Darwin's writing, nothing was known of modern genetics. The union of traditional Darwinian evolution with subsequent discoveries in classical and molecular genetics is termed the *modern evolutionary synthesis*. Natural selection remains the primary explanation for adaptive evolution.

Genetic drift is the change in the relative frequency in which a gene variant (allele) occurs in a population due to random sampling and chance: The alleles in offspring are a random sample of those in the parents, and chance has a role in determining whether a given individual survives and reproduces. A population's allele frequency is the fraction of the gene copies that share a particular form.

Genetic drift is an important evolutionary process which leads to changes in allele frequencies over time. It may cause gene variants to disappear completely, and thereby reduce genetic variability. In contrast to natural selection, which makes gene variants more common or less common depending on their reproductive success, the changes due to genetic drift are not driven by environmental or adaptive pressures, and may be beneficial, neutral, or detrimental to reproductive success.

The effect of genetic drift is larger in small populations, and smaller in large populations. Vigorous debates wage among scientists over the relative importance of genetic drift compared with natural selection. Ronald Fisher held the view that genetic drift plays at the most a minor role in evolution, and this remained the dominant view for several decades. In 1968 Motoo Kimura rekindled the debate with his neutral theory of molecular evolution which claims that most of the changes in the genetic material are caused by genetic drift.

Mutations are changes in the DNA sequence of a cell's genome and are caused by radiation, viruses, transposons and mutagenic chemicals, as well as errors that occur during meiosis or DNA replication. Errors are introduced particularly often in the process of DNA replication, in the polymerization of the second strand. These errors can also be induced by the organism itself, by cellular processes such as hypermutation.

Mutations can have an impact on the phenotype of an organism, especially if they occur within the protein coding sequence of a gene. Error rates are usually very low — one error in every 10 million–100 million bases — due to the 'proofreading' ability of DNA polymerases. Without proofreading, error rates are a thousand-fold higher. Chemical damage to DNA occurs naturally as well, and cells use DNA repair mechanisms to repair mismatches and breaks in DNA. Nevertheless, the repair sometimes fails to return the DNA to its original sequence.

In organisms that use chromosomal crossover to exchange DNA and recombine genes, errors in alignment during meiosis can also cause mutations. Errors in crossover are especially likely when similar sequences cause partner chromosomes to adopt a mistaken alignment; this makes some regions in genomes more prone to mutating in this way. These errors create large structural changes in DNA sequence—duplications, inversions or deletions of entire regions, or the accidental exchanging of whole parts between different chromosomes (called translocation).

Mutation can result in several different types of change in DNA sequences, these can either have no effect, alter the product of a gene, or prevent the gene from functioning. Studies in the fly *Drosophila melanogaster* suggest that if a mutation changes a protein produced by a gene, this will probably be harmful, with about 70 per cent of these mutations having damaging effects, and the remainder being either neutral or weakly beneficial. Due to the damaging effects that mutations can have on cells, organisms have evolved mechanisms such as DNA repair to remove mutations. Therefore, the optimal mutation rate for a species is a trade-off between costs of a high mutation rate, such as deleterious mutations, and the metabolic costs of maintaining systems to reduce the mutation rate, such as DNA repair enzymes. Viruses that use RNA as their genetic material have rapid mutation rates, which can be an advantage since these viruses will evolve constantly and rapidly, and thus evade the defensive responses of e.g. the human immune system.

Mutations can involve large sections of DNA becoming duplicated, usually through genetic recombination. These duplications are a major source of raw material for evolving new genes, with tens to hundreds of genes duplicated in animal genomes every million years. Most genes belong to larger families of genes of shared ancestry. Novel genes are produced by several methods, commonly through the duplication and mutation of an ancestral gene, or by recombining parts of different genes to form new combinations with new functions.

Here, domains act as modules, each with a particular and independent function, that can be mixed together to produce genes encoding new proteins with novel properties. For example, the human eye uses four genes to make structures that sense light: three for colour vision and one for night vision; all four arose from a single ancestral gene. Another advantage of duplicating a gene (or even an entire genome) is that this increases redundancy; this allows one gene in the pair to acquire a new function while the other copy performs the original function. Other types of mutation occasionally create new genes from previously non-coding DNA.

Gene Flow

Gene flow is the exchange of genes between populations, which are usually of the same species. Examples of gene flow within a species include the migration and then breeding of organisms, or the exchange of pollen. Gene transfer between species includes the formation of hybrid organisms and horizontal gene transfer.

Migration into or out of a population can change allele frequencies, as well as introducing genetic variation into a population. Immigration may add new genetic material to the established gene pool of a population. Conversely, emigration may remove genetic material. As barriers to reproduction between two diverging populations are required for the populations to become new species, gene flow may slow this process by spreading genetic differences between the populations. Gene flow is hindered by mountain ranges, oceans and deserts or even man-made structures such as the Great Wall of China, which has hindered the flow of plant genes.

Depending on how far two species have diverged since their most recent common ancestor, it may still be possible for them to produce offspring, as with horses and donkeys mating to produce mules. Such hybrids are generally infertile, due to the two different sets of chromosomes being unable to pair up during meiosis. In this case, closely related species may regularly interbreed, but hybrids will be selected against and the species will remain distinct. However, viable hybrids are occasionally formed and these new species can either have properties intermediate between their parent species, or possess a totally new phenotype. The importance of hybridization in creating new species of animals is unclear, although cases have been seen in many types of animals, with the gray tree frog being a particularly well-studied example.

Hybridization is, however, an important means of speciation in plants, since polyploidy (having more than two copies of each chromosome) is tolerated in plants more readily than in animals. Polyploidy is important in hybrids as it allows reproduction, with the two different sets of chromosomes each being able to pair with an identical partner during meiosis. Polyploids also have more genetic diversity, which allows them to avoid inbreeding depression in small populations.

Horizontal gene transfer is the transfer of genetic material from one organism to another organism that is not its offspring; this is most common among bacteria. In medicine, this contributes to the spread of antibiotic resistance, as when one bacteria acquires resistance genes it can rapidly transfer them to other species Horizontal transfer of genes from bacteria to eukaryotes such as the yeast *Saccharomyces cerevisiae* and the adzuki bean beetle *Callosobruchus chinensis* may also have occurred. An example of larger-scale transfers are the eukaryotic bdelloid rotifers, which appear to have received a range of genes from bacteria, fungi, and plants. Viruses can also carry DNA between organisms, allowing transfer of genes even across biological domains. Large-scale gene transfer has also occurred between the ancestors of eukaryotic cells and prokaryotes, during the acquisition of chloroplasts and mitochondria.

Migration into or out of a population may be responsible for a marked change in allele frequencies. Immigration may also result in the addition of new genetic variants to the established gene pool of a particular species or population.

There are a number of factors that affect the rate of gene flow between different populations. One of the most significant factors is mobility, as greater mobility of an individual tends to give it greater migratory potential. Animals tend to be more mobile than plants, although pollen and seeds may be carried great distances by animals or wind.

Maintained gene flow between two populations can also lead to a combination of the two gene pools, reducing the genetic variation between the two groups. It is for this reason that gene flow strongly acts against speciation, by recombining the gene pools of the groups, and thus, repairing the developing differences in genetic variation that would have led to full speciation and creation of daughter species.

For example, if a species of grass grows on both sides of a highway, pollen is likely to be transported from one side to the other and vice versa. If this pollen is able to fertilise the plant where it ends up and produce viable offspring, then the alleles in the pollen have effectively been able to move from the population on one side of the highway to the other.

The Mendelian and biometrician models were eventually reconciled, when *population genetics* was developed. A key step was the work of the British biologist and statistician R.A. Fisher. In a series of papers starting in 1918 and culminating in his 1930 book *The Genetical Theory of Natural Selection*, Fisher showed that the continuous variation measured by the biometricians could be produced by the combined action of many discrete genes, and that natural selection could change gene frequencies in a population, resulting in evolution. In a series of papers beginning in 1924, another British geneticist, J.B.S. Haldane, applied statistical analysis to real-world examples of natural selection, such as the evolution of industrial melanism in peppered moths, and showed that natural selection worked at an even faster rate than Fisher assumed.

The American biologist Sewall Wright, who had a background in animal breeding experiments, focused on combinations of interacting genes, and the effects of inbreeding on small, relatively isolated populations that exhibited genetic drift. In 1932, Wright introduced the concept of an adaptive landscape and argued that genetic drift and inbreeding could drive a small, isolated subpopulation away from an adaptive peak, allowing natural selection to drive it towards different adaptive peaks. Fisher and Wright had some fundamental disagreements and a controversy about the relative roles of selection and drift continued for much of the century between the Americans and the British. The Frenchman Gustave Malécot was also important early in the development of the discipline.

The work of Fisher, Haldane and Wright founded the discipline of *population genetics*. This integrated natural selection with Mendelian genetics, which was the critical first step in developing a unified theory of how evolution worked.

John Maynard Smith was Haldane's pupil, whilst W.D. Hamilton was heavily influenced by the writings of Fisher. The American George R. Price worked with both Hamilton and Maynard Smith. American Richard Lewontin and Japanese Motoo Kimura were heavily influenced by Wright.

In the first few decades of the 20th century, most field naturalists continued to believe that Lamarckian and orthogenic mechanisms of evolution provided the best explanation for the complexity they observed in the living world. However, as the field of genetics continued to develop, those views became less tenable. Theodosius Dobzhansky, a postdoctoral worker in T.H. Morgan's lab, had been influenced by the work on genetic diversity by Russian geneticists such as Sergei Chetverikov. He helped to bridge the divide between the foundations of microevolution developed by the population geneticists and the patterns of macro-evolution observed by field biologists, with his 1937 book *Genetics and the Origin of Species*.

Dobzhansky examined the genetic diversity of wild populations and showed that, contrary to the assumptions of the population geneticists, these populations had large amounts of genetic diversity, with marked differences between sub-populations. The book also took the highly mathematical work of the population geneticists and put it into a more accessible form. In Great Britain E.B. Ford, the pioneer of ecological genetics, continued throughout the 1930s and 1940s to demonstrate the power of selection due to ecological factors including the ability to maintain genetic diversity through genetic polymorphisms such as human blood types. Ford's work would contribute to a shift in emphasis during the course of the modern synthesis towards natural selection over genetic drift.

15 Conservation of Nature

Nature, in the broadest sense, is equivalent to the *natural world, physical world,* or *material world* 'Nature' refers to the phenomena of the physical world, and also to life in general. It ranges in scale from the subatomic to the cosmic.

The term 'nature' may refer to living plants and animals, geological processes, weather, and physics, such as matter and energy. The term is often refers to the 'natural environment' or wilderness—wild animals, rocks, forest, beaches, and in general areas that have not been substantially altered by humans, or which persist despite human intervention. For, example, manufactured objects and human interaction are generally not considered part of nature, unless qualified as, for example, 'human nature' or 'the whole of nature'. This more traditional concept of "nature" implies a distinction between natural and artificial elements of the Earth, with the artificial as that which has been brought into being by a human consciousness or a human mind.

Earth (or, 'the earth') is the only planet presently known to support life, and its natural features are the subject of many fields of scientific research. Within the solar system, it is third nearest to the sun; it is the largest terrestrial planet and the fifth largest overall. Its most prominent climatic features are its two large polar regions, two relatively narrow temperate zones, and a wide equatorial tropical to subtropical region. Precipitation varies widely with location, from several metres of water per year to less than a millimetre. 71 per cent of the Earth's surface is covered by salt-water oceans. The remainder consists of continents and islands, with most of the inhabited land in the Northern Hemisphere.

Earth has evolved through geological and biological processes that have left traces of the original conditions. The outer surface is divided into several gradually migrating tectonic plates, which have changed relatively quickly several times. The interior remains active, with a thick layer of molten mantle and an iron-filled core that generates a magnetic field.

The atmospheric conditions have been significantly altered from the original conditions by the presence of life-forms, which create an ecological balance that stabilizes the surface conditions. Despite the wide regional variations in climate by latitude and other geographic factors, the long-term average global climate is quite stable during interglacial periods, and variations of a degree or two of average global temperature have historically had major effects on the ecological balance, and on the actual geography of the Earth.

Earth is estimated to have formed 4.54 billion years ago from the solar nebula, along with the Sun and other planets. The moon formed roughly 20 million years later. Initially molten, the outer layer of the planet cooled, resulting in the solid crust. Outgassing and volcanic activity produced the primordial atmosphere. Condensing water vapor, most or all of which came from ice delivered by comets, produced the oceans and other water sources. The highly energetic chemistry is believed to have produced a self-replicating molecule around 4 billion years ago.

Continents formed, then broke up and reformed as the surface of Earth reshaped over hundreds of millions of years, occasionally combining to make a supercontinent. Roughly 750 million years ago, the earliest known supercontinent Rodinia, began to break apart. The continents later recombined to form Pannotia which broke apart about 540 million years ago, then finally Pangaea, which broke apart about 180 million years ago.

Land-based plants and fungi have been part of nature on Earth for about the past 400 million years. These have needed to adapt and move many times as the continents and climates changed.

There is significant evidence, still being discussed among scientists, that a severe glacial action during the Neoproterozoic era covered much of the planet in a sheet of ice. This hypothesis has been termed the 'Snowball Earth', and it is of particular interest as it precedes the Cambrian explosion in which multicellular life forms began to proliferate about 530-540 million years ago.

Since the Cambrian explosion there have been five distinctly identifiable mass extinctions. The last mass extinction occurred some 65 million years ago, when a meteorite collision probably triggered the extinction of the non-avian dinosaurs and other large reptiles, but spared small animals such as mammals, which then resembled shrews. Over the past 65 million years, mammalian life diversified.

Several million years ago, a species of small African ape gained the ability to stand upright. he subsequent advent of human life, and the development of agriculture and further civilization allowed humans to affect the Earth more rapidly than any previous life form, affecting both the nature and quantity of other organisms as well as global climate. By comparison, the oxygen catastrophe, produced by the proliferation of algae during the Siderian period, required about 300 million years to culminate.)

The present era is classified as part of a mass extinction event, the Holocene extinction event, the fastest ever to have occurred. Some, such as E.O. Wilson of Harvard University, predict that human destruction of the biosphere could cause the extinction of one-half of all species in the next 100 years. The extent of the current extinction event is still being researched, debated and calculated by biologists.

Ecosystems are composed of a variety of abiotic and biotic components that function in an interrelated way. The structure and composition is determined by various environmental factors that are interrelated. Variations of these factors will initiate dynamic modifications to the ecosystem. Some of the more important components are: soil, atmosphere, radiation from the sun, water, and living organisms.

Central to the ecosystem concept is the idea that living organisms interact with every other element in their local environment. Eugene Odum, a founder of ecology, stated: "Any unit that includes all of the organisms (ie: the 'community') in a given area interacting with the physical environment so that a flow of energy leads to clearly defined trophic structure, biotic diversity, and material cycles (ie: exchange of materials between living and non-living parts) within the system is an ecosystem." Within the ecosystem, species are connected and dependent upon one another in the food chain, and exchange energy and matter between themselves as well as with their environment. The human ecosystem concept is grounded in the deconstruction of the human/nature dichotomy and the premise that all species are ecologically integrated with each other, as well as with the abiotic constituents of their biotope.

A smaller unit of size is called a microecosystem. For example, a microsystem can be a stone and all the life under it. A *macro-ecosystem* might involve a whole ecoregion, with its drainage basin.

Wilderness

Wilderness is generally defined as areas that have not been significantly modified by human activity. The wild Foundation goes into more detail, defining wilderness as: "The most intact, undisturbed wild natural areas left on our planet — those last truly wild places that humans do not control and have not developed with roads, pipelines or other industrial infrastructure." Wilderness areas can be found in preserves, estates, farms, conservation preserves, ranches, National Forests, National Parks and even in urban areas along rivers, gulches or otherwise undeveloped areas. Wilderness areas and protected parks are considered important for the survival of certain species, ecological studies, conservation, solitude, and recreation. Some nature writers believe wilderness areas are vital for the human spirit and creativity, and some Ecologists consider wilderness areas to be an integral part of the planet's self-sustaining natural ecosystem (the biosphere). They may also preserve historic genetic traits and that they provide habitat for wild flora and fauna that may be difficult to recreate in zoos, arboretums or laboratories.

Although there is no universal agreement on the definition of life, scientists generally accept that the biological manifestation of life is characterized by organization, metabolism, growth, adaptation, response to stimuli and reproduction. Life may also be said to be simply the characteristic state of organisms.

Properties common to terrestrial organisms (plants, animals, fungi, protists, archaea and bacteria) are that they are cellular, carbon-and-water-based with complex organization, having a metabolism, a capacity to grow, respond to stimuli, and reproduce. An entity with these properties is generally considered life. However, not every definition of life considers all of these properties to be essential. Human-made analogs of life may also be considered to be life.

The biosphere is the part of Earth's outer shell – including air, land, surface rocks and water – within which life occurs, and which biotic processes in turn alter or transform. From the broadest geophysiological point of view, the biosphere is the global ecological system integrating all living beings and their relationships, including their interaction with the elements of the lithosphere (rocks), hydrosphere (water), and atmosphere (air). Currently the entire Earth contains over 75 billion tons (150 *trillion* pounds or about 6.8×10^{13} kilograms) of biomass (life), which lives within various environments within the biosphere.

Over nine-tenths of the total biomass on Earth is plant life, on which animal life depends very heavily for its existence. More than 2 million species of plant and animal life have been identified to date, and estimates of the actual number of existing species range from several million to well over 50 million. The number of individual species of life is constantly in some degree of flux, with new species appearing and others ceasing to exist on a continual basis. The total number of species is presently in rapid decline.

Although humans currently comprise only a minuscule proportion of the total living biomass on Earth, the human effect on nature is disproportionately large. Because of the extent of human influence, the boundaries between what humans regard as nature and 'made environments' is not clear cut except at the extremes. Even at the extremes, the amount of natural environment that is free of discernible human influence is presently diminishing at an increasingly rapid pace.

The development of technology by the human race has allowed the greater exploitation of natural resources and has helped to alleviate some of the risk from natural hazards. In spite of this progress, however, the fate of human civilization remains closely linked to changes in the environment. There exists a highly complex feedback loop between the use of advanced technology and changes to the environment that are only slowly becoming understood. Man-made threats to the Earth's natural environment include pollution, deforestation, and disasters such as oil spills. Humans have contributed to the extinction of many plants and animals.

Humans employ nature for both leisure and economic activities. The acquisition of natural resources for industrial use remains the primary component of the world's economic system. Some activities, such as hunting and fishing, are used for both sustenance and leisure, often by different people. Agriculture was first adopted around the 9th millennium BCE. Ranging from food production to energy, nature influences economic wealth.

Although early humans gathered uncultivated plant materials for food and employed the medicinal properties of vegetation for healing, most modern human use of plants is through agriculture. The clearance of large tracts of land for crop growth has led to a significant reduction in the amount available of forestation and wetlands, resulting in the loss of habitat for many plant and animal species as well as increased erosion.

Index

Y

Z